THE NATIONAL TRUST GUIDE TO

ART DECO
IN AMERICA

DAVID GEBHARD

Damage Noted
p. 215-220 4/97

PRESERVATION
PRESS

JOHN WILEY & SONS, INC.

New York · Chicago · ... · Singapore

This text is printed on acid-free paper.

Copyright © 1996 by David Gebhard.

Published by John Wiley & Sons, Inc.

A cooperative publication with the National Trust for Historic Preservation, Washington, D.C., chartered by Congress in 1949 to encourage the preservation of sites, buildings, landscapes, and communities significant in American history and culture.

This publication is designed to provide accurate and authoritative information in regard to the subject matter covered. It is sold with the understanding that the publisher is not engaged in rendering legal, accounting, or other professional services. If legal advice or other expert assistance is required, the services of a competent professional person should be sought.

All photographs not specifically credited are by David Gebhard.

Library of Congress Cataloging-in-Publication Data:

Gebhard, David.
    The National Trust guide to Art Deco in America / David Gebhard
      p. cm.
    Includes bibliographical references and index.
    ISBN 0-471-14386-3 (paper : alk. paper)
      1. Art deco (Architecture) — United States.   2. Architecture,
  Modern — 20th century — United States. I. National Trust for Historic
Preservation in The United States. II. Title.
NA712.5.A7G4   1996
720'.973 — dc20
          96-19948
          CIP

Printed in the United States of America

10 9 8 7 6 5 4 3 2 1

Dedicated to John Beach, who brought the Art Deco and the Streamline Moderne to life for so many of us.

CONTENTS

South

Midwest

Southwest

West

PREFACE

The Preservation Press approached David Gebhard about writing this book early in 1988, and the manuscript was completed late in 1991. The writing, however, was seemingly the easy part, for verifying information on the individual sites and then locating photographs and obtaining permission to reproduce them was a monumental task requiring endless correspondence. It is regrettable that the author will not be able to see the results of these labors or hold the finished book in hand.

David Gebhard's enthusiasm for the architectural styles of the 1920s and 1930s began in the early sixties—anticipating by many years the current interest in and study of those styles. Growing up in the thirties, he understood that Art Deco and Moderne buildings were making a distinct architectural statement not always appreciated by contemporary enthusiasts of the Colonial Revival. When he became an architectural historian and critic, he was able to see these styles as a large and important part of the total output of the period, and not as a footnote to the International Style then being championed by the architectural establishment.

This book reflects its author's preferences and his particular knowledge of individual sites and thus offers a personal view of the styles. If it opens an observer's eyes to an appreciation of Art Deco in all its manifestations and helps place the styles in proper perspective, he would have been most gratified. Now, after viewing again the images together with the text, I feel sure that every reader will be struck with enthusiasm for the distinctiveness, idiosyncracies, and creativeness of the styles.

Patricia Gebhard
Santa Barbara, California
April, 1996

Editors' Note: We very much regret David Gebhard's passing on March 3, 1996. Patricia Gebhard, his wife, generously assisted in the final stages of bringing this book to print.

ACKNOWLEDGMENTS

The first historical look at the Art Deco and the Streamline Moderne was undertaken at the end of the 1960s. From that moment on, these Moderne styles have enjoyed a vogue among curators and collectors as well as art and architectural historians. Numerous books, magazine articles, and museum catalogs published on the subject have been consulted for this guide, and a great debt is owed to their authors. Among the many individuals who have kindly made suggestions and contributed information and photographs are: Carla Breeze, David Bricker, Lauren Weiss Bricker, David De Long, Jean R. France, Esley Hamilton, Cynthia Howk, Chuck Kaplan, Jerome Kotas, Chester Leibs, Richard Longstreth, John Margolies, Tom Martinson, Henry Matthews, Kathy Church Plummer, Michael Shellenbarger, Paul Sprague, Wilson Stiles, Richard Striner, Harriette Von Breton, Marcus Whiffen, Dennis Wilhelm, Robert Winter, and Sally Woodbridge.

Finally, I wish to thank Diane Maddex, who suggested this volume when she was director of the Preservation Press, and Buckley C. Jeppson, the next director of the Preservation Press, who so strongly supported the project, and finally Janet Walker, who did the original editing. Thanks must also go to Jan Cigliano and David Sassian for bringing the book to completion.

David Gebhard
Santa Barbara, California

ART DECO AND STREAMLINE MODERNE ARCHITECTURE IN THE UNITED STATES, 1920 TO 1949

A recurring theme of the 1920s and 1930s, both in traditional design and architecture and in the various avant-garde movements, was the desire to seek out new forms or modifications of old forms to express the continually changing character and accelerated tempo of the new age. The machine and technology, especially the automobile, were seen as new nontraditional sources for architecture. "The black bottom and the Charleston typify the new rhythm of modern life," wrote the Austrian architect Adolf Loos in the mid-1920s. "An architect of today," he noted, "to be successful must be able to translate that rhythm into something of beauty in brick and stone."

Without question the two most pervasive and most popular modes that expressed the prevailing attitude toward change were the Art Deco and the Streamline Moderne. While other architectural styles also emerged in these years—Constructivism, Expressionism, Futurism, and, perhaps most significantly, the International Style—it was the Art Deco and the Streamline Moderne that caught the eye and held the attention of most Americans. These two styles permeated virtually every facet of the design world; their influence was manifest in everything from hairstyles and clothing to Hollywood films, to science fiction illustrations, to furniture, and finally, to architecture.

Although the Art Deco and the Streamline Moderne were almost universally embraced in their time, the limits of their popularity are worth noting. Untold numbers of commercial and public buildings adopted a stylish image in the decades following World War I, but only rarely did the Moderne penetrate the realm of domestic architecture. In the 1930s by far the most

1

popular image for single-family housing in the United States was the colonial Cape Cod cottage (or its West Coast equivalent, the California ranch house), and while tubular metal furniture might appear in a sunroom, screened porch, or breakfast nook, it would not replace the maple reproductions of colonial chairs, tables, and cupboards that occupied the principal rooms of the average American house. In a fundamental sense, most Americans perceived the Art Deco and the Streamline Moderne as fashions of the moment. The American middle class would never abandon its belief that permanency, or at least the illusion of permanency, was preferable to a world of continual change.

For many Americans who lived during the Jazz Age of the 1920s and the Depression years of the 1930s, the open contradiction between the imagery of permanence and the imagery of the transitory helped to create a delightful visual richness and complexity. At the end of the 1930s, middle-class Americans could leave their Colonial Revival suburban homes, climb into their streamlined cars, and dart off to their Streamline Moderne supermarkets or neighborhood movie theaters. Or they could tend to public business in a Public Works Administration (PWA) Moderne or Colonial Revival post office or government office building.

Modern or Moderne?

In a guidebook such as this, it is useful to set forth with all possible precision the characteristics of each style under consideration. The terms used to denote architectural styles are, however, notoriously slippery, and in this regard *Art Deco* and *Streamline Moderne* are not exceptional. Like the labels attached to many other styles of the past or near past—*Gothic, Baroque, Rococo*—the terms *Art Deco* and *Streamline Moderne* came into being decades after the modes to which they respectively refer held sway. In retrospect, *Art Deco* may seem an almost inevitable term to choose, given that the Exposition Internationale des Arts Décoratifs et Industriels Modernes which took place in Paris in 1925, was widely acknowledged as one of the principal sources of the "new look" in American architecture and design in the late 1920s and the 1930s. But what we today know as the Art Deco went by many names before the term was coined in the 1960s by the British critic and historian Bevis Hillier. In his 1968 book *Art Deco* Hillier took a careful look at the various terms employed in the 1920s and 1930s and also at the labels that had cropped up in the intervening years. He selected *Art Deco* partly because it could easily be paired off against *Art Nouveau*, the term used to denote a pervasive turn-of-the-century stylistic movement. *Art Deco* seemed apt also because at the time interest in the style was focused primarily on the decorative arts. Not incidentally, Hillier's chosen term provided art dealers and collectors with a label that carried overtones of lineage and respectability.

The second wave of the Moderne, which emerged in the 1930s and drew its primary inspiration from the aerodynamic teardrop, almost immediately acquired the term *Streamline*. The coupling of *Streamline* with *Moderne* occurred decades later when the first Art Deco/Streamline Moderne exhibition was mounted in the United States. This exhibition and its catalog, organized and written by Harriette Von Breton and myself, were devoted to the work of Kem Weber. The exhibition was presented in 1969 at the University Art Museum at the University of California, Santa Barbara. Since the designs and architecture of Kem Weber encompassed both phases of the popular Moderne, the distinction was drawn between the designer's work of the 1920s, which was labeled "Zigzag Moderne" (Art Deco), and his later work, which expressed the Streamline Moderne.

In the 1920s and 1930s casual observers of the architectural scene seldom focused on the differences between works that would today be perceived as exemplifying contending styles. Such terms as *Functional, Modernistic, Modernesque,* and *Modern* were used virtually interchangeably to refer to any and all works designed in the "new" style. But practitioners of what is generally called "International Style" or simply "modern" architecture, which developed in the 1920s and 1930s primarily in Europe and on America's West Coast, tended to object to being grouped with the designers who worked in the popular Moderne modes. Following the lead of the German architect Walter Gropius, the modernists played a semantic game, arguing that they were not creating a style at all but, rather, were merely responding to the new social, economic, and material conditions of the 20th century. Henry-Russell Hitchcock and Philip Johnson called the modernists' bluff in their 1932 exhibition and book, *The International Style: Architecture since 1922,* but the American high-style modernists continued to disclaim any interest in forging a new style.

Another discomfort experienced by the International Style modernists was that their avowed affinity for the North American concrete grain elevator, the automobile, the airplane, and the ocean liner was openly shared by the designers of Moderne objects and architecture. The elitist poetry of Le Corbusier's ode to the transportation machine in his 1923 manifesto *Towards a New Architecture* became, in the hands of Sheldon Cheney, Paul T. Frankl, and others, one of the arguments in support of the popular Moderne. Echoing Le Corbusier, Cheney wrote in his 1930 book *The New World Architecture,*

> We sometimes wonder why our dwelling-place couldn't have been conceived and built as cleanly, as efficiently—and as beautifully—as our automobile: THAT has just the combination of mechanical efficiency and comfort, of cleanli-

ness and pleasurable brightness, of mechanically perfect shelter and of beauty out of proportioning and structure, that we should relish in a house.

The line separating works in the popular Moderne styles from works of International Style modernism is in some cases so fine as to be invisible. A significant percentage of the buildings and monuments listed in this book are hybrids—either combinations of the Moderne and the International Style or admixtures of various Moderne styles. Still, it is useful when studying modern or Moderne architecture to retain certain distinctions. While each of the styles that emerged in the 1920s and 1930s was to some extent expressive of the new age, the Moderne styles were based upon fashion and taste, not upon any functional or moral imperative; and whereas the modernists eschewed traditional forms in their search for entirely new forms, the Moderne designers played freely with historical precedent, sometimes abstracting traditional forms beyond recognition.

The Art Deco

In 1928 an observer of the new Moderne architecture described the Art Deco as characterized by "Straight lines; it is angular, geometric and tends to follow cubic proportions. . . . The lines are unvaryingly plain and severe, with touches of decoration in the way of color, wrought iron and glass work, for relief." As a description of the Art Deco, this is a good starting point. What should also be noted as primary are the importance the style placed on ornament, especially sculptural ornament, and the direct manner in which the Art Deco was nourished by historical roots.

Insofar as most of America's Art Deco structures were produced by architects directly or indirectly educated within the Parisian Beaux-Arts system, it should not be surprising that when these architects turned their attention to the "new" language of design (as almost all of them did after 1925), the forms they produced were, to a considerable degree, derived from classical precedent. Whether the project was a PWA-funded post office or public school building in a small Midwestern community or a towering slab skyscraper in New York City, the classical ideals of solidity and mass remained paramount. So too remained the predilection for classical-inspired proportions and axial, balanced, symmetrical plans and elevations. The architect might look to the classical traditions of Western Europe—to the Greek, the Gothic, the Romanesque, or the Renaissance—or to the architecture of ancient Egypt, ancient Assyria in Mesopotamia, or the pre-Columbian world of the Aztecs and Mayans in Mexico and Central America. Whatever historical sources the Art Deco designer drew from, the forms, surfaces, and details were maneuvered within a classical Beaux-Arts framework.

Thus the typical Art Deco building represented a bringing up to date, a modernization, of one or another of the architectural traditions. For this reason, it is sometimes difficult to separate the buildings that represent a slowly evolving phase of a particular historical language from those that were consciously intended to be responded to as Moderne. A case in point would be Paul P. Cret and Alexander B. Trowbridge's Folger Shakespeare Library (1932) in Washington, D.C., which Cret himself cited as an example of the "new classicism." Cret would certainly have rejected the idea that this building, or any of his designs, could be cataloged as Art Deco. Yet for us today, Cret's buildings of the late 1920s and 1930s comprise some of the most impressive examples of abstraction of the classical tradition—a quality intimately associated with the Art Deco.

What separates the Art Deco from other contemporaneous modes is, above all, its approach to ornament and surface sheathing. The Art Deco building often played a sort of game, contrasting the earthbound, even monumental, nature of the structure with the fragility and thinness of its exterior surfaces. The general tendency, from the mid-1920s on into the early 1940s, was to exhibit exterior walls that expressed little depth or projection. Such abstraction would dissolve the traditional link between architecture and sculpture; the result was buildings less sculptural and more like drawings on a drafting board.

The Moderne skyscrapers that captured the upward-soaring quality of the Gothic belong to a subset of the Art Deco generally referred to as the American Vertical style. These tall urban buildings articulated their thin stone-veneered or terra-cotta–clad surfaces with attenuated vertical shafts alternating with vertical bands, usually recessed, containing windows and spandrels.

In many Art Deco buildings the style's characteristic emphasis on verticality was manifest in a row of piers or pilasters that subtly represented a classical portico or temple front. Most such Art Deco designs alluded to a traditional base, but typical of the style was the absence of a cornice or other device to provide a vertical conclusion. While an attic or a band of ornament might imply a conclusion, such features were at best highly abridged versions of a cornice. Even in those instances where a classical-inspired low dome or pyramidal hipped roof was used, the form was customarily recessed behind a parapet and sprang, not from the building's outside walls, but from the rooftop itself (thus reading principally as a pure geometric shape, only incidentally as a traditional roof).

The thin panels of stone or brick that sheathed many Art Deco buildings were meant to appear as an appliqué, abstractly (as in a drawing) suggesting traditional masonry. (By a similar token, the interior public spaces of many large Art Deco buildings employed thin sheets of rare and expensive polished stone, whose effect was like that of wallpaper or a painted mural: just a skin covering the frame of the structure.) Terra-cotta was a material frequently employed, both for the overall sheathing of a building and for its ornament. Sometimes the terra-cotta was treated so as to be indistinguishable from stone; on other occasions it was made to resemble porcelain or glass—fragile, with brilliant colors and gleaming glazed surfaces. Another popular material for sheathing Art Deco buildings was cast stone (a fine-surfaced concrete), in some cases so similar to stone that it is difficult to identify as concrete.

The 1920s styles, especially the Art Deco, delighted in experimenting with the numerous metal alloys introduced in the course of the decade. All sorts of mixtures of steel, bronze, nickel, silver, platinum, lead, and zinc were used for elevator doors, window frames, spandrels, decorative panels, and sculpture. Lightweight aluminum also came into its own in these years, and the Art Deco architects were obviously fascinated with it, both as a material in its own right and, with plating applied, as a substitute for other materials: bronze, nickel, silver, even gold.

"The automobile with its firm but soft coloring and its flashes of bright metal may again afford us a clue," wrote Sheldon Cheney in discussing the Moderne's relation to color. Such a scheme—"firm but soft color" contrasted with "bright metal"—was certainly one of the hallmarks of the Art Deco, employed in the production of objects both large (skyscrapers) and small (perfume bottles and cigarette lighters). The Art Deco typically contrasted warm tans and pale shades of green and blue either with shiny metals or with accents of strong "pure" color—vehement reds, cobalt blues, or golden yellows. The style also exploited the drama of light and shadow through the adroit use of electric lighting. The Art Deco's most dramatic employment of artificial lighting was the nighttime illumination of building exteriors. For here architects could come close to transferring light-and-shadow renderings (such as the drawings of the famed Hugh Ferriss) into the real three-dimensional world. In a critical discussion of the buildings of Rockefeller Center, Lewis Mumford wrote, "Here, at night, is what Ferriss meant: something large, exciting and romantic . . . again, life has imitated art."

The architectural details associated with a particular historical style often underwent a reductive process when subsumed into the Art Deco. The slender column (or cluster of slender columns) traditionally associated with the Gothic was commonly employed on the exterior of American Vertical–style skyscrapers. In their Moderne incarnation, such columns might become narrow vertical bands without bases or capitals. Similarly, the Art Deco might reduce the Doric column to the barest vestige of a pilaster, its surface a continuation of the adjacent wall. In many Art Deco buildings vertical fluting along an exterior surface constituted the only residue of a classical column.

The Art Deco took two approaches to ornament: the first was to make ornament integral to the surface upon which it was placed; the second was to confine the ornament to a panel that hovered (or seemed to hover) in front of the wall surface. Favorite motifs in Art Deco ornament included spirals, sunflowers, steps, zigzags, triangles, double triangles, hexagons, fragmented circles, and seashells. The patterns containing these motifs were generally rendered in low relief with sharp angular contours.

The Art Deco frequently enlisted sculpture and inscriptions in its game of playing tradition against modernity. Figures and events from classical mythology, from the bible, or from ancient and "primitive" cultures (Near Eastern, Native American, pre-Columbian, etc.) were represented in Art Deco sculpture. Such sculpture transported the middle-class audience to which it was addressed not only into the past but also around the globe. The figures and the ideas they personified were often maneuvered to comment on the modern world of commerce and industry—hence the inclusion of gears, propeller blades, automobile headlights, or whole airplanes, dirigibles, trucks, steamships, radio towers, and oil rigs in so much Art Deco sculpture.

Three methods were typically employed for integrating sculpture into an Art Deco building. In the Goodhue-esque approach (originated by the architect Bertram G. Goodhue and widely emulated) three-dimensional figures were made to spring forth in primeval fashion from the surface and mass of the structure. A second route was to project a rectangular panel out from the building's surface and then to place relief sculpture on the panel. An opposite tack was to place low-relief sculpture within a recessed panel; figures or decorative patterns contained in such recesses seldom broke out beyond the plane of the adjacent surface. On the whole, Art Deco figurative sculpture (of humans, animals, birds, and plant forms) reflected trends in the parallel world of modern art: the reemergence of the classical human figure, the influence of primitive and folk art, and the impulse toward abstraction evident in the work of cubist and postcubist artists of the 1910s and 1920s.

The Art Deco was employed in the design of all kinds of buildings, large and small—banks, retail stores, motion picture theaters, apartment houses, even service stations—but without question the style's favorite building type was the skyscraper. Perhaps the least well-known of America's Art Deco treasures are the tombstones and mausoleums in cemeteries and memorial parks across the country. Some of these were designed by noted architects (Reginald D. Johnson and Thomas Tallmadge, for instance); others were produced by anonymous designers who obviously kept abreast of the latest architectural trends. With the onset of the Depression, commercial construction ground to a halt and public buildings, many of them funded by the PWA and built by WPA labor, became one of the principal vehicles for the Art Deco. These buildings, which constitute a subset of the Art Deco known as the PWA Moderne, included courthouses, schools, armories, water treatment plants, bridges, and dams. PWA Moderne structures generally assumed a demeanor of stripped classicism, with an emphasis on the monumental (reminiscent of the "Fascist" architecture espoused in the same years by totalitarian rulers in Europe). The style was employed also for several private-sector building projects, most notably the office buildings constructed throughout the United States by the regional Bell Telephone companies; these late Art Deco skyscrapers typically also incorporated elements of the Streamline Moderne and the International Style.

It could convincingly be argued that several of the most lively Art Deco buildings constructed in the United States at the end of the 1920s and in the 1930s were churches. The various Protestant denominations, as well as certain factions within the Roman Catholic Church, sought to express their modernity and their compatibility with the 20th-century world through buildings that appeared at once traditional and modern. By 1940 an impressive number of Art Deco churches in exposed reinforced concrete had been constructed on the West Coast. In the central United States, churches designed by Barry Byrne and Bruce Goff commingled the Gothic, Expressionism, and the Moderne; and the New York architect Henry J. McGill (working in some instances with Talbot F. Hamlin) designed churches that seemed to carry on Goodhue's exploration of architecture as sculpture.

Sources of the Art Deco

In the United States the Art Deco began as a "smart" urban style, the latest fashion among a small contingent of upper-middle-class sophisticates in New York, Chicago, San Francisco, and other major cities. From these centers the style rapidly spread to smaller communities throughout the country. If the Art Deco was the mode of the moment in New York, then there was no reason that it shouldn't be emulated posthaste in Fresno or Peoria. By the end of the 1920s virtually all facets of American design—advertising, fashion, the decorative arts, and architecture—were following the example of Paris.

Although the French capital was the acknowledged fountainhead of the Art Deco, the style's sources were varied and complex. The foundation for much post–World War I Parisian design was the work of the Austrian and German designers Joseph Hoffman, Joseph Olbrich, and Peter Behrens. The 1925 exposition had in fact originally been planned in 1914, as the French answer to Vienna's perceived preeminence in architecture and design, and the war had caused its postponement. By the mid-1920s several well-established Central European designers had emigrated to the United States and set up practice, including Kem Weber in California and Joseph Urban and Paul T. Frankl in New York. These designers helped to establish the Moderne in the United States in the years immediately before and after the 1925 Paris exposition.

Many American architects also created buildings and furniture that helped to establish the style. Frank Lloyd Wright designed some splendid (but unbuilt) Art Deco skyscrapers in the late 1920s. Claude Bragdon wrote a sharp-edged essay entitled "Ornament from Platonic Solids" that enjoyed wide circulation. Lloyd Wright, Barry Byrne, and Bruce Goff produced designs that have much in common with the Parisian-influenced mode. Even a "futurist" such as R. Buckminster Fuller registered the impact of the Art Deco in his Dymaxion houses of the late 1920s.

Among the architects who made the most significant contributions to the early development of the Art Deco in the United States were: Eliel Saarinen, who arrived in this country from Finland in the 1920s; the Franco-American Paul P. Cret, an advocate of the Beaux Arts who opened an office in Philadelphia; and the New York architects Bertram G. Goodhue and Cass Gilbert, both of whom in the 1910s and 1920s turned from a preoccupation with the Gothic to a monumental version of the Moderne mode. Saarinen's widely published design for the Helsingfors Railroad Terminal (1904–14) illustrated how sculpture and architecture could be integrated in a dramatic new manner; his universally admired entry in the 1922 Chicago Tribune Tower competition was a pioneering exploration of the vertical vocabulary through which the American Vertical style developed. Cret's contribution can be seen in his Folger Shakespeare Library in Washington, D.C. (1928–32). Cass Gilbert's United States Army Supply Base (1918) in Brooklyn, New York, demonstrated that an abstracted classicism could be achieved in exposed concrete. Goodhue took this theme and elaborated on it in his design for the Nebraska State Capitol (1922–26).

The Streamline Moderne

If the Art Deco captured the spirit of the moment, the modern age, the Streamline Moderne offered a glimpse of the future. What it portended was a fully automated world in which machines, controlled by man, were every-where—and everywhere invisible. The style evinced an intense fascination with speed—speed of transportation and communication. Its visual vocabu-lary (the curve, the teardrop, the uninterrupted horizontal line) was derived largely from the form of high-speed modern transportation machines: the air-plane, the automobile, the ocean liner.

Another fundamental difference between the Streamline Moderne and the Art Deco was the economic climate in which the two styles flourished. The Streamline Moderne conjured up an exciting vision of the future partly in order to help lift the American public out of the gloom of the Depression. In striking contrast to the skyscrapers and large-scale public buildings that constitute the great monuments of the Art Deco, Streamline

Moderne structures were relatively small. As a consequence of increasing surburbanization throughout the United States, Streamline Moderne buildings also tended to be street- or highway-oriented (service stations, motels, drive-in restaurants and theaters, supermarkets), not confined to urban environments to the extent that Art Deco buildings were. The Streamline Moderne was also commonly employed in remodeling, or repackaging, existing buildings (storefronts, bars and cafés), since new construction was beyond the means of most American entrepreneurs in the 1930s. As yet another point of distinction, the typical Art Deco building argued for permanence in its forms and materials, while the Streamline Moderne structure, with its "flash-and-gleam beauty," implied a built-in impermanence akin to the need to replace one's automobile every year due to Detroit's annual ritual of restyling.

What the Art Deco and the Streamline Moderne had in common was that each came close to being a universal style, employed for everything from airplanes, ships, trains, and automobiles to children's toys, to household appliances, to buildings. In the case of the Streamline Moderne, no matter how an object was produced, it was meant to be read as machine-made. The style's evocation of machine imagery was in a sense indirect: that is, the machine aspect of a Streamline Moderne object was not set out before us to see and comprehend. Rather, the object's smooth flowing "skin," its sheathing, served to symbolize that the object was produced by a machine and/or was itself a machine. "Simple lines are modern," wrote Paul T. Frankl in 1928. "They are restful to the eye and dignified and tend to cover up the complexity of the machine age. If they do not completely do this, they at least divert our attention and allow us to feel ourselves master of the machine."

The visual language of the Streamline Moderne was realized through a limited number of highly effective motifs. In architecture, the designer's attention focused primarily on the building's skin. Structure was seldom revealed. Similarly, there was no outward assertion of a building's mechanical systems. Plumbing pipes, ducts, electrical conduits, together with furnaces or air-conditioning units, were hidden away behind a smooth exterior.

In its form the ideal Streamline Moderne building was a horizontal rectangular container, usually with dramatic rounded corners and occasional semicircular bays, surmounted by parapeted or projecting thin-slab roofs. The image projected was that of a scientifically advanced, effortlessly hygienic world. A sense of rapid movement was imparted by narrow horizontal bands of windows that often wrapped around corners and by horizontal layering in the building's facade (via changes in colors or material). The sense of speed was often enhanced by projecting or recessed bands (or groups of bands) disposed on the facade, by metal ship's railings, and by horizontal window mullions. Although terraces and screened porches might extend a building out over its site, the ideal Streamline Moderne structure was meant (like its International Style counterpart) to be experienced as an object independent of its environment.

Two prominent characteristics of the style were glass brick (for windows and even entire walls) and small round windows reminiscent of the portholes on yachts and ocean liners. Window frames and doorframes, and even the doors themselves, were metal or appeared to be metal—products of the Machine Age. White cement stucco was a close to universal sheathing material. Thin rectangular sheets of opaque colored glass—Vitrolite and Carrara glass—were extensively used on smaller commercial buildings, as were steel panels coated with porcelainized enamel. Stainless steel and aluminum were employed for detailing and hardware; linoleum and Formica were the preferred materials for interior floors and countertops. By the end of the 1930s plywood had also entered into the Streamline Moderne vocabulary. It was employed for walls, ceilings, and furniture; its typical finish was bleached white, sealed with a coat of matte lacquer.

That the Streamline Moderne embraced its own built-in obsolescence also set the style apart from the Art Deco. In place of the elegant and expensive (or at least expensive-looking) materials encountered in Art Deco buildings, the Streamline Moderne favored mass-produced, easy-to-install components—in short, materials perfect for use in remodeling projects. A colorful new facade of Vitrolite or Carrara glass (available in black, white, green, blue, red, and other colors), a few curved walls or glass-brick windows, a bit of stainless-steel trim, and some bands of neon signage could effectively and dramatically repackage any existing structure. By 1940 almost every city and small town in the United States had acquired an array of commercial buildings remodeled in the Streamline Moderne mode.

Those architects who were fortunate enough to continue their practice in the Depression years occasionally sallied forth into the Streamline Moderne. For them the Streamline was a new language, employed to convey a sense of ultramodernity. Even such "space age" designers as R. Buckminster Fuller and Frederick Kiesler absorbed the Streamline language into their work of the 1930s. Many of the style's foremost exponents belonged to an entirely new breed of professionals. While a few may have been trained as engineers or architects, several of the major figures came to this new profession with backgrounds in theater design or the graphic arts. Between 1926 and 1930 Norman Bel Geddes, Walter Dorwin Teague, Raymond Loewy, Henry Dreyfuss, Kem Weber, Paul T. Frankl, and Harold Van Doren brilliantly performed their first act of repackaging, namely reinventing themselves in the newly created role of "industrial designer." Their paramount task in the bleak years of the Depression was to repackage the old and package the new so that the American public would be stimulated to buy products ranging from houses to electric toasters.

National chains of retail stores and service stations were especially fond of the Streamline Moderne. In the mid-1930s such chains began to realize the sales advantage not only of establishing a uniform and instantly recognizable image but also of cultivating an image that the middle-class public perceived as modern, up-to-date. Sears, Roebuck & Company advanced their sales by utilizing the Art Deco image in the 1920s, and by the late 1930s they had turned to the Streamline Moderne. Service stations built by the regional and national oil companies ranged from Frederick Frost's Streamline Moderne oil-drum design for Mobil to Walter Dorwin Teague's porcelainized-enamel-clad stations for Texaco.

The single-family house, as a machine for living, also occasionally assumed a Streamline Moderne image. For the limited number of Americans who could afford to build, a Streamline Moderne dwelling established them in their own eyes and in the eyes of their neighbors as progressive, scientific, avant-garde. Advances in construction technology offset some of the effects of the Depression, and manufacturers of prefabricated building components took advantage of the opportunity to catch the public's eye with a strikingly designed object. Magazines such as *American Home* and retail stores such as W. J. Sloane & Company sponsored the construction of Streamline Moderne model houses across the country. Frederick Kiesler's "Space House" of 1933, built within the showrooms of the Sloane & Company store in New York City, was perhaps the most sophisticated Streamline Moderne dwelling built in the country. Just as there were subdivisions whose images were limited to the Colonial Revival or the California ranch house, there were a few developments restricted to the Streamline Moderne, among them Swan Acres near Pittsburgh (1934–38) and the Park Moderne in Los Angeles (1929–34).

Alfred Barr, director of the Museum of Modern Art from 1929 to 1943, claimed always to be able to distinguish between works in the International Style and those in the populist Streamline Moderne mode. Barr decried the Moderne for its "desire for 'styling' objects for advertisement. Principles such as 'streamlining,'" he said, "often secured homage out of all proportion to their adaptability." Yet many International Style buildings of the 1930s utilized design elements that are commonly associated with the Streamline Moderne. This is true of buildings designed by such notable architects as Richard Neutra and R. M. Schindler on the West Coast, George Fred Keck in the Midwest, William Lescaze and Edward D. Stone in the Northeast, and others. It might even be argued that the most splendid and original Streamline Moderne building in the United States is Frank Lloyd Wright's Johnson Wax Company Administrative Building (1936). Although purely Wrightian and highly individualistic, this streamlined structure and its interior spaces are remarkably similar to buildings depicted in illustrations by Frank Paul that graced the cover of *Amazing Stories* magazine in the 1930s.

As one might expect, elements of the Streamline Moderne—rounded corners, corner windows, glass brick, metal ship's railings, circular staircases, even portholes—are often found in buildings that we would today call Art Deco. They even crop up in some Monterey Revival and Colonial Revival buildings of the 1930s. One of the most suave and sophisticated styles of the day, the Regency Revival, delighted in incorporating outright Moderne traits. One often feels today that a coin could be tossed as to whether certain structures should be labeled Streamline Moderne or Regency Revival.

The high point of the Streamline Moderne, which turned out also to be the style's swan song, was reached in the buildings of the 1939 New York World's Fair. While the Trylon and the Perisphere, designed by the New York architects Harrison & Fouilhoux, served as the symbolic center of the fair, the buildings that attracted the most attention were those produced by the industrial designers Norman Bel Geddes, Walter Dorwin Teague, and Raymond Loewy. Bel Geddes's Futurama and his exhibition for General Motors entitled "Highways and Horizons," with its multilayered streets and sidewalks, were masterpieces of the Streamline Moderne.

Sources of the Streamline Moderne

The visual imagery of the Streamline, for architecture as well as for transportation machines, originated in the world of science fiction. The genre itself reaches far back into the 19th century, past such classics as H. G. Wells's 1896 novel *The Time Machine* and E. M. Forster's "The Machine Stops" (1909), past Jules Verne's depiction of Captain Nemo and his streamlined submarine in *Twenty Thousand Leagues Under the Sea* (1870) and his *Journey to the Center of the Earth* (1864), all the way to Edgar Allan Poe's "Hans Phael—A Tale" (1835). But science fiction came into its own—in books, pulp magazines, and films—in the 1920s and 1930s, and the image of the Streamline was an essential ingredient of its futuristic world. The term *science fiction* was coined in 1928 by Hugo Gernsbeck, who three years earlier had commenced publication of the magazine *Amazing Stories*; by early 1929 the illustrator Frank Paul (whose fame rests on his illustrations for *Amazing Stories* in the 1930s and 1940s) was sharing with readers of *Science Wonder Stories* his glorious vision of Streamline cities of the future. Comic strips and Hollywood movies brought images of Streamline Moderne buildings into the everyday world of middle-class America. The comic strip "Buck Rogers of the 25th Century" began appearing in 1929, and five years later it was joined by the popular "Flash Gordon." Several feature-length science fiction films were also created in these years, among them such classics as *Just Imagine* (1933) and *Things to Come* (1938).

The speed of modern transportation was a theme of avant-garde architecture as early as the beginning of the 20th century. The low-lying and expansive California bungalows that seemed almost to hover over their sites were often called "airplane bungalows." Frank Lloyd Wright's Robie House and other Prairie School works were sometimes satirically referred to as beached ocean liners. But the architectural evocation of fast-moving transportation machines is probably most accurately traced to the sketches and drawings produced in the 1910s by several European modernists, among them the Italian Antonio Sant'Elia and the Germans Kem Weber and Eric Mendelsohn. In 1921 some of Mendelsohn's drawings were published in the United States under the title *Dynamic Architecture: New Forms of the Future.* Mendelsohn's realized European work, with its frequent commitment to the curve and horizontality, did much to set the stage for the Streamline Moderne. The designers and architects who took up the Streamline Moderne in the 1930s also borrowed from the International Style, particularly in their use of rectangular flat-roofed boxes articulated by smooth stucco surfaces and horizontal bands of windows.

To these sources within the world of architecture should be added the influence of the painters, sculptors, and graphic artists whose fondness for the curve and for organically derived forms was expressed in much of the art produced from the 1930s onward. And, of course, the contribution of engineering design must not be overlooked. The airplane—in spite of the fact that commercial airliners were not fully streamlined until the early 1930s—assumed the position as the dominant icon of the age.

Finally, it should be noted that the popularity of Streamline Moderne architecture was probably enhanced by the redesign and repackaging of many everyday household products and appliances in the 1930s. For example, the streamlined Hoover vacuum cleaner (Henry Dreyfuss, 1936) and the child's Tot Bike (Harold Van Doreen, 1937) familiarized most middle-class Americans with the style and helped to pave the way for acceptance of Streamline Moderne buildings.

The Continuation of the Art Deco and Streamline Moderne After 1945

When building activity in the United States resumed after World War II, a populist version of the International Style, rather than either the Art Deco or the Streamline Moderne, emerged as the dominant mode. While many Streamline Moderne buildings were constructed after 1945, the style no longer embodied the image of the moment. The new image of the here-and-now machine, the metal-and-glass rectangular box hovering on stilts over its urban or suburban site, came to express the modernity of the moment. The

Streamline Moderne's vision of the future faded, and the style itself was nudged aside by Corporate Modernism.

The imagery of the Art Deco and Streamline Moderne did not, however, disappear from the scene after World War II. Frank Lloyd Wright created a number of major monuments in the Streamline Moderne style in the late 1940s and 1950s: his Guggenheim Museum in New York, his Annunciation Greek Orthodox Church in Wauwatosa, Winsconsin, and his Marin County Civic Center in San Raphael, California. With the advent of Post Modernism in the late 1960s, the Art Deco and Streamline Moderne became new, much used sources for architects. The interest of these Post Modern architects was not in the richness of Art Deco ornamentation; rather it was the simplification and abstraction of form that had come to typify these two popular modern styles. Parapeted towers with pyramidal roofs, windows and doors with corbeled arches, and curved walls of glass brick formed a repeated vocabulary of many Postmodernist buildings. The image of the streamlined transportation machine emerged once more in the form of new (now quite fashionable) diners. And even the early Expressionist verticalism emerged as a dominant motif in major monuments of the early 1990s, such as the Mormon Temple in San Diego. With their references to the Classical tradition and at the same time to modernity, the Art Deco and Streamline Moderne will undoubtedly continue to be rich sources that architects of the future can plagiarize. They also continue to hold a fascination for the middle class, as is evident in a recent real estate ad in the *Los Angeles Times* (June 11, 1994), which announced the opening of an "Art Deco Jewel," Kelton Place, a new condominium complex in the heart of Brentwood.

ART DECO AND STREAMLINE MODERNE: PRESERVING THE BEST

Being a relatively recent style, the Art Deco has fared reasonably well in terms of preservation. The major financial investment that most Art Deco structures represent (by virtue of their size and materials) has generally encouraged their retention. The interiors as well as the exteriors of the majority of Art Deco public buildings remain largely intact. On the whole, the damage that has been done to Art Deco commercial skyscrapers—through insensitive remodeling of storefronts, entrances, and lobbies—has been confined to their ground floors. In some cases, however, windows on higher floors have also been indifferently replaced. Many smaller Art Deco buildings have either been remodeled beyond recognition or torn down. The Art Deco interiors of retail stores have been especially susceptible to remodeling. Bullock's Wilshire Department Store in Los Angeles (Parkinson & Parkinson, 1929) boasts one of the few intact Art Deco interiors in the country.

Even among the large-scale Art Deco buildings there have been significant losses: the gleaming black-and-gold-sheathed Richfield Building in Los Angeles (Morgan, Walls & Clements, 1928), the auto-oriented Sunkist Building in Los Angeles (Walker and Eisen, 1935), the streamlined Airline Terminal in New York (John B. Peterkin, 1939–40), and that splendid enlarged perfume bottle, the Café Dewitt in Syracuse, New York (W. C. Walker, 1931).

Streamline Moderne buildings, although more recent than Art Deco buildings, have on the whole fared far worse. There are numerous reasons for the continual loss of these structures. The Streamline Moderne acknowledged its own transitory nature, and it therefore seems almost fitting that

17

Richfield Building, Los Angeles, Caifornia. Demolished. Marvin Rand, photographer, 1968.

Streamline buildings have been replaced with structures in more recent styles. While many Streamline Moderne buildings were solidly constructed and well detailed, the mode did not lend itself to physical longevity. Like its contemporaneous counterpart, the International Style, the Streamline Moderne produced buildings that do not age well; their appearance suffers appreciably unless they are continually refurbished. And, like discarded rusting automobile chassis, Streamline Moderne buildings do not make traditionally romantic ruins.

Probably upward of three-quarters of the Streamline Moderne buildings erected in the 1930s are now gone. Of the hundreds of service stations designed in the style, only a handful remain, and even these few isolated sur-

NBC Building, Hollywood (Los Angeles), California. Demolished. *Architectural Concrete.*

vivors—in California, in Iowa, in Massachusetts, and in other states—are being removed one by one. The street facades of glass brick, Vitrolite, and neon that adorned cafés, bars, and motion picture theaters on almost every main street in the United States have largely vanished. Also fast disappearing are the distinctive supermarkets and other roadside attractions of the late 1930s and the 1940s. The Streamline Moderne bus depot was once a landmark common to most American cities; now only a few remain. Two significant losses have been the NBC Building (Austin & Co., 1938–39) and Coulter's Department Store (Stiles Clements, 1938), both in Los Angeles. In the realm of domestic architecture, the most notable loss is Richard Neutra's landlocked Streamline Moderne ship, the Von Sternberg House (Northridge, California, 1936).

Old postcards, back issues of magazines, and other printed material must now evoke for us the aura of stylishness that was embodied in the Art Deco and the Streamline Moderne buildings at Chicago's 1933 Century of Progress Exposition, at New York's World's Fair of 1939, and at San Francisco's 1939 Golden Gate International Exposition. Fortunately, the principal buildings at the Dallas site of the Texas Centennial Exposition of 1936 still exist, and through them we are afforded a glimpse of the ways in which the legendary expositions of the 1930s derived grandeur and visual excitement from the Art Deco and the Streamline Moderne.

GUIDE TO THE GUIDE

The following selection of Art Deco and Streamline Moderne buildings and monuments is the result of various games that one is inevitably forced to play when compiling such a list. The first, and in many ways the most severe, limitation has to do with the number of buildings and monuments that could be included. There are 500-plus works listed here; the number could just as easily have been 5,000. Although an effort has been made to demonstrate the nationwide occurrence of each style, this was not an entirely simple task. Both Moderne modes were indeed national in their geographic reach, but the principal centers for both styles were the major urban centers: New York, Philadelphia, Chicago, Los Angeles, San Francisco. (New York was and still is the center for Art Deco buildings; Los Angeles emerged in the mid- to late 1930s as the country's Streamline Moderne capital.) Another consideration affecting the choice of examples has to do with providing an indication of the range of building types encountered within each of the Moderne styles. Finally, the author has intentionally ventured into both the rarefied realm of architectural "high style" and the more commonplace world of America's main streets and highways.

The reader should bear in mind that many of the buildings listed are private, and in most cases permission must be obtained before entering them.

NEW ENGLAND

CONNECTICUT

NEW BRITAIN

World War I Memorial

Walnut Hill Park, W. Main Street at
    Lexington Street
1928–32

H. VAN BUREN MAGONIGLE

Each corner of this tapered 12-sided shaft is accentuated by a pair of vertical bands, producing the effect from a distance of a fluted column. Near the top of the shaft are four rows of slightly projecting stars. The culmination of the design is a gigantic eagle, whose wings project upward and back. The shaft occupies the center of a raised circular platform surrounded by a low wall; a pair of open basins stands beside each of the two staircases. Like many Art Deco monuments, this memorial appears most impressive at night, when it is bathed in brilliant light and the details of the great eagle are dramatically emphasized.

World War I Memorial, New Britain, Connecticut.
New Britain Public Library.

Merritt Parkway

Highway 15, especially between
　Norwalk and Greenwich
1934–42

GEORGE DUNKELBERGER; W. THAYER CHASE,
　LANDSCAPE ARCHITECT

A good number of the original bridges over the parkway's pre-1942 section are excellent examples of the late Art Deco, occasionally accompanied by references to the Streamline Moderne. The character of the Art Deco component of these bridges is wonderfully captured in the relief sculpture that occurs on the Milford connector, Milford. This relief depicts a speeding streamlined car passing over one of the Parkway's bridges. With the exception of the River Road overpass in Stratford, the Art Deco/Streamline Moderne decoration of these bridges was realized in cast concrete. Low relief and freestanding sculpture by Edward Ferrari occur on several of the bridges. The parkway was placed on the National Register of Historic Places in 1991.

The most important of the Art Deco/Streamline Moderne–inspired Merritt Parkway bridges are:

Burr Street overpass, Fairfield (relief sculpture by Edward Ferrari)

Comstock Hill overpass, Norwalk (relief sculpture by Edward Ferrari)

East Rocks Road overpass, Norwalk

James Farm Road overpass, Stratford (a pair of six-foot-high Nike wings by Edward Ferrari)

Lapham Road overpass, New Canaan

Long Ridge Road overpass, Stamford

Madison Avenue overpass, Trumbull

Milford connector, Milford

Morehouse Highway overpass, Fairfield

North Avenue overpass, Westport

North Street overpass, Trumbull

River Road underpass, Stratford (elaborate ornament in metal)

Sport Hill Road overpass, Fairfield

MAINE

ELLSWORTH

Grand Theater

167 Main Street
1938

KROKYN AND BROWNE

A stepped gable—a recurring Art Deco theme suggestive of Assyrian or pre-Columbian architecture—provides what amounts to a central tower for this theater, whose design combines elements of the Art Deco and the Streamline Moderne. The rectangular marquee sports the name of the theater in wide, bold, uppercase letters.

MASSACHUSETTS

BOSTON

New England Telephone and Telegraph

6 Bowden Square
1930

DENSMORE, LECLEAR AND ROBBINS

During the late 1920s and on through the 1930s, telephone company buildings across the United States adopted the vertical skyscraper version of the Art Deco for their larger downtown buildings. The 11-story Boston building exhibits the usual stepped-back top, accompanied by curved balconies.

Suffolk County Courthouse

Somerset Street and Ashburton Place
1939

DESMOND & LORD

In the fall of 1939 the editors of the *Architectural Record* conducted polls in several cities as to what were consid-

Suffolk County Courthouse, Boston, Massachusetts. Diana Rhudick, photographer.

First National Bank Building, Northampton, Massachusetts. Massachusetts Historical Commission.

ered the best new buildings. One of the works singled out was the recently completed Suffolk County Courthouse. This 25-story building to some extent carried on the American Vertical skyscraper style of the late 1920s, but this building is both more refined and more delicate than earlier examples, and its abstracted references to the classic tradition are more apparent than in other buildings in this style. The building's four sides project out from the central core of the structure almost as discrete pavilions. The upper section of the building is recessed, and the stepped top section is covered by a low-pitched roof. The vertical bands of metal-frame windows and their spandrels, as well as the exterior ornament, are kept close to the surface of the granite and gray-glazed brick walls. As

with most public buildings of the 1930s, the construction of this courthouse was funded through the Public Works Administration.

NORTHAMPTON

First National Bank Building

1 King Street
1928

J. WILLIAM BEALE & SONS

This two-story building beautifully embodies the delicate sophistication that one associates with the Art Deco. The building's two street facades are essentially sheets of thin stone upon which ornament and fluted pilasters have been drawn. The ornament and the pilasters are slightly recessed into the surface of the stone; the only projections from the surface plane are highly stylized wing-spread eagles at the corners of the parapet. The orna- ment around the central arched opening, above the second-floor windows, and above the pilasters employs motifs derived from the 1925 Paris Exposition of Decorative Arts.

RHODE ISLAND

Pawtucket

City Hall

137 Roosevelt Avenue
1938–39

John F. O'Malley

The Pawtucket City Hall was an early Depression project funded by the PWA. The H-shaped plan of the building is pure Beaux Arts, and the low-pitched gable roof has an almost Colonial Revival feeling. But the Art Deco asserts itself in the lower portion of the build-

Pawtucket City Hall, Pawtucket, Rhode Island. Erik Gould, photographer; Rhode Island Historic Preservation Commission.

ing in the pattern of fluted pilasters and in the row of sculptured plaques above the pilasters. The building's strongest Art Deco statement is its narrow tower, which projects six stories above the building's three-story base. The corners of the tower are contained by slender buttresses; above the buttresses is a sculptural frieze that wraps itself around the tower; higher still are four sculptured eagles, one to each face; and, finally, the tower is surmounted by a stepped pyramid of gleaming stainless steel.

MID-ATLANTIC

DELAWARE

WILMINGTON

Kalmar Nyckel Monument

Fort Christina

7th Street northwest of Church Street

1938

CARL MILLES, SCULPTOR; WHEELWRIGHT &
STEVENSON, LANDSCAPE ARCHITECTS

Kalmar Nyckel Monument, Wilmington, Delaware. *Architectural Forum* (1938).

Working in polished black granite, the sculptor placed a highly stylized rendition of the Swedish ship *Kalmar Nyckel* on top of a shaft. The shaft has concave sides in which bold-relief sculpture is set. The sculptured figures and a plan of Fort Christina float on the surface of the shaft. The ship, with its swelling sails and its abstract depiction of a wave, resembles early 20th-century Surrealist sculpture. Milles's work of the 1930s, like that of Paul Manship and others, lies partly within and partly without the Art Deco/Streamline Moderne sensibility.

DISTRICT OF COLUMBIA

For other Art Deco and Streamline Moderne buildings in and around Washington, D.C., see Hans Wirz and Richard Striner's *Washington Deco* (1984).

Chesapeake and Potomac Telephone Company Building

730 12th Street, N.W.
1928

RALPH T. WALKER (VOORHEES, GMELIN & WALKER)

This New York architecture firm was responsible for several impressive telephone company buildings in the northeastern United States. The firm's designs of the mid- to late 1920s illustrate the manner in which many architects of the period worked toward an abstraction of the classical tradition and sought to enrich basic geometric forms with episodes of rich ornamentation. For the telephone company's Washington offices, the architects turned for inspiration to medieval illuminated manuscripts and to turn-of-the-century European Art Nouveau. Naturalistic, curvilinear patterns of vines and leaves—which occur within the spandrels and as capitals for the pilasters—sometimes spill over onto adjoining surfaces. The ground-floor pilasters play an inventive visual game: their thin vertical shafts suggest at one moment classical fluting and at the next moment elongated medieval clustered colonnettes. On the interior, the green marble walls of the vestibule exhibit a stepped pattern as well as zigzags and sunrays; metal grillework contains a delicate floral motif.

Folger Shakespeare Library

201 E. Capitol Street, S.E.
1930–32

PAUL P. CRET AND ALEXANDER B. TROWBRIDGE

Cret viewed the design of the Folger Shakespeare Library as a step on the road to the "new classicism." He certainly did not think it an example of the Art Deco. Yet, like the work of Bertram G. Goodhue, Cret's designs of the 1920s and 1930s beautifully exhibit the same abstraction of classicism that characterized the principal buildings at the 1925 Paris Exposition of Decorative Arts. In his 1933 article "Ten Years of Modernism," published in the *Architectural Forum,* Cret argued that the contemporary architect should cast aside the decorative elements of the antique and return to a basic "system of structural construction." The Folger Shakespeare Library follows this dictum to a T. While the building is classical in its calm proportions, its smooth undecorated surfaces, reinforced by the narrow recessed band of the parapet, suggest the bridge of a modern ship. Between the fluted piers (which have neither bases nor capitals) and below the windows are rectangular blocks of sculpture (by John Gregory) that read as decoration separate from the building itself. The pairs of griffins that flank the two entrance staircases are set within recessed frames. While Cret may well have been accurate in asserting that the design was classical-inspired, its visual sensibility sets it fully within the Art Deco.

Greyhound Bus Terminal

New York Avenue between 11th and
  12th Streets, N.W.
1939

WILLIAM S. ARRASMITH (WISCHMEYER,
  ARRASMITH & ELSWICK)

Glass doors led from the street to an entrance lobby that in turn flowed into a semicircular waiting room. The waiting room was lighted by a low dome and lantern, supplemented by clerestory windows of glass brick and by glass doors that led out to the bus concourse. Curved walls articulated with horizontal lines and banded windows paid homage to the Streamline Moderne and its evocations of speed. The reinforced-concrete walls of the building were sheathed in buff-colored Indiana limestone, while shimmering black terra-cotta provided a horizontal base and an accent around the entrance. The concourse side of the building boasted a glazed gray-colored brick trimmed with black brick. Like several other bus terminals designed by this firm, the building was planned as a small shopping center that included shops and a restaurant.

After 1976, when the terminal was remodeled and partly hidden behind a mansard roof, the Art Deco Society of Washington took the building on as a cause. In 1990–91 the Washington architecture firm of Keyes Condon Florance Eichbaum Esocoff King restored and incorporated the bus terminal as the lobby of a new high-rise office building at 1100 New York Avenue, N.W. The new building employs some of the hallmarks of the Streamline Moderne—horizontally banded surfaces, curved walls with corner windows—and materials and colors that harmonize with the 1939 terminal.

Greyhound Bus Terminal, Washington, D.C. National Trust for Historic Preservation.

Hecht Company Warehouse

1401 New York Avenue, N.W.
1936–37

ABBOTT, MERKET & COMPANY

Each of the Hecht Company Ware-house's six floors is composed of horizontal bands, and the building's rounded corner reads as the prow of a spaceship. Like many Streamline Moderne buildings, this one works most dramatically at night, when the narrow horizontal bands of pale buff brick appear dark and the intervening glass-brick-and-metal-frame windows become brilliant streaks of light. The most theatrical note occurs at the northwest corner, where the brick bands are like rubber bands holding a glass brick cylinder. At the top of this cylindrical tower, two layers of glass brick assume a pattern of concave surfaces that suggests an abbreviated fluted column. Although openly committed to the popular Streamline Moderne, the Hecht warehouse exhibited enough high-art leanings to be included in the Museum of Modern Art's 1940 publication *Guide to Modern Architecture, Northeast States,* edited by John McAndrews.

Kennedy-Warren Apartment Hotel

3133 Connecticut Avenue, N.W.
1932

JOSEPH YOUNGER

The central tower, characterized by setbacks and a pyramidal roof, is reminiscent of earlier designs by Bertram G. Goodhue, especially his 1922–26 Los Angeles Public Library. The basic composition of the building, with its balanced symmetry and abstracted fluted pilasters, refers to the classical tradition. Much of the ornament, however, looks to pre-Columbian art, to ancient Assyrian architecture, or to the rich ornament of Byzantium. Near the summit of the tower is a pair of griffins in high relief; pairs of eagles surmount the ground-floor windows adjacent to the entrance. Lacelike cast-aluminum grillework surrounds the entrance, whose curved marquee corresponds to the curved bay above. The recessed cast-aluminum spandrel panels of the projecting tower exhibit a hexagonal pattern. In the entrance lobby, solid semicircular piers of marble play off delicate metal railings that contain an Indian pinwheel design

Hecht Company Warehouse, Washington, D.C. *Pencil Points.*

and the popular Art Deco motif of paired spirals centered on an open sunflower.

Majestic Apartments

3200 16th Street, N.W.
1937
ALVIN AUBINOE AND HARRY L. EDWARDS

The dominant note of this eight-story U-shaped apartment building is sound-ed by the elongated bays that project toward the street from each of the arms. The Streamline Moderne effect created by these bays, the corner windows, and the glass-brick-enclosed metal entrance is offset by Art Deco vertical ribs that penetrate the uppermost parapets. The exterior walls are sheathed in light-colored brick with accents of stone and metal. Farther down 16th Street, at 1530, are the High Tower Apartments (1927), another eight-story building designed by Aubinoe that combines elements of the Art Deco and the Streamline Moderne.

MARYLAND

BALTIMORE

For other Art Deco and Streamline Moderne buildings in Baltimore see Sheryle R. Cucchiella's *Baltimore Deco* (1984).

Church of Saint Katherine of Sienna

1222 N. Luzerbe Avenue
1933
HENRY D. DAGIT & SONS

At the end of the 1920s and on into the 1930s, various dioceses of the Roman Catholic Church openly encouraged innovative architecture, ornament, and art. The Philadelphia firm responsible for this church had begun in the late 1890s to design a wide variety of church buildings. (The senior Dagit died in 1929, so this design was the work of his three sons, Henry D., Jr., Alfred F., and Charles E.) The church exhibits the principal elements of the Italian Romanesque—a corbeled gable front with a rose window and groups of arched windows—but these elements have been abstracted. The blue, gray, and tan stone walls are treated as interlocking planes, and the fenestration is kept close to the surface. Near the entrance three carved figures emerge from the smooth cut stone, and the lettering and ornament are almost linear in quality.

On the interior, a mildly Goodhue-esque approach is taken. The walls provide a neutral backdrop for the polychrome painted roof trusses, the glass mosaic stations of the cross, and the primarily red-and-blue central altar panel. The suspended cylindrical light fixtures of polished aluminum have gleaming winglike ribs, and the stone floor of the nave exhibits an almost Mondrian-like pattern. The red-and-blue stained glass windows, which contain faintly Art Deco motifs, were designed by Henry Lee Willett.

Church of Saint Katherine of Sienna, Baltimore, Maryland. *American Architect* (1934).

Hutzler Brothers Department Store

212 N. Howard Street
1931–32

JAMES R. EDMUNDS, JR.

Three pairs of vertical bands ascend the full eight stories to the parapet. The spandrels between these bands are sheathed in glazed black brick that strongly contrasts with the adjacent surfaces of light red brick. The entrances occur on either side of the building's polished black granite base. These entrances are emphasized by deeply recessed two-story windows, above which are located the building's vertical signs. The two entrances are recessed within the black granite base, and above their revolving doors is abundant Art Deco ornament. The store's original interiors remain largely intact.

Maryland National Bank Building

Baltimore Street at Light Street,
    northeast corner
1929

TAYLOR & FISHER; SMITH & MAY

Like many other skyscrapers of the late 1920s, this 500-foot-high building conveys an Art Deco sensibility via its rich borrowing of forms and decoration from the past. The building's high-pitched hipped roof might be seen as derived from the French Chateauesque tradition or as resembling a pre-Columbian temple platform. Other details, such as the tall arched windows and the grouping of colonnettes, seem medieval (Byzantine, Romanesque, or Gothic). The buttresses of the building's central tower project above the parapet, and from a distance they sug-

gest the prows of a Viking ship. The richly decorated entrances and interiors reveal a play of classical, medieval, and Art Deco motifs.

Pikes Theater

1001 Riverstone Road
1937

JOHN F. EYRING

The upper portion of the theater exhibits rounded corners that are strongly emphasized by parallel bands of dark brick. A central pavilion with its large glass-brick window slightly projects forward at the center; below the glass brick window is the marquee, whose sides curve upwards. The lower part of the facade, containing the ticket booth, entrance doors, and advertising windows, is sheathed in dark Vitrolite. Eyring also designed other Art Deco/Streamline Moderne theaters in Baltimore, including the Earle Theater (1937) at 4847 Belair Road and the Uptown Theater (1941) at 5010 Park Heights Avenue.

Senator Theater

5904 York Road
1939

JOHN J. ZINK (ZINK, ATKINS & CRAYCROFT)

The Art Deco, brought up to date by occasional references to the Streamline Moderne, was frequently employed in the design of motion picture theaters in the 1930s. The front facade of this theater assumes a classic Art Deco pose: a segmented bay is held in place at each side by a heavy pierlike member. In contrast, the cladding of the upper portion of the building in white stucco, the use of glass bricks for the bay windows, and the narrow windows within the buttresses are hallmarks of the Streamline Moderne. The circular two-story lobby and the theater proper are almost pure Art Deco. The mural by Paul M. Roche on the upper walls of the lobby is entitled *The Progress of Visual Entertainment.* Zink designed some 200 motion picture theaters. His other theaters in the Baltimore area include the Ambassador Theater (1935) at 4604 Liberty Heights Road and the Colony Theater (1949) at 8123 Harford Road. Several of Zink's theaters in Washington, D.C., have also survived, among them the Uptown (1936) at 3426 Connecticut Avenue, N.W.

White Tower

Erdman Avenue at Belair Road
1945, 1948

CHARLES J. JOHNSON

The earliest White Tower hamburger shops—circa 1926—were shimmering white Art Deco castles (see Paul Hirshorn and Steven Izenour's 1979 book *White Towers*). By the late 1930s, the restaurants had assumed a Streamline Moderne image. After World War II, as the design of this particular White Tower suggests, the Streamline had been made less insistent. Projecting lights brilliantly illuminate the white porcelain walls of the structure, and through the broad windows one can see the interior counter and displays of food.

CAMBRIDGE

Cambridge Yacht Club

South shore of the Lower Choptank
    River
1938

VICTORINE AND SAMUEL HOMSEY

In the 1930s the ideal image for a yacht club was a Streamline Moderne ship. As the editors of the *Architectural Forum* indicated in an article on this building published in October 1938, "Inside as well as out, by night as well as day, resemblance to a ship afloat is

Cambridge Yacht Club, Cambridge, Maryland. *Architectural Forum* (1938).

architecturally maintained." Within the T-shaped plan, the lounge projects out as the curved prow of a ship; above is the bridge, bordered by a nautical metal railing. Round portholes, together with a thin canopy supported by metal pipes, complete the composition. As in other designs by the Homseys, the architects here took the idiom of the Streamline Moderne into the realm of high-art modernism.

CATONSVILLE

Melvin Avenue Reservoir

Melvin Avenue

1937–38

This brick cylinder with stone trim contains a four-million-gallon steel water tank. An Art Deco theme is asserted by the rhythmic pattern of the limestone buttresses, which terminate below the entablature/cornice in a stepped pattern suggesting capitals. The strongest Art Deco element of the structure is the horizontal band of deeply cut zigzags around the entablature/cornice. At the base, the small entrance door is treated monumentally; pilasters at either side support a V-shaped lintel.

GREENBELT

Greenbelt Center Elementary School and Community Building

Crescent Road

1936–37

DOUGLAS D. ELLINGTON AND REGINALD D.
    WADSWORTH

The architects of this brick-sheathed white-painted school would appear, as Hans Wirz and Richard Striner have pointed out in their book

Washington Deco (1984), to have looked carefully at Paul P. Cret's Folger Shakespeare Library as a source for their design, but they have moved it one or two steps further toward the Streamline Moderne. The scale of their building, its painted-brick surfaces, and its details transformed Cret's library into a more informal structure. The fluted piers of the school's buttresses, with their angled tops, and the building's two lower wings (one of which houses the entrance) are almost domestic in scale. As in Cret's library, sculptured panels appear below the windows— in this case, below the bank of five large windows that admit light to the combined auditorium and gymnasium. The high-relief sculpture within these panels (works by Lenore Thomas depicting aspects of the preamble to the Constitution) display the primitive childlike quality associated with American Scene painting of these years. The two-story classroom wing to the west contains stairways lighted by vertical bands of glass brick. In addition to this school and the middle school, Ellington and Wadsworth designed most of the original buildings of Greenbelt, the first of the New Deal towns of the mid-1930s.

WHEATON

WTOP (WJSV) Radio Transmission Station

2021 University Boulevard

1939

E. BURTON CORNING

As a reflection of their technological sophistication, radio stations and facilities for radio transmission built in the 1930s often assumed a Streamline

Moderne image. For this station, the architect composed a series of ascending white stucco volumes whose horizontality is emphasized by bands of glass-brick windows. The highest volume of this two-story building curves dramatically at one end; the intermediate volume, with its single curved end, cantilevers out over the entrance and is in part supported by two round metal columns. The reference in this design is to International Style modernism transformed into a streamlined object.

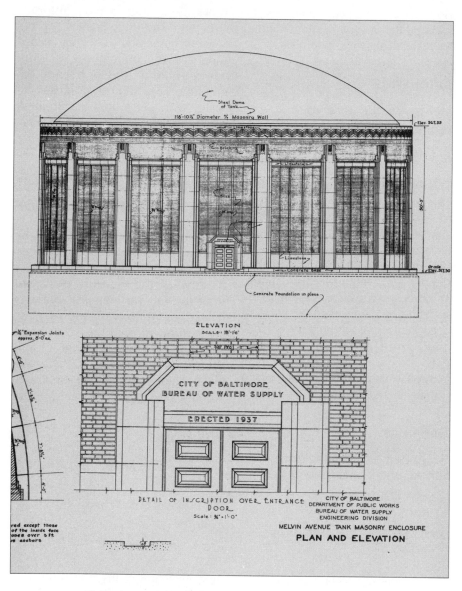

Melvin Avenue Reservoir, Catonsville, Maryland. City of Baltimore.

NEW JERSEY

MENLO PARK

Edison Tower

Wood Avenue north of Lincoln
  Highway (Highway #27)
1937

GABRIEL MASSENA (MASSENA & DU PONT);
  JOHN J. EARLEY, SCULPTOR

The Edison Tower is located on the site where Thomas A. Edison produced the first practical incandescent bulb. A steel-framed tower was built in 1929 to commemorate the site, and in 1937 the present tower replaced the original structure. Like many Art Deco monuments, the Edison Tower is essentially an abstracted tapered shaft. The shaft, rising 118 feet, is articulated by vertical buttresses that curve inward as they ascend, forming a base for the gigantic replica (in Pyrex) of the first incandescent light bulb. At ground level a speaker grille of cast concrete projects from each of the eight buttresses. The tower itself is built of concrete and sheathed in precast concrete panels with a high degree of quartz aggregate. The panels are a dark buff color near the ground and fade toward white at the top of the shaft. Inside the tower is the "Eternal Light Room," which houses a lighted replica of Edison's original 1879 bulb. Above this room is the Amplifier Room, from which sound is broadcast through the eight speakers. During daylight hours the soaring quality of the ribs is emphasized by intervening deeply cut shadows. At night the effect is reversed, with the recessed spaces lighted by floodlights and the faces of the ribs reading as dark upward-thrusting bands.

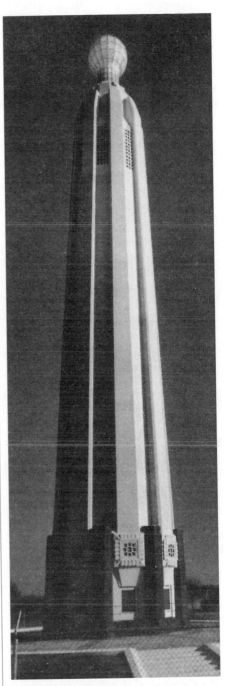

Edison Tower, Menlo Park, New Jersey.
Architectural Concrete (1938).

NEW YORK

ALBANY

Home Savings Bank Building

N. Pearl Street and James Street
1927

DENNISON & HIRONS

Though narrow, this building asserts its presence both at the street level and in its roofscape. Above the deeply recessed entrance is a large-scale model of an 18th-century galleon. Rich patterns of Art Deco ornament—spirals, leaves, flowers in terra-cotta—occur as capitals on pilasters, as lintels over the windows, and in a horizontal band between windows on the second floor. At the top of the building, a band between windows contains images of Indians and Euro-pean explorers realized in orange, blue, black, and green glazed terra-cotta.

BUFFALO

Buffalo City Hall

65 Niagara Square
1929–31

GEORGE J. DIETEL AND JOHN J. WADE;
    SULLIVAN W. JONES

The sculptural and monumental quality of works by Bertram G. Goodhue seems combined in this building with Hugh Ferriss's vision of the skyscraper's essential image. The central 28-story tower is terminated by a modern version of a drum and dome. Projecting forward on either side of the tower is a 14-story wing; between the wings, at ground level, is a 3-story portico consisting of 8 columns that support a lintel bearing a frieze of high-relief sculpture.

This Art Deco sculpture is by Albert T. Stewart; René Chambellan designed the remaining exterior and interior sculpture. The murals in the lobby, which depict scenes from local history, are by William de Leftwich Dodge.

New York Central Railroad Terminal

Memorial Drive at Paderewski Drive
1929

FELLHEIMER & WAGNER

This 17-story tower, with its truncated corners and tiered setbacks, appears to be an Art Deco version of Howells and Hood's 1922–24 Chicago Tribune Tower. The building also recalls Eliel Saarinen's 1904–13 railroad station in Helsinki, Finland. The architects of this railroad terminal markedly increased the scale of Saarinen's building, but they retained the barrel vaults and great semicircular windows, the vertical arrangement of the fenestration, and the suggestion of buttresses.

Vars Building

344–352 Delaware Avenue
1929

BLEY & LYMAN

This four-story structural open-cage building asserts its smartness via its Art Deco ornament. The vertical piers pose as fluted pilasters. Above these are abstracted volutes set within a band of low-relief sculpture. Additional ornament occurs on the vertical and horizontal members of the second- and third-floor windows and at the top of the building.

City Hall, Buffalo, New York. Buffalo & Erie County Historical Society.

NEW YORK CITY: MANHATTAN

In the 1920s and on into the 1930s, New York was the epitome of the 20th-century metropolis. Although innovative and impressive examples of Art Deco occurred across the country, New York became the undisputed center for the "smart" Art Deco style. The Empire State Building, the Chrysler Building, and the Rockefeller Center complex were the stylesetters of their time, and even today our view of the Art Deco conjures up these and other New York monuments of the style. Within New York City examples of the Art Deco abound, not only in major monuments but also in literally hundreds of small buildings, shops, and apartment houses.

New York City was not, however, the center for the Streamline Moderne; that honor goes to Los Angeles. New York did, of course, make its commitment to the Streamline in the World's Fair of 1939, but the buildings that housed this exposition have not survived. Most of the storefronts throughout the city that were remodeled in the Streamline Moderne style in the Depression years of the 1930s have also disappeared.

Listed here are only a few of New York City's major Art Deco monuments. Anyone who wishes to sample the city's rich Art Deco heritage should consult such volumes as Cervin Robinson and Rosemarie Haag Bletter's *Skyscraper Style: Art Deco New York* (1975), the special edition of *Architecture and Urbanism* entitled "New York Art Deco Skyscrapers" (1987); and Carla Breeze's *New York Deco* (1993).

American Radiator Building

40 W. 40th Street
1924

RAYMOND M. HOOD

Hood's name, more than that of any other architect, is closely associated with the passion for skyscrapers as the surpassing achievement of American civilization. During the 1920s and early

American Radiator Building, New York, New York.

1930s Hood shifted from one architectural style to another with great rapidity: from the Gothic mode of the 1922–24 Chicago Tribune Tower (with John Mead Howells) to the Streamline Moderne in the McGraw-Hill Building of 1931 in New York City. The American Radiator Building was a midway point, still somewhat Gothic but with Art Deco overtones. Hood conceived this small (for New York) 20-story building as a freestanding tower that steps back to its final open crown. The facades are treated in a perpendicular fashion, but it is above all the tower's massing that emphasizes verticality. At the ground level large windows provide views into the building from the street. The entrance itself is Gothic, as are the sculptured brackets that support the false cornice above the second floor. What attracted the most attention at the time the building was constructed was Hood's original and provocative use of color on the exterior. The building is clad in black brick, with polished black granite at its base. Most of the detailing is in highly contrasting gold terra-cotta, and against the black background the gold gleams mysteriously at night when the upper reaches of the tower are illuminated.

Barclay-Vesey Telephone Building

140 West Street
1923–26

RALPH T. WALKER (MCKENZIE, VOORHEES, GMELIN & WALKER)

The Barclay-Vesey Telephone Building is an immense brick pile that is on its way to the Art Deco. The building emphasizes the vertical via the typical Art Deco arrangement of pilasters and recessed window-and-spandrel panels, but its verticality is really only lukewarm. The program of ornament, which in design is highly original, is generally based upon plant, flower, animal, seashell, and occasionally human forms, not classical but not really classic Art Deco either. Ornament of a similar nature, located around entrances and on facades, would emerge within a year or two as a hallmark of the new skyscraper style known as the American Vertical. The architect, Ralph T. Walker, wrote in *American Architect:* "In sharp contrast with the vertical rigidity of the buff brick piers of the Telephone Building the ornamental stonework is carved with a free and flowing ornament so designed to be an integral part of the wall it decorates. . . . The ornament of a skyscraper should be so complicated in its structure as not to be readily apparent; it should be hidden as the steel structure itself."

Barclay-Vesey Telephone Building, New York, New York. *The American Architect* (1936).

Chanin Building

122 E. 42nd Street
1927–29

SLOAN & ROBERTSON; IRWIN S. CHANIN; JACQUES L. DELAMARRE; RENÉ PAUL CHAMBELLAN, SCULPTOR

The fame of this 56-story building rests on its "cubist" mass, its buttressed crown, and the absolutely lush ornament at its base and on its interior. At the level of the fourth floor is one of the building's unique and outstanding features: a band of intertwined spirals, leaves, flowers, and semicircles. Much of the decoration in the lobby and throughout the building was designed by René Chambellan and Jacques Delamarre.

Chrysler Building

405 Lexington Avenue
1930

WILLIAM VAN ALEN

The Chrysler Building is the skyscraper that people most frequently associate with the Art Deco style. For a matter of months the building, which rises 1,046 feet, was the world's tallest structure (it lost its preeminence in this regard to the Empire State Building). Although in its early years the Chrysler Building was highly regarded by the middle-class American public, many architects remained ambivalent. In 1930 Kenneth M. Murchison wrote in *American Architect:* "The Chrysler Building has probably earned more publicity during its short but lurid career than even its own instigators hoped for. And as it is a commercial proposition, embodying the emblazonment of automotive progress, why should the architect have hesitated a moment in being the Ziegfield of his profession and glorifying American mechanical genius and incidentally, Mr. Chrysler's output of cars, trucks and boats?"

The program for ornamenting the building takes a number of different directions: from the stepped, stainless-steel, perfume-bottle top to abstracted automobile parts to near-cubist patterns of wall, ceiling, and floor surfaces. The building's well-known metal top, the "vortex," was an afterthought, appended at the last moment to add 180 feet and make the building as tall as possible. As Murchison observed, "Like a glistening mirror, the brilliant metal of the tower catches the rays of the sun and is visible for many miles."

Chrysler Building, New York, New York.

Daily News Building

220 E. 42nd Street
1929–30

HOWELLS & HOOD

In 1928 John Mead Howells set forth in the pages of *American Architect* an argument for the American Vertical style: "The simple composition of verticals, which some like to call modernistic, seems to me 'indicated', as the doctors say, for the design of steel cage buildings. . . . First, the verticals are accentuated just as in the steel cage itself. . . . Second, the grouping of vertical lines holds the windows in place naturally in the composition. . . . Third, the verticals can terminate naturally against the sky. . . . in the same way that a growth of pine trees or a palisade or cliff ends up against the sky." Howells & Hood's Daily News Building expresses this full commitment to the vertical. The vertical bands of masonry are simply that; they do not contain even the slightest hint of pilasters or buttresses. The ingenious setbacks allowed the building to assume the form of a free-standing tower. The minimal ornament takes typical Art Deco motifs and abstracts them even further. The entrance frontispiece (by René Paul Chambellan) with its linear sculpture, together with the central globe and other features of the lobby, take one from the Art Deco to the Streamline Moderne.

Empire State Building

350 5th Avenue
1930–31

WILLIAM LAMB (SHREVE, LAMB & HARMON); INTERIORS BY B. ALTMAN AND COMPANY

Following its completion in 1931, the Empire State Building was for four

Empire State Building, New York, New York.

decades the world's tallest building (102 stories, rising a total of 1,250 feet). Although the building is indeed tall, its fenestration (in vertical bands that are kept very shallow) does not emphasize the building's height. The street entrances are sophisticated but not grand. The best parts of the interior are the metal bridges crossing over at a second level (echoing in small scale the layered streets and pedestrian ways depicted in the drawings of Hugh Ferriss). The building's most assertive element is its metal crown, with a symbolic dirigible mooring that can be seen from far and wide. At nighttime the building's upper floors are bathed in brilliant colored light.

Film Center Building

630 9th Avenue
1928–29

ELY KAHN (BUCKMAN & KAHN)

Unquestionably, the lobby of this skyscraper is a must to visit. While the feeling of the space is Art Deco, especially in the elegant use of metals and polished stone, its forms seem derived from one of H. G. Wells's science fiction

stories. Sections of the ceilings are stepped up, and a vertical band of polished red stone cylinders (perhaps some type of symbolic control knobs?) project out of the elevator walls. The elevator doors are framed by fluted pilasters that support a thin metal shelf; below is a motif of six red cylinder knobs. The elevator doors exhibit an elaborate geometric pattern, and at one end of the lobby a stone mosaic embraces the elevator call-button panel.

Film Center Building, New York, New York.
Architectural Record (1929).

Fuller Building

41 E. 57th Street
1928–29

WALKER & GILLETTE

The exterior surfaces of this towered building are relatively plain except for its top and its ground floor. The stepped-back upper stories exhibit a sharp angled pattern of horizontal bands, zigzags, triangles, and stars. These designs are realized in black and white stone. The tall entrance at the base of the building has vertical lines suggesting the flutes of a column. The capitals are a row of elongated triangles. Above the name of the building in low relief is a miniature cityscape of skyscrapers. In front of this cityscape are two male figures by the sculptor Elie Nadelman.

Solomon R. Guggenheim Museum

5th Avenue, between 88th and 89th
  Streets
1942–59

FRANK LLOYD WRIGHT

None of Wright's buildings easily fit into the modes current at the time of their design, yet each of his buildings always ends up entailing what was the latest fashion of the moment. His turn-of-the-century Prairie houses reflect the then-prevalent Arts and Crafts movement, while his pre-Columbian designs for Arizona and California mirror the widely admired Period Revivalism of the decades of the 1910's and 1920's. The Guggenheim Museum is no exception to Wright's continued reflection of his times. Along with the Johnson Wax Company building at Racine, Wisconsin, and such later buildings as the Annunciation Greek Orthodox Church at Wauwatosa, Wisconsin, and the Marvin County Civic Center at San Raphael, California, the Guggenheim Musuem provides an ending note to the Streamline Moderne fashion of the late 1930s and early 1940s. Its dramatic exterior spiral form and its interior balconied space convey the atmosphere one associates with the 1930's science fiction covers of Frank R. Paul for the magazine *Amazing Stories*. The image

of the streamlined ocean liner is conveyed in the Guggenheim Museum by the bridge-like form of the circular administrative offices and is reinforced by the large porthole windows. As with many of Wright's designs, the strongest design element was first used in a much earlier, unrealized project: the spiral ramp appeared in the 1925 Gordon Strong Planetarium on Sugar Loaf Mountain, Maryland.

Lescaze House

211 E. 48th Street
1934

WILLIAM LESCAZE

Lescaze continually wavered between the Streamline Moderne and International Style modernism. His own town house strongly tends toward the Streamline Moderne, particularly with its curved wall leading one's eyes toward the entrance and in its extensive use of glass brick.

Lowell Apartments

28 E. 63rd Street
1926

HENRY S. CHURCHILL AND HERBERT LIPPMANN

The glory of this modest brick-clad apartment building is its entrance. The doors are encased in polished stone, and to each side are stylized pilasters. Mounted on the face of the pilasters are long narrow lights whose surface is like that of overlaid leaves. Swelling out from the red terra-cotta surface above the entrance is a bold double spiral. Below this is a brightly colored hexagonal mosaic panel by Bertram Hartman on which a skyscraper is hidden behind trees.

McGraw-Hill Building

330 W. 42nd Street
1931

RAYMOND M. HOOD; GODLEY & FOUILHOUX

As in his Beaux-Arts apartment build-ing (1930) at 307–310 E. 44th Street, Hood here turned from American Vertical perpendicularity to the hori-zontality of International Style mod-ernism and the Streamline Moderne. The horizontal bands of the building are established by the windows; the intervening surfaces are clad in glazed blue-green tile. The entire structure comes close to being a horizontally grooved base for a large (also horizon-tally oriented) sign atop the building. The massing, which consists of four receding volumes plus a crown, almost gives the impression of discrete struc-tures. The theme of the Streamline Moderne is effectively carried out in the lines of the roof sign and also in the wonderful banding around the en-trance and along the walls of the lobby.

New School for Social Research

66 W. 12th Street
1929–30

JOSEPH URBAN

Urban was one of a small group of central Europeans who introduced modernism into this country after World War I. Influences evident in his work range from Viennese

McGraw-Hill Building, New York, New York. Raymond Hood, photogra-pher; *Contemporary American Architects* (1931).

Secessionism to the Art Deco to various Mediterranean styles. In the New School for Social Research he combined elements of International Style modernism and the Streamline Moderne. The street facade of the building contains a rectangular six-story bay articulated by bands of wraparound windows and horizontally grooved spandrels. The curve also asserts itself inside the building, especially in the auditorium. The wonderful space-age auditorium has recently been restored (1994).

Panhellenic Tower, New York, New York. *The Book of the Boston Architectural Club for 1929.*

Panhellenic Tower

Northeast corner of 1st Avenue at 49th
  Street
1928

JOHN MEAD HOWELLS

In its early years the Panhellenic Tower
was often invoked as an example of the
emerging American Vertical skyscraper
style. The pilasters appear almost as
buttresses, with the intervening window-and-spandrel sections sunk
deeply into the building. The pilasters
are themselves recessed relative to the
solid angled corner blocks. The walls of
the building rise from the street without any setbacks until they reach the
series of stepped volumes that comprise the upper floors. There is sparse
terra-cotta ornament on the lower
three floors and near the top; otherwise
the building establishes its character
solely through its play of orange-
brick–sheathed volumes.

RCA Victor Building (later the General Electric Building)

570 Lexington Avenue
1931

CROSS & CROSS

This skyscraper, which culminates in a
freestanding tower, strongly asserts its
presence via its terra-cotta ornament.
The theme of electricity is conveyed in
radiating zigzag lines that flow across
the ground-floor wall surfaces, as well
as across the spandrels. Near street
level is an angled stepped pier that terminates in a clock face. The crown of
the building, its unquestionable focal
point, entails an open work of terra-
cotta that represents electricity. The
building assumes its most dramatic
pose when its exterior is illuminated at
night.

Rockefeller Center

For more information about the art and
architecture of Rockefeller Center see
Carol Herselle Krinsky's *Rockefeller
Center* (1978).

  Associated Press Building
  British Empire Building
  International Building
  Maison Française Building
  Palazzo D'Italia Building
  Radio City Music Hall
  RCA Building
  Time-Life Building
  United States Rubber Company
    Building

5th Avenue between W. 48th and W.
  51st Streets
1931–40

REINHARD & HOFMEISTER; CORBETT, HARRISON
  & MACMURRAY; HOOD & FOUILHOUX

The first of the pre–World War II buildings of Rockefeller Center do not fit
with ease into either the Art Deco or
the Streamline Moderne, and they certainly are not International Style. If they
have any point of strong similarity to
other images of the 1930s, it is with the
PWA Moderne. The individual low-rise
and slab skyscrapers (as they were
referred to in the 1930s) that make up
Rockefeller Center were meant to be
read as monumental pieces of
masonry, something they admirably
succeed in accomplishing. They have a
feeling of traditional permanence that
one can experience as strongly today
as when the buildings were new; at the
same time, however, they asked their
audience in the 1930s to respond to
them as modern.

  The light touch of verticality of
their walls is similar to the Chrysler
Building, but they become much more
vertical with their composition of
ascending slabs and thinness of profile.

Within Rockefeller Center there are variations in imagery: the RCA Building and the smaller Maison Française and British Empire Buildings exhibit Art Deco tendencies in their fenestration and their use of sculpture, whereas the Radio City Music Hall (especially the interiors by Donald Deskey) moves over to the Streamline. The (original) Time-Life Building and the Associated Press Building come close to reading as PWA Moderne structure. An impressive array of artists associated with the Art Deco and the Streamline Moderne were involved with this project: Lee Lawrie, René Chambellan, Paul Manship, Carl Milles, Leo Friedlander, Gaston Lachaise, Isamu Noguchi, Margaret Bourke-White, and Diego Rivera (whose *Man at the Crossroads* has been removed from the lobby of the RCA Building. The buildings have been kept in excellent repair, and most of the sculpture still gleams as it did originally. The Rainbow Room within the RCA Building was restored in 1985.

RCA Victor Building, New York, New York.

RCA Building, Rockefeller Center, New York, New York. *Architectural Forum* (1933).

60 Wall Street Tower

60 Wall Street
1930–32

CLINTON & RUSSELL, HOLTON & GEORGE

One does not even have to step back to take in this American Vertical–style skyscraper (built for the City Services Corporation), for a large model of the building greets the visitor inside the lobby. The model both portrays the building and serves as decoration in the form of an obelisk. The pattern of ornament is quite unusual, combining classical motifs such as the Ionic column with Art Deco zigzags, triangles, and sunbursts. The stepped summit of the building is exuberant, with ornamental metal grillework and a glass pinnacle.

Two Park Avenue Building

2 Park Avenue, between 32nd and
33rd Streets
1927

JACQUES KAHN

The exterior is sheathed in horizontal bands of cream, red, and blue-green terra-cotta, which are played off against areas of brick. The ornamentation is agressively sharp and angular, almost primitive in nature. The interior is richly decorated, though in a more delicate fashion.

United States Post Office, Madison Square Station

149 E. 23rd Street
1936

LORMIER RICH AND LOUIS A. SIMON

This small midblock post office is one of the most elegant examples of the PWA Moderne. Its street face is a sheet of gleaming, polished, mahogany-colored granite. Cut into this face is a central five-bay portico, at the ends of which are small doors. The piers between the bays maintain the wall plane and bear only a slight suggestion of molded capitals. Above the lintel is a single molding, and the cap of the parapet has a single line hinting at a cornice. The two rows of letters above the central cornice are incised into the granite surface and then painted in gold leaf. The metal spandrels above the recessed bays feature cast-iron sculpture. The three central works are by Edmund Amateis; those to either side are by Louis Slobodkin. In the lobby are eight murals by Kindred McLeary depicting New York City street life.

U.S. Post Office, Madison Square Station, New York, New York. *Architectural Forum* (1941).

NEW YORK CITY: BROOKLYN

Ingersall Memorial, Brooklyn Public Library

Grand Army Plaza at Flatbush Avenue and Eastern Parkway
1941

GITHENS AND KEALLY; C. PAUL JENNEWEIN AND THOMAS H. JONES, SCULPTORS

The modernity of the Streamline Moderne is here rendered through the refinement one associates with the Regency Revival of the 1930s. The entrance poses as a rectangular cutout that penetrates the plain undecorated wall. Within the recessed entrance rectangle are a pair of columns covered by gilded bas relief figures by C. Paul Jennewein. The metal screen above the doors, with figures and Art Deco motifs, is by Thomas H. Jones.

United States Army Supply Base

End of 58th Street to 65th Street, facing Upper New York Bay
1918

CASS GILBERT

This row of immense eight-story reinforced-concrete warehouses helped to set the stage for the American Vertical

U.S. Army Supply Base, Brooklyn, New York. *The Book of the Boston Architectural Club for 1929.*

skyscraper style that emerged in the mid-1920s. Gilbert took a number of the lessons that he had learned in designing the Woolworth Building (1913) and applied them to these utilitarian structures. The facades exhibit a pattern of narrow and wide piers, pilasters, and pavilions set between massive corner blocks. The U.S. Army Supply Base was often invoked in the 1920s as a prototype for the development of a new architecture as, in a sense, it turned out to be.

NEW YORK CITY: QUEENS

Church of the Most Precious Blood

32–30 37th Street north of Broadway, Astoria
1932

HENRY J. MCGILL (MCGILL AND HAMLIN)

In the late 1920s and early 1930s the New York architect Henry J. McGill designed a number of Roman Catholic churches that reveal a highly imaginative interpretation of the Art Deco. The scheme of this church is traditional, a sanctuary with a high gabled roof accompanied by a freestanding campanile, but the abstract approach to the volumes and the treatment of their surfaces, fenestration, and ornament are distinctly Moderne. The exterior of the church is smooth cut granite; the openings are simply and sharply incised into the stone. The octagonal campanile terminates in an aluminum drum decorated with a highly abstracted peacock pattern. The interior of the sanctuary forcefully carries on the Art Deco theme in metal, terracotta, and colored glass. The stations of the cross, occupying panels beneath the windows, were designed by

Church of the Most Precious Blood, Queens, New York. *American Architect* (1932).

D. Dunbar Beck. The sculpture, which employs Art Deco motifs, is by Hazel Clere. The suspended light fixtures appear to be miniaturized Chrysler Buildings; the bright chrome wall fixtures and sanctuary lamp are akin to what one would expect to find inside an expensive Art Deco penthouse apartment. Another McGill Art Deco church is the Blessed Sacrament Church located on 35th Avenue in Queens. The first part of this church was designed in 1933 in association with Talbot Hamlin. McGill later added to the church complex in 1937 and 1949.

NEW YORK CITY: STATEN ISLAND

The Healy Mausoleum

Oceanview Cemetery

Amboy Road at Hopkins Avenue, northwest corner (between Richmond and Great Kills)

1929

ARTHUR K. HEALY

The Healy Mausoleum is a highly abstract version of the Art Deco. Its basic form is that of a solid rectangular volume, with chamfered corners and a two-tiered recessed top. Quartered

The Healy Mausoleum, Oceanview Cemetery, Staten Island, New York. *Architectural Forum* (1930).

fluted columns flank the recessed entry, with its sculptured bronze doors. The relief sculpture on the doors displays a pair of angels standing at the base of a cross.

ROCHESTER

Ashbury Methodist Church

1040 East Avenue
1952–55

A. HENSEL FINK

The Art Deco architect's preoccupation with abstracting traditional forms continued into the years after World War II. The design of this stone-clad Gothic church by a Philadelphia architect reflects the approach that Goodhue and others might have taken in the 1920s. The linear complexity that one associates with the Gothic results here in sharp rectangular volumes. Gothic tracery occurs as decoration throughout the building, just as Art Deco ornament would have been used. The

commanding, 150-foot high entrance tower accomplishes a series of setbacks; the lantern and spire are turned at a 45-degree angle, thus emphasizing their open-work corner buttresses.

Gustaf Fassin House

217 Wisner Road (Irondequoit)
1939

GUSTAF FASSIN

The Streamline Moderne reaches near perfection in this stucco-sheathed two-story concrete block house. Horizontal banding and horizontally oriented windows, with their strong suggestion of speed, characterize the design. A low curved wall leads toward the entrance, and a circular staircase is housed in a curved glass-brick bay. The Streamline Moderne's nautical theme crops up in porthole windows as well as metal ship's railings and ladders. The living room centers on a blue Vitrolite fireplace surround, which is accented with built-in red and blue lights. The house was designed by an industrial engineer who worked for the Bausch and Lomb Company.

Fire Academy Building, Rochester Fire Department Headquarters

185 North Street
1936

JOSEPH FLYNN

The narrow entrance end of this two-story Art Deco structure presents an effective programmatic frontispiece. Two helmeted firefighters with their heads tilted slightly toward the door emerge from the stone screen in char-

Gustaf Fassin Residence, Rochester, New York. Landmark Society of Western New York.

Fire Academy Building, Rochester Fire Department Headquarters, Rochester, New York. Ira Srole, City of Rochester, 1984.

acteristic Goodhue-esque fashion. The expressions on the faces hint that these figures are exhausted, having just returned from fighting a fire. Thin, slightly tapered shafts that protrude upward frame the three sets of signage and the second-floor window. Below the window is a horizontal band containing the wheels of a firetruck.

Genessee Valley Trust Company Building (now the Times Square Building)

Exchange Street at Broad Street, northwest corner
1929

RALPH T. WALKER (VOORHEES, GMELIN, & WALKER)

Rows of projecting and receding piers place this 19-story building squarely within the American Vertical skyscraper style of the late 1920s. The building's fame, however, rests in its tower, with its sculptured *Wings of Progress*: four upward-projecting wings, 42 feet high and manufactured of cast aluminum. Behind the patterned aluminum grille at the center of the tower are spotlights that dramatically illuminate the wings. The effect, especially at night, is that of an elegant René Lalique perfume bottle.

Hallman's Chevrolet Building

200 East Avenue
1936

JOHN TRIEPEL

In 1936 the Buffalo architect John Triepel remodeled a 1911 brick building into this impressive example of the

Genessee Valley Trust Company Building, Rochester, New York. Ira Srole, City of Rochester.

Streamline Moderne. He sheathed much of the building in black Carrara glass, which stands in sharp contrast to the stainless steel pilasters and other details. The dominant note of the design is the curve, present in the quarter-curve corner and the large half-circle display window. The metal pilasters are fluted, and instead of having capitals they exhibit semicircular metal housing for lights (which shine down and accentuate the flutes of the pilasters). Projecting above the curved corner of the building is a neon-lighted metal clock on which letters spelling out "Superservice" are substituted for numbers. Much of the large showroom remains intact, including a fireplace encased in Carrara glass.

Hallman's Chevrolet Building, Rochester, New York. Ira Srole, City of Rochester.

"Jalna" House

2331 Westfall Road

c. 1940

The street facade of this two-story stucco-sheathed house presents a symmetrical Art Deco composition. The entrance with its canopy and the window above it are contained within a U-shaped frame; over the window is a horizontal band exhibiting a zigzag pattern. The pairs of first- and second-floor windows to either side of the entrance are treated as vertical bands via vertical strips of wood. The angled canopy over the entrance, together with its pair of stepped supporting brackets and its layered fascia, suggests the sort of monumentality most often associated with a large public or commercial structure. The house was originally painted pink.

Henry Lomb Memorial

Saint Paul Boulevard at Upper Falls
 Boulevard

1932

LEWIS J. BREW AND WALTER CASSEBEER

The Henry Lomb Memorial presents the essential Art Deco structure. The 48-foot-high, slightly tapered octagonal shaft stands at the center of the boulevard as one approaches Bausch Memorial Bridge. The shaft and its base are sheathed in polished black Minnesota granite, with details in contrasting pink granite. Four of the shaft's narrow sides contain flutes of cast aluminum. At the apex is a rectangular silver screen behind which light pours forth at night. The monument is dedicated to Henry Lomb, one of the founders of the Bausch and Lomb Optical Company of Rochester.

Henry Lomb Memorial, Rochester, New York. The Landmark Society of Western New York.

RYE

Playland

Playland County Recreation Park
Off Playland Parkway and Forest
Avenue
1927–28

WALKER & GILLETTE, ARCHITECTS; GILMORE D.
CLARKE, LANDSCAPE ARCHITECT; JAY
DOWNER, ENGINEER; FRANK M. DARLING,
DIRECTOR OF AMUSEMENT PARKS

As is often the case with the architecture of amusement parks, it is not easy to pin down the imagery utilized for Playland. The first published drawings for the park showed a design that was predominantly Mediterranean-inspired, with various details revealing Oriental and Art Deco influences. In

Playland County Recreation Park, Rye, New York. Rye Historical Society.

the final design, however, the Art Deco element emerges with great strength. The Art Deco high point of the park buildings is the Music Tower and its accompanying bandstand. The tower's main shaft has layered buttresslike corners, and each face of the shaft is indented at the top in a steplike pattern. Surmounting the shaft is a smaller tower and, above this, a tall slender metal lantern, all articulated in an Art Deco fashion. Polychrome stucco panels exhibit a variety of Art Deco motifs, ranging from zigzags and Greek key patterns to stylized flowers and interwoven spirals.

SYRACUSE

Syracuse Lighting Company Building (Niagara Mohawk Power Company)

300 Erie Boulevard W.
1932

MELVIN L. KING (KING & KING); BLEY &
LYMAN

As befits the offices of an electric power company, this six-story Art Deco structure pays homage to light. During daylight hours the stainless-steel detailing shimmers in the sunlight; at night not only is the building dramatically lighted by floodlights but beacons of light, emanating from fixtures situated atop the central tower, project up into the sky. At the center of the building is a standing male figure from whose outstretched hands bolts of light project upward. This 28-foot-high stainless-steel sculpture, *Spirit of Light,* was designed by Clayton B. Frye.

WANTAGH

Jones Beach State Park

Meadowbrook Parkway at Ocean
  Parkway
1928–29

HERBERT A. MAGOON AND AYMAR EMBURY II

The entire facility—comprising bath houses, a recreation building, concession stands, viewing terraces, stairs and platforms, pools, and a water tower—was designed in the Art Deco style. The centerpiece is the 200-foot-high water tower, which consists of a pale sandstone base and a shaft of pink brick interrupted by bright green terra-cotta. At the top of the tower the corners return to stone and support a pyramidal roof of green weathered copper. The principal recreation building has two low towers that appear almost Hindu in inspiration. The rich and at times bewildering complexity of buildings, terraces, and staircases is matched by the rich texture of brick, stone, and blue and green detailing.

PENNSYLVANIA

ERIE

West Ridge Greyhound Bus Terminal

28 N. Park Row
1940

WISCHMEYER, ARRASMITH, & ELSWICK

In this Streamline Moderne design a pylon bearing the "Greyhound" sign and a connected canopy over the entrance form an L-shaped composition that continues across the facade and encompasses the "West Ridge" sign. A band of blue terra-cotta at the base of the building is carried into the curved walls flanking the entrance. In the second story a horizontal band of windows concludes in a half-circle. Originally a restaurant with a curved glass wall looked onto the foyer, and the two-story waiting room had a metal staircase and balcony at one end.

West Ridge Greyhound Bus Terminal, Erie,
Pennsylvania. University Lithoprinters.

HARRISBURG

Armory for the 107th Pennsylvania Artillery

19th Street, between Pine and
Sycamore Streets
1935–37

EDMUND GEORGE GOOD, JR.

This armory presents a late Art Deco design, somewhat simplified and cleaned up by Streamline Moderne details. Pairs of first- and second- floor windows are contained within slightly recessed vertical panels and are separated by two-story-high panels suggesting fluted pilasters. Among the building's other Art Deco motifs are the recessed squares over the entrance piers, a horizontal band of vertical lines just below the parapet, and chevron patterns adjoining the stairs. Mirror-image cannons are cast into the wall at the base of the entrance platform.

PHILADELPHIA

N. W. Ayer & Son Building

204–212 S. 7th Street
1927–29

RALPH B. BENCKER

The 15-story Ayer Building well reflects the concern for current fashion that might be expected of a major advertising firm. The smooth limestone walls of this American Vertical–style skyscraper stress modernity, monumentality, and permanence. The building is abundantly decorated within and without, but the decoration in stone, metal, and paint is all highly reserved. The spandrels are decorated with zigzags, layered horizontal curved planes, and low-relief sculptured figures. A number of the intervening piers terminate in heroic human figures, above which are stylized wings in low relief. The interior, especially the ceilings and the upper

Armory for the 107th Pennsylvania Artillery, Harrisburg, Pennsylvania.
Architectural Concrete (1939).

portions of the walls, contains a variety of Art Deco ornament. Slightly convex fluted piers line the walls of the lobby, and the metal elevator doors feature highly decorated recessed panels.

Federal Building (William Penn Annex, Post Office, and the Federal Courthouse)

Market Street at 9th Street, southeast
corner
1934–41

BALLINGER COMPANY AND HARRY STERNFIELD

A five-story block of offices contains courtrooms at its center and, on the ground floor, a post office. As with many PWA Moderne buildings, the Federal Building was originally conceived as a classical temple on a base.

The base contains the deep-set entrances and the adjoining rectangular windows and sculptured panels. Above, the image of a columned temple has been reduced to fluted piers and vertical recesses containing windows and spandrels. There is an occasional hint of the Streamline Moderne in this design, but the basic theme is abstracted classicism. Large, very bold sculptural panels in granite occur on either of the building's four entrances. The panels that flank the entrances to the courthouse (on Market and Chestnut streets) symbolize Law and Justice; they were carved by Donald De Lue. The panels flanking the 9th Street entrances to the post office depict the activities of the postal service and were produced by Edmund Amateis. The interior sculpture was executed by Louis Milione.

Federal Building, Philadelphia, Pennsylvania. *Pencil Points* (1941).

Federal Reserve Bank

10th Street at Chestnut Street, northeast corner
1931–35, 1940

PAUL P. CRET

With respect to form as well as detail, this building is Art Deco at its most restrained. Cret took a rectangular block of Vermont Blue marble and, on the ground level, projected into it a classical portico. Except at the ends, the entire entablature is a simple plane; above this, the cornice and its sparse details project in an abbreviated fashion. The building's top three floors contain nine narrow vertical bands of windows and spandrels; on either side of these bands two sets of three windows reinforce the corners of the classical box. The exterior sculpture is by Alfred Boittau.

Integrity Trust Company Building

1528 Walnut Street
1928

PAUL P. CRET

In this 22-plus-story building, Cret developed the Art Deco theme as far as he ever would. Its elegent Art Deco features include doors, lanterns, and grilles of bronze. In addition, wall panels by the French sculptor Alfred Boittau depict scenes relating to agriculture, trade, industry, transportation, and navigation. After passing through richly decorated exterior doors and a set of revolving doors, one arrives at the two-story banking room. The public passage in this space is terminated in an octagon space that centers on an elaborate round check-writing table.

Integrity Trust Company Building, Philadelphia, Pennsylvania. *Architectural Record* (1929).

Lasher Printing Company Building

1309 Noble Street
1927

PHILIP TYRE

The architect of this seven-story Art Deco tower obviously looked closely at the buildings at the 1925 Paris Exposition of the Decorative Arts, and then elongated them. A dramatic zigzag pattern rides across the lower part of the facade and connects with the dark brick entrance screen. The building's central tower, which terminates in a masonry covering, is reminiscent of an Egyptian pylon.

WCAU Radio Station Building

162 Chestnut Street
1931–35

GABRIEL ROTH AND HARRY STERNFIELD

The first published design for this building showed a modest, two-story Art Deco/Streamline Moderne struc-

ture of dark rose-colored brick and stainless steel. The final design, in blue and silver, focused on a tall, narrow, layered glass tower atop which the call letters of the radio station were arranged. Vertical bands running parallel to the glass tower contain Art Deco vinelike motifs. The building has been substantially altered on the interior, and to a lesser degree on the exterior. The building was altered and in part restored in 1983.

PITTSBURGH

Cathedral of Learning, University of Pittsburgh

5th Avenue at Bigelow Boulevard
1925–37

CHARLES Z. KLAUDER

Although this 42-story skyscraper reads as a Gothic tower, the atmosphere of the Art Deco permeates the design. Gothic vertical shafts are here abstracted in a Goodhue-esque fashion, and traditional Gothic ornament takes on a flat linear quality. The focal point of the interior is the great Commons Room, which measures 200 by 100 feet and rises four stories to its vaulted ceiling. As on the exterior, the theme inside is Gothic, but Gothic reworked through the eyes of an architect who was obviously well acquainted with innovative American and European architecture of the 1910s and 1920s. Klauder also designed several other college and university buildings across the country (see Charles Klauder and Herbert Wise's *College Architecture in America*, 1929).

WCAU Radio Station Building, Philadelphia, Pennsylvania. Pennsylvania Historical and Museum Commission.

Gulf Refining Company Building

7th Avenue at Grant Street, northwest
corner
1931–32

TROWBRIDGE & LIVINGSTON; E. P. MELLON

One of the recurring themes in American architecture is the conjectural reconstruction of the classical Mausoleum of Halicarnassus. In the Gulf Building, the architects' interest in this theme is manifest in the building's top floors, which take the form of a stepped structure surmounted by a small lantern with arched openings. Although vertically articulated, the 600-foot-high Gulf Building reads more as a solid classical pile than does the nearby Koppers Building, which is of comparable height. The ground-floor lobby also leans more toward 1920s Beaux-Arts classicism, even if the intense dark colors (especially the reds and deep yellows) are outright Art Deco. The mystery as well as the modernity of the Gulf Building were enhanced by its nighttime illumination: bands of neon tubes outlining the building's stepped summit and floodlights trained on the terminal lantern.

Koppers Building

7th Avenue at Grant Street, southwest
corner
1927–29

GRAHAM, ANDERSON, PROBST & WHITE; E. P.
MELLON

The architects of this skyscraper, the Chicago firm of Graham, Anderson, Probst & White, were well aware not only of Eliel Saarinen's entry in the 1922 Chicago Tribune Tower competition but also of Bertram G. Goodhue's design for the Nebraska State Capitol, which was then under construction. This 34-story building is topped by a recessed high-pitched hipped roof of copper. The exterior walls are treated in the fashion referred to in the 1920s as the American Vertical style, that is, they exhibit a pattern of narrow vertical grooves containing the windows and spandrels. The three-story high lobby displays rich designs in polished stone and metal; inspiration for the building's ornament was drawn from Egypt, from the classical world of Greece and Rome, from Byzantium, and from the pre-Columbian civilizations of Mexico and Central America.

Koppers Building, Pittsburgh, Pennsylvania.

Swan Acres

Babcock Boulevard at Three Degree
    Road, Sewickley Heights
1934–37

HARRY C. CLEPPER

This 35-acre subdivision was initially
laid out to accommodate 33 houses. It
was the first subdivision to boast
"homes all of modern design." By "modern design" was here meant a rectangular version of the popular Streamline
Moderne. The first 12 houses were of
concrete (i.e., "Haydite block") construction and featured steel casement
corner windows and glass brick. The
utilitarian aspects of these houses, their
kitchens, bathrooms, and garages,
strongly announce their presence.

READING

Band Shell

Penn's Commons (City Park), 11th
    Street at Penn Street
1934

MILES DECHANT (WILLIAM H. DECHANT &
    SONS)

Concrete band shells were a favorite
building type for the Art Deco and the
Streamline Moderne. In this example,
the wide arch composed of four bands
contains a gunite shell. At the ends of
the arch, small but monumental-appearing buildings establish the Art
Deco theme. The Streamline Moderne
is expressed by the vertical expanses of
glass block and by the horizontal band-

Model house, Swan Acres, Pittsburgh, Pennsylvania. *Architectural Forum* (1937).

Penn's Commons (City Park) band shell, Reading, Pennsylvania. *Architectural Concrete* (1939).

ing of the base. A stone-clad wall separates the front of the band shell from the adjoining lily pond.

Soldiers' and Sailors' Memorial Bridge

Penn and Front Streets
1930

WILLIAM GEHRON (GEHRON & ROSS); LEE LAWRIE, SCULPTOR

At the eastern end of this 17-span limestone bridge are two pylons 147 feet in height. Each of the pylons is surmounted by a stylized eagle clasping a bunch of arrows in one claw. At the base, Lawrie has provided panels of relief sculpture depicting tanks, swords, gunbelts, helmets, hand grenades, and other miliary as well as nonmilitary motifs.

SCRANTON

Masonic Temple and Scottish Rite Cathedral

420 Washington Avenue
1927–30

RAYMOND HOOD

Hood employed the abstracted Gothic in his winning entry in this Scranton competition, the same imagery that he and John Mead Howells had used in their famed 1922 Chicago Tribune Tower. Hood's approach to the Gothic owes an obvious debt to earlier designs by Bertram G. Goodhue; as in Goodhue's work, episodes of ornament are played off against plain wall surfaces. The building poses as a massive piece of scuptured masonry.

Thin, vertical compositions of Gothic tracery and niches occur between the buttresses on either side of the entrance and also out of the three buttresses of the theater lobby wall. The low-relief geometric sculpture on the small corner tower, the lettering panel, and the serpentlike pattern of ornament above the entrance are the building's most openly Art Deco features.

Masonic Temple and Scottish Rite Cathedral, Scranton, Pennsylvania. *Contemporary American Architects* (1931).

SOUTH

ALABAMA

BIRMINGHAM

Alabama Power Company Building

600 N. 18th Street
1925

WARREN, KNIGHT & DAVIS; SIGMUND
   NESSELROTH, ASSOC.

The central section of each facade of this building is dominated by elongated piers; the slightly recessed dark bands between the piers contain windows and black glass spandrels. The corners of the building read as heavy masonry blocks holding the composition of piers in place. Above the piers and the corners of the building are decorative bands of marble, colored terra-cotta, and brick. The patterns feature circles, crosses, and repeated and alternating squares. The building is

Alabama Power Company Building, Birmingham, Alabama. *The Book of the Boston Architectural Club for 1929.*

surmounted by a recessed block containing the water tanks and, at the rear, an elevator tower. A steeply pitched hipped roof, in the fashion of Bertram G. Goodhue, tops the water-tank portion of the building. The ridge of the roof boasts a gleaming figure of Electra in gold-leafed bronze. Above the tall, deep-set entrance is a composition of three sculptured figures representing Power, Heat, and Light. These three figures and Electra are the work of the New York sculptor John Field Stanford, Jr. Nearby and also of interest is a somewhat similar skyscraper, also designed by Warren, Knight & Davis. The 14-story Protective Life Building, built in 1928, is located at the southwest corner of 1st and 21st Streets.

Birmingham City Hall

710 20th Street
1950

CHARLES MCCAULEY

This 10-story building offers evidence that the PWA Moderne, the stripped-down version of the Art Deco, did not die out after World War II. Below the building's alternating vertical bands of piers and recessed window-and-spandrel panels lie axially aligned pools of water. At the base of the tall central section are four attenuated piers within which the entrance doors are set. The building is sheathed in limestone and granite, and its figurative sculpture, framed within deeply recessed panels, conveys a strong 1930s flavor.

Birmingham City Hall, Birmingham, Alabama. Birmingham Public Library.

ARKANSAS

FORT SMITH

Sebastian County Courthouse and Fort Smith City Hall

East side of 6th Street between Parker
and Rogers Avenues
1936–37

TROY E. BASSHAM, CARNALL WHEELER, AND
E. CHESTER NELSON

A three-story wing projects forward on either side of the central six-story volume. The first four floors of the central mass are surmounted by the dominant feature of the design: a two-story jail. The vertical recesses containing windows and spandrels are kept close to the surface so that the structural mass of the building is not overly apparent. The delicacy of the Art Deco ornament within the spandrels, adjoining the entrance and at the top of the parapets, is matched by the elegance of the tile acroteria along the edge of the eaves of the jail.

LITTLE ROCK

Monkey House, Little Rock Zoo

Fair Park Boulevard at 8th Street,
Fair Park
1940

HARRY D. WAGNER

Four tall, massive pylons stand before the low stone building. The pylons have the appearance of primitive piers waiting for an entablature and pediment. Groups of four windows occur low in the stone walls at the ends of the building; these windows are connected at their tops and bottoms by a continuous horizontal masonry band. Although sheathed in stone, the building seems almost fragile compared to the four pylons announcing the entrance. The design is abstracted Art Deco tempered by subtle references to the Streamline Moderne.

Sebastian County Courthouse and Fort Smith City Hall (window and spandrel detail), Fort Smith, Arkansas. Lynn Riebow, photographer.

FLORIDA

ISLAMORADA

Florida Keys Memorial

Highway 1, south of Islamorada
1937

FLORIDA DIVISION OF THE FEDERAL ARTS
    PROJECT

This WPA Art Deco memorial was erected to commemorate the veterans of World War I who lost their lives in the violent hurricane of 1935. The monument is composed of three distinct parts: a raised rectangular concrete base (reminiscent of the base of a classical temple); a stone-clad mausoleum in the form of a simple rectangular block; and adjoining the mausoleum, an 18-foot-high stone shaft. Carved into one side of the extended base of the shaft is a relief panel on which waves and inclined palms recall the intensity of the winds of the hurricane.

Florida Keys Memorial, Islamorada, Florida.

JACKSONVILLE

Assembly and Repair Shop, United States Naval Air Station

Wasp Street at Yorktown Avenue

1940

ROBERT & COMPANY

The central pavilion, with its curved and banded corners, its low stepped roof, and its central lantern, resembles an enlarged plastic radio of the 1930s. The single-story wings to either side contain deep bands of windows. The intervening sections of wall are recessed, banded, and painted a dark color. Nearby, the large opening of the hangar is visually anchored by a pair of Art Deco ornamented towers, glass bricks and all.

Elephant House, Jacksonville Zoological Park

8605 Zoo Road

1935

ROY A. BENJAMIN

Although this octagonal dwelling for elephants exhibits a low-pitched tile roof, its basic design is Art Deco. A curved banded canopy with ab-stracted columns defines the entrance. On the remaining sides of the building are slightly recessed panels displaying highly stylized palm trees in low relief. Running around the building and forming part of the entablature are two horizontal bands of glass brick.

A. L. Lewis Mausoleum

Memorial Cemetery, Moncrief Road at Edgewood Avenue

1939

LEROY SHEFTALL

A white marble cube indicates its adherence to the Art Deco by emphasizing the horizontal joints of its marble surfaces and by recessing a narrow band at the top. The band is broken by a single block of stone that projects slightly above the parapet on the front facade. To either side of the recessed bronze doors, which feature various Art Deco motifs, are curved fluted walls. An abstracted classical urn stands on either side of the entrance. The mausoleum was designed for A. L. Lewis, who was one of Florida's most prominent black businessmen in the early decades of this century.

U.S. Naval Air Station, Assembly and Repair Shop, Jacksonville, Florida. U.S. Naval Air Station.

Elephant House, Jacksonville Zoological Park, Jacksonville, Florida. Jacksonville Zoological Park.

Gulf Service Station, Miami, Florida.

MIAMI

Gulf Service Station

1240 W. Flagler Drive

1941

From a rounded white stucco volume spring the three service bays to one side, and, toward the front, over the pump area, a cantilevered canopy supported by a single column. A series of increasingly slender drums rises over the station office. The tallest of these contains eight narrow glass-brick windows, which, together with the neon sign wrapped around the drum, announced (especially at night) the presence of the station. On the exterior, a dark band unites the station proper with the service bays. A single round window interrupts the wall between the service bays and the office.

Miami City Hall (formerly the Terminal Building, Pan American Airway Base)

3500 Pan American Drive

1928–31

DELANO & ALDRICH

The New York architects Delano & Aldrich were best known for their many sophisticated Period Revival country houses. But like many other Beaux-Arts designers, they were able to move over into the Art Deco and the Streamline Moderne with great ease. The former Pan American seaplane terminal in Miami is essentially a classical design modernized by the simple articulation of volumes; by the organization of the surfaces so that they read as thin, light walls; and by the introduction of curves and, of course, glass brick. A

Miami City Hall (Pan American Airway Base Terminal Building), Miami, Florida.

gold and green frieze featuring winged globes, underscored by a band of waves, terminates at each corner in a gold eagle. The airline terminal was adapted as a city hall in 1945.

MIAMI BEACH

Art Deco Historic District

From 22nd Street south to 1st Street, from Ocean Drive west to Pennsylvania Avenue

1930–42

Between 1934 and 1942, Miami Beach experienced a rash of construction of hotels and apartment buildings. Most of the new structures were relatively small and were built to accommodate winter visitors to Florida. Virtually all of them embraced the Art Deco and Streamline Moderne styles. The particular version of the Moderne employed in these buildings tended on the whole to be conservative, that is, instead of being forthright Streamline Moderne designs the buildings were based on late 1920s Art Deco designs and were updated by Streamline flourishes. An overriding theme that places all of these buildings in the 1930s is their general nautical atmosphere. In varying degree the buildings give the impression of being Streamline ocean liners pulled up on shore and now posing on the white sands of Miami Beach. Most of the hotels, such as the Savoy Plaza (1935) and the Whitelaw (1936), were three stories tall; a few, such as the eight-story New Yorker (1940), began to cultivate the Art Deco skyscraper image. All of the buildings are rendered in white stucco, with contrasting painted, terra cotta, or stone ornament.

Themes that recur in relief sculpture, etched glass, or wall murals include underwater scenes, palm trees, and pink flamingos. Alongside the hotels and apartment buildings rose a number of commercial buildings (such as the Paddock Grill of 1934) and public buildings (like the 1931 Miami Beach Public Library and the Post Office Building of 1938) that also employed the Moderne styles. This group of private and public buildings constitutes the largest surviving cache of Moderne buildings in the country. The following are some of the most assertive of these Art Deco/Streamline Moderne buildings.

Albion Hotel
1650 James Avenue
1939

POLEVITSKY & RUSSELL

This seven-story hotel expresses its debt to the Streamline ocean liner via an upper bridge, horizontal bands, rounded corners, and portholes.

Albion Hotel, Miami Beach, Florida.

Beach Patrol Headquarters

East end of 10th Street at Ocean Drive

c. 1939

A small Streamline Moderne ship has been beached. Its semicircular bridge, bordered by nautical railings, looks out to sea. Portholes dominate the first floor; above are more ship's railings and metal vents.

Beacon Hotel

720 Ocean Drive
1936
HARRY O. NELSON

Beach Patrol Headquarters, Miami Beach, Florida.

The street facade exhibits a play of horizontal and vertical banding; triangles and half-circles extend down from the parapet. Grilles containing highly stylized plant forms occur above the first-floor openings.

Berkeley Shore Hotel

1610 Collins Avenue
1940
ALBERT ANIS

Beacon Hotel, Miami Beach, Florida.

The Berkeley Shore Hotel is one of the most frequently photographed of the Miami Beach hotels. Like several of its neighbors, it plays a game between the Art Deco and the Streamline Moderne. A round central shaft rises above the marquee, penetrates through the upper two canopies, and then forms a banded tower.

Cardoza Hotel

1300 Ocean Drive
1939
HENRY HOHAUSER

This Streamline Moderne design features horizontal bands of canopies and circular shields high on the parapets.

Berkeley Shore Hotel, Miami Beach, Florida.

Carlyle Hotel

1250 Ocean Drive
1941

KIEHNEL & ELLIOTT

The center of the building develops a vertical theme: three recessed bands rise and are interrupted near the top by semicircular canopies.

Century Hotel

140 Ocean Drive
1939

HENRY HOHAUSER

The strong Streamline Moderne elements include the lettering, glass bricks, rows of portholes, and the stylized central mast.

Haddon Hall

1500 Collins Avenue
1940

L. MURRAY DIXON

This three-story Streamline Moderne hotel is organized around an open front court. A vertically oriented central panel over the entrance marquee relieves the building's otherwise insistent horizontality.

Hoffman's Cafeteria

1450 Collins Avenue
1940

HENRY HOHAUSER

The dramatic theme of the circle and the drum is repeated throughout this

Carlyle Hotel, Miami Beach, Florida.

Century Hotel, Miami Beach, Florida.

Haddon Hall, Miami Beach, Florida.

Hoffman's Cafeteria, Miami Beach, Florida.

structure. At the corner, curved walls lead toward the entrance, above which is an assertion of major and minor drums. The stepped parapets on either side of the corner pavilion contain decorative concentric circles.

House

5959 La Gorce Drive
1935

ROBERT LAW WEED

The architect was one of Florida's most gifted designers of the era. His early work drew inspiration from Mediterranean and Hispanic sources. In the 1930s he produced traditional- ist designs based loosely upon the architecture of the Caribbean region. In addition, he designed buildings in the Art Deco and Streamline Moderne styles. For the 1933 Century of Progress Exposition held in Chicago, he designed a Streamline Moderne "tropical house" constructed of concrete with steel- and aluminum-frame windows and doors. A few years later he produced this Streamline Moderne house on La Gorce Drive, which features curved walls and an extensive amount of glass brick. The most unusual aspect of the design is the entrance surround of local Keystone; the surface of the stone is carved in a complex pattern of interlocking Art Deco motifs.

House, Miami Beach, Florida.

House, (doorway detail), Miami Beach, Florida.

Miami Beach Public Library (now the Bass Museum of Art)

Collins Avenue at 21st Street, northwest corner
1930

RUSSELL T. PANCOAST

This is pure Art Deco, with its commitment to the building as a monumental piece of sculpture. The entrance is contained between two solid projecting blocks, and the building's upper reaches become a series of receding

Bass Museum of Art (Miami Beach Public Library), Miami Beach, Florida.

volumes. The entire structure is sheathed in coral stone. The sculptured ornament by Gustav Bohland includes references to the pre-Columbian world of Mexico and to the age of modern transportation machines: ocean liners and flying boats.

Surf Hotel

444 Ocean Drive
1936

HENRY HOHAUSER

The central panels of this three-story hotel boast wonderful relief sculpture: a pair of flamingos between the second- and third-story windows; a higher panel dominated by a palm tree; and, finally, at the parapet, two female nudes.

United States Post Office

Washington Street at 13th Street, northwest corner
1938–39

HOWARD LOVEWELL CHENEY

The Miami Beach post office has more to do with Swedish Modern of the 1930s than with the PWA Moderne or the Streamline. A corner rotunda with a narrow circular lantern is the centerpiece of the design. A door of exaggerated height set within picture-frame molding faces out to the intersection of the two streets. Overall, the design exhibits a delicacy of surfaces and details, especially in the various metal railings. Within the rotunda is a three-panel mural entitled *Florida History;* the mural was executed in 1940–41 by Charles Hardman under the U.S. Treasury Fine Arts Program.

U.S. Post Office, Miami Beach, Florida.

MOUNTAIN LAKE

Bok Singing Tower

Two miles north of Lake Wales on Highway CR 17A, one mile east of the junction with U.S. Route 27A
1929

MILTON B. MEDARY, ARCHITECT; FREDERICK LAW OLMSTED, JR., LANDSCAPE ARCHITECT; LEE LAWRIE, SCULPTOR

Situated atop Iron Mountain, the highest point in Florida, this tower is one of the most exotic Art Deco structures in the country. It was commissioned by Edward William Bok, editor of the *Ladies' Home Journal*. The landscape architect Frederick Law Olmsted, Jr., transformed the 130-acre site into a romantic man-made jungle. Under certain conditions of mood and light, the tower comes off strongly as an Art Deco artifact; at other moments,

Bok Singing Tower, Mountain Lake, Florida.

though, it seems equally related to the Spanish Colonial Revival or to medieval architecture. The tower's upward thrust is enhanced by projecting ribs of Georgian marble at each change of the wall planes. The marble of the ribs contrasts with the salmon-pink coquina stone employed for the body of the building. The upper openings are covered by elaborate window grilles (by Lee Lawrie) featuring a central human form against a backdrop of intertwined stems, leaves, and birds. Projecting above the parapet are eight stylized stone birds. At the base of the south facade is a wall sundial, surrounded by 12 small square relief panels depicting the signs of the zodiac. The tower sits within a moat. Two small bridges lead across the water to the entrance, which is deeply recessed within a pointed Gothic arch. The room at the base of the tower, with its large fireplace and iron balcony, suggests the great hall of a medieval castle. The bronze doors into the great medieval hall (on which the six days of creation are depicted), the wrought iron gates leading to the bridges over the moat, and all of the other metalwork were executed by the preeminent metal craftsman of the day, Samuel Yellin of Philadelphia. The architect of the tower, Milton B. Medary, was a prominent figure in Philadelphia and Washington, D.C., and was fluent in a wide variety of architectural styles, from the Art Deco to the classical Beaux Arts, the medieval, and the Colonial Revival. As a member of the Philadelphia firm Zantzinger, Borie & Medary, he designed the classical-inspired Justice Department Building in Washington, D.C. (1934).

ORLANDO

Kress Building

15–17 W. Church Street

1935

EDWARD F. SIBBERT

The consistent quality of the designs prepared by the New York office of Edward F. Sibbert for the nationwide chain of Kress department stores is remarkable. Although almost all of his 1930s designs for Kress are Art Deco rather than Streamline Moderne, they nonetheless convey the light decorative quality more commonly associated with the 1930s than the 1920s. The three-story Kress store in Orlando exhibits six vertical bands rising from the storefront canopy. The colorful facade is composed of polished granite accented with polychrome terracotta.

PALM BEACH

Mar-a-Lago (Edward F. Hutton House)

1100 S. Ocean Boulevard

1927–28

JOSEPH URBAN; WYTH, KING & JOHNSON; LEWIS AND VALENTINE, LANDSCAPE ARCHITECTS; WALTER AND FRANZ BARWIG, SCULPTORS

Although Joseph Urban can be considered one of the major promoters of the Art Deco, none of his work fits easily into a single stylistic category. The winter house Mar-a-Lago, designed for the stockbroker Edward F. Hutton, is primarily Mediterranean in style, but with strong overtones of Vienna (c. 1910) and of Urban's own version of the 1920s Art Deco. Masonry sculpture, painted decoration, and ironwork are the strongest Moderne elements of the design. The curved second-story loggia seems both Assyrian and Art Deco. The entrances to the three pavilions looking toward the west face a circular court; with their pattern of intertwined stems, leaves, flowers, and birds, these entrances refer to the Islamic decorative tradition as well as to the Art Deco. While much of the house's sculptured ornament looks to the medieval, its mode of abstraction is distinctly Moderne.

PANAMA CITY

Ritz (Martin) Theater

409 Harrison Street
1940

DESIGNED IN-HOUSE BY THE RITZ MOTION PICTURE CO.

The attention-grabbing facade is made of brilliant red, green, orange, white, and tan Vitrolite. A series of vertical panels dominates the center of the building, while to each side a vertical chevron motif is played off against vertical and horizontal bands of colored glass. The marquee is angled, with its Streamline Moderne lettering ("Martin") recessed in the center. Small retail stores occur at either side.

Mar-a-Lago (Edward F. Hutton House), Palm Beach, Florida.

GEORGIA

SAVANNAH

Atlantic Greyhound Bus Station
W. Broad Street
c. 1938
GEORGE D. BROWN

Here, near the center of a city that one associates with Colonial architecture of the 18th and early 19th centuries, is an impressive statement of the Streamline Moderne. The architect, who designed several bus stations in the South, poses a street facade of dark blue Vitrolux, below which is a band of ivory Vitrolite. A long horizontal window skims across this surface, terminating at one end in the glass doors and at

Atlantic Greyhound Bus Station, Savannah, Georgia. University Lithoprinters.

the other end in a half-circle. A stainless-steel canopy curves out from the top of the ivory Vitrolite wall and then curves and turns upward into a vertical neon sign.

KENTUCKY

FORT KNOX

Fort Knox Water Treatment Plant
Vine Grove Road, Pershing Drive, and
    Bullion Boulevard
1938
QUARTERMASTER GENERAL'S OFFICE

The army's employment of the Art Deco for this utilitarian structure indicates just how popular and pervasive this Moderne style was. The designers of this reinforced-concrete building played a low mass at one side against a larger towerlike form. The horizontality of the lower part of the building is emphasized by a band of wavy zigzags that cross over the upper sections of the vertically oriented windows. The vertical bands on the tower are the

design's tour de force; one contemporary critic described them as a "series of slender grilles [that] taper off into deep receded reveals at the parapet walls giving a symbolic effect of tall fountains."

United States Bullion Depository
Bullion Boulevard
1935–36
OFFICE OF THE SUPERVISING ARCHITECT OF THE
    TREASURY DEPARTMENT

This is PWA Moderne at its sternest. A low symmetrical block, with a recessed second floor, is approached by a driveway, walkway, and steps. Small fortresslike gatehouses stand on

United States Bullion Depository, Fort Knox, Kentucky. U.S. Government Printing Office

either side of the main entrance gate. A narrow band of Greek fretwork occurs over the windows of the gatehouses; above this band the stone and concrete angle back toward their roofs. The main building has been placed on a low earth terrace. At the four corners of the terrace, adjacent to the building, are low, stone-clad octagonal monitors that pose as defensive gun turrets. With the exception of the black polished marble around the entrance, these reinforced-concrete buildings are all sheathed (appropriately) in a cool, somewhat forbidding, gray granite.

LOUISIANA

BATON ROUGE

Louisiana State Capitol

Riverside Street at Capitol Lake Drive,
    southeast corner

1930–32

WEISS, DREYFOUS & SEIFERTH; LEE LAWRIE AND
    ADOLPH A. WEINMAN, LORADO TAFT,
    ULRIC ELLERHUSEN, SCULPTORS; JULES
    GUERIN, MURALIST

If the architects of the Louisiana State Capitol to some extent emulated Bertram G. Goodhue's famed capitol at Lincoln, Nebraska (1922–32), they must also have been inspired by other civic buildings modeled on skyscrapers, such as the Los Angeles City Hall (1926–28). This 28-story tower overlooks the Mississippi River and the nearby Capitol Lake. The building's monumentality, the richness of its mate-

Louisiana State Capitol, Baton Rouge, Louisiana. Historic New Orleans Collection.

rials, and the lavish use of sculpture were all specifically endorsed by Louisiana's governor at the time, Huey P. Long. The result was certainly an impressive monument, both to him and to his political machine.

The base and wings of this white Alabama limestone building exhibit features typical of an Art Deco building: smooth stone walls that play off plain and fluted buttresses, as well as a rich array of stone ornament and sculpture. On each side of the monumental granite steps leading to the main entrance on the south side are sculptural groups by Lorado Taft. The overscaled entrance incorporates relief sculpture by Lee Lawrie, who also produced the row of sculpture above the entrance (*Dominations of Louisiana*), as well as the building's crown, the "spiritual temple." To one side of the entrance is a frieze by Ulric Ellerhusen, who also produced the cornice frieze of the central block.

The solidity of the tower's corners is offset by recessed vertical bands of windows that terminate at their setback in stylized plant and animal motifs (sugar cane, magnolias, and cattails; pelicans, raccoons, minks, and crawfish) and by four colossal figures by Ulric Ellerhusen that emerge from the corners of the tower and that represent Law, Science, Art, and Philosophy. At the very top of the tower, Lee Lawrie posed an eagle at each corner. The wings of these freestanding eagles project upward and back into the building, forming a version of medieval flying buttresses.

The plan is classical and axially arranged, with the Senate chambers on one side and the House of Representatives on the other. Between these chambers is the large Memorial Hall, with its luxurious red Levanto marble strip and pilasters. The east and west ends of the hall exhibit paintings by Jules Guerin. Bronze is used extensively for light fixtures and for decorated doors and doorframes.

The architects' intent in their employment of many of America's foremost sculptors and muralists is said to have been "a modern interpretation of classical motifs" (*Architectural Forum*, December 1932). In this regard, the designers were highly successful, for the capitol is a beautiful marriage of 1920s Beaux-Arts classicism and Art Deco skyscraper style.

NEW ORLEANS

Bridges

City Park
  Baseball Drive
  Diagonal Drive
  Harrison Avenue
  Lagoon Drive
  Zachary Taylor Drive
1934–36
RICHARD KOCH, ARCHITECT; GEORGE RICE,
  ENGINEER

These five small reinforced-concrete bridges were built during the Depression by the Works Progress Administration. The architect was a well-known exponent of regionalism and an advocate of historic preservation. Like many Beaux-Arts–trained designers, he was sympathetic to the Art Deco. The gentle curve of the arched opening beneath each of the bridges springs from pylonlike forms. These pylons always have bases, but on the top was employed the usual Art Deco device of indenting the final surface. All of the bridges contain ornament incorporating the human figure. Above the arch on the Harrison Avenue Bridge is the figure of a nude female floating on waves; a similar female figure seems to be reclining in a tropical jungle on the sides of the Lagoon Drive Bridge. Cast into the abutments of the Baseball Drive Bridge are a nude female carrying a jar on her head and a partially clothed male. The Zachary Taylor Drive Bridge depicts a girl and a boy reading books, with their backs against the trunk of a tree. The interior of the Diagonal Drive Bridge presents seven workingmen. All of the sculpture was produced in negative molds and was then poured in place during construction.

Feibleman House

12 Nassau Drive (Metairie)
1938
WEISS, DREYFOUS & SEIFERTH

This sophisticated exercise in the Streamline Moderne was supposedly inspired by the designs of Walter Gropius. Laid out as a series of interlocking, horizontally oriented volumes, the house exhibits bands of windows (some very long and shallow), glass brick, curved corners and bays, and round portholes.

"The Lone Star Home"

55 S. Claiborne Avenue
1935
WEISS, DREYFOUS & SEIFERTH

Developers, home-design and architecture magazines, and producers of building supplies sponsored the construction of numerous model houses during the Depression years of the 1930s. This nationally advertised house was sponsored by the Lone Star Cement Company to illustrate the viability of concrete as a structural mater-

Harrison Avenue Bridge, New Orleans, Louisiana.

Feibleman House, New Orleans, Louisiana. Historic New Orleans Collection.

ial in houses for America's upper-middle class. The windows to the left of the entrance were composed as bands that wrap around the corner. The spandrel between the first- and second-floor windows is divided into horizontal bands. Originally the concrete between the windows was colored black, as were the vertical fluted panels over the entrance. The concrete walls of the house are ribbed and hollow. The house's traditional low-pitched hipped roof was added to the architects' original design by the sponsors. (For more information see Karen Kingsley's *Modernism in Louisiana: A Decade of Progress, 1930–1940* (1984).

Port Allen High School, West Baton Rouge, Louisiana. *Architectural Concrete* (1938).

WEST BATON ROUGE

Port Allen High School

3553 Rosedale Road (Port Allen)

1937

BODMAN & MURRELL

This school was described at the time of its construction as an example of the "conservative-modern style," that is, Art Deco rather than Streamline Moderne. The centerpiece of the 320-foot-long poured-in-place concrete building is its central 58-foot-high tower. Four rising corner piers hold the vertical center of the tower. Much of the building's ornamentation consists of horizontal grooved lines, which are occasionally interrupted by pilasters. Motifs such as the round shield and the inverted V provide Art Deco accents. In relief above the tower's second-floor windows is a shield surrounded by pelicans; above the entrance door of the combined gymnasium and auditorium is a recessed panel depicting a male athlete.

MISSISSIPPI

COLUMBIA

Columbia High School

1101 Broad Street

1937

N. W. OVERSTREET AND A. H. TOWN

Four thick rectangular pylons and a band of freestanding concrete letters, reading "Columbia High School," announce the entrance of this two-story building. At the opposite end of the front facade a deep porch, defined by curved walls and by four massive round pillars, provides the entrance to the combined auditorium and gymnasium. Horizontal bands of metal-frame windows race across the facade, occasionally halted by vertical bands of glass brick or by circular windows. The architect, A. H. Town, described the design as "ultra-modern," as opposed to the "conservative-modern" Art Deco.

Columbia High School, Columbia, Mississippi. *Architectural Forum* (1938).

JACKSON

Edward L. Bailey School (now Bailey Alternative School)
1900 N. State Street
1937

N. W. OVERSTREET AND A. H. TOWN

A five-story tower composed of vertical layered buttresses forms the centerpiece of this large Art Deco school complex. To each side of the tower, the school's exterior walls are treated in classic Art Deco fashion, with windows and spandrels recessed between low-relief pilasters that rise undecorated to

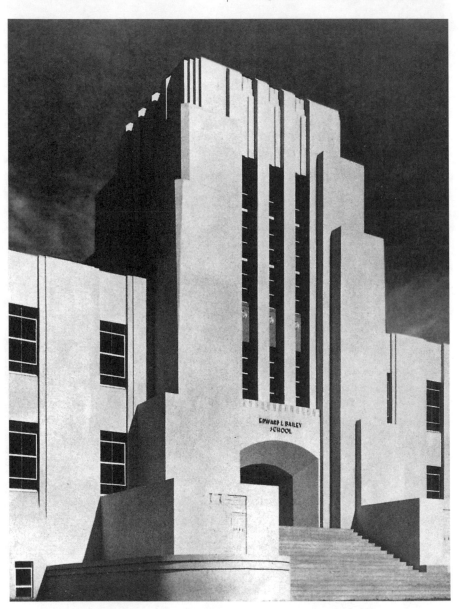

Edward L. Bailey School Building, Jackson, Mississippi. *Architectural Concrete* (1937).

the top of the parapets. Touches of the Streamline Moderne are evident in the bands of windows that cut corners at a 45-degree angle and in the segmented curve of the auditorium entrance. Low-relief panels occur on either side of the main entrance steps; a pair of stylized tigers (the school's symbol) is situated near a secondary entrance and again in a high-relief panel at the center of the auditorium entrance. At the rear of the building a canopied automobile entrance features a "bas-relief plaque of a modern automobile with the inscription 'auto porch.' The architects wrote that they "well know that the current tendency in architecture is towards a more functional, possibly more severe design than that adopted, but we did not feel that a building of that style would be as fully appreciated as a more conservative structure of monumental character."

OXFORD

Oxford City Hall

107 S. LaMar Boulevard
1938

J. T. CANIZARO

The Oxford City Hall is essentially a two-story rectangular concrete box; from one side of the box extends a one-story, three-garage fire department. The building has a deeply recessed porch whose formality is exaggerated by a pair of black granite columns. Horizontality is emphasized by shallow bands of lettering, by a thin concrete canopy above the letters, and by a strip window that extends around a corner. Other Moderne decorative features include a clock face on the front of the building and a rectangular panel of black concrete on which the history of the community is recounted in sculpture and text.

TUPELO

Church Street Elementary School

445 N. Church Street
1936–37

N. W. OVERSTREET AND A. H. TOWN

Like other schools designed by these Mississippi architects, the primary school in Tupelo moves back and forth between the late Art Deco and the Streamline Moderne. In typical Art Deco fashion, wide buttresses flank the school's main entrance. Ribbed walls curve inward toward the doors, and above the entrance is a clock face. Massive blocks hug the entrance steps; flat relief sculpture on the fronts of these blocks depicts historic scenes. To the left of the entrance pavilion is a segmented curved bay with a band of metal-frame windows; to the right are three groups of horizontally oriented windows separated by recessed horizontal bands. Other Moderne elements include square wall grilles, round windows, glass brick, and thin cantilevered roofs over the entrances.

Church Street Elementary School, Tupelo, Mississippi. *Architectural Concrete* (1939).

Asheville City Building (detail of roof and lantern), Asheville, North Carolina. *Architectural Record* (1928).

NORTH CAROLINA

ASHEVILLE

City Building

County City Plaza, Spruce Street at
  College Street
1926–27

DOUGLAS D. ELLINGTON

This nine-story building conveys the
feeling that its central shaft has been
substantially reduced in height, but this
was apparently the intent of the architect, for he wrote in 1928 that "there was
a desire to have the structure emerge
from the ground in a fortress-like
strength." The architect further pointed
out that his design was meant to convey a sense of tradition as well as a feeling of the modern age; the building
thus combines classical and Art Deco
elements. Above the central five-story
shaft the structure becomes a series of
receding octagons that terminate in an
open lantern. The sloping roofs of the
lantern and the layered octagons are
ribbed in green, blue, and gold terra-
cotta tile.

While Ellington was designing the
City Building, his First Baptist Church
(1927; southeast corner of Oak and
Woodfin Streets), which also combined
classical and Art Deco features, was
under construction a few miles away.
The church's domed auditorium contains an abundance of Art Deco ornament.

Hiwassee Dam, Hiwassee,
North Carolina. *Architectural
Forum* (1941).

HIWASSEE

Hiwassee Dam

Northeast of Hiwassee
1940

ROLAND A. WANK; TENNESSEE VALLEY
  AUTHORITY

Like other Tennessee Valley Authority
projects of the 1930s and early 1940s,
the Hiwassee Dam incorporates elements of both the International Style
and the Streamline Moderne. The
drama of this 307-foot-high, 1,287-foot-
long dam recalls the grandiose architecture envisioned in 1930s science-
fiction illustrations. Specific features,
such as the hydroelectric power plant
and its accompanying gantry crane,
bear a strong resemblance to designs
by Norman Bel Geddes. Other TVA
dams in the Streamline Moderne style
include   Wheeler   Dam   (Elgin,

Alabama), Guntersville Dam (northwest of Guntersville, Alabama), Watts Bar Dam (Watts Bar, Tennessee), and Pickwick Landing Dam (Pickwick Landing, Tennessee).

KITTY HAWK

Wright Brothers National Memorial

Kill Devil Hill, south of Kitty Hawk; west on Government Road
1930–32
ROBERT B. ROGERS AND ALFRED E. POOR

In late 1929 a nationwide competition was held for the design of a monument to commemorate the site upon which Wilbur and Orville Wright flew the first motor-powered airplane. Thirty-four designs were submitted, and the jury awarded first prize to the New York firm of Robert B. Rogers and Alfred E. Poor. Poor, who had Beaux-Arts training and had worked in the office of John

Russell Pope, produced here one of the country's most abstract Art Deco monuments. Upon a star-shaped platform he placed a slightly tapered 60-foot-high rectangular block that, at its top, steps in on one side. Projecting upward from this stepped section is a beacon tower. The granite block with low relief wings carved into two of its sides is in fact a highly stylized eagle. At its base is a pair of bronze doors that lead into a cryptlike room sheathed in pink marble. Opposite this entrance is a niche containing a model of the first engine-powered airplane. The walls on either side contain niches with busts of the Wrights. A romantic contrast is created between the sophisticated Art Deco design of the monument, with its refined materials and craftsmanship, and the desolate sand hills and dunes that surround it. The monument reads most dramatically at night when its rectangular shaft is illuminated and the beacon tower emits sharp slivers of light.

Wright Brothers National Memorial, Kitty Hawk, North Carolina. Wright Brothers National Memorial.

WINSTON-SALEM

R. J. Reynolds Tobacco Company Building

N. Main Street at 4th Street, northeast
    corner
1928–29

SHREVE, LAMB & HARMON

The New York firm that designed the Empire State Building provided a set-back Art Deco design for this 22-story skyscraper. Vertical bands of windows and spandrels are contained by the building's solid masonry corners. The top three setbacks become even more sculptural by virtue of deep-set windows and wide pilasters that project above the parapets. The building's entrance and its lobby exhibit a rich array of polished stone (walls) and polished metal (light fixtures and elevator doors). Exterior and interior ornament tends to the abstracted classical—suggestions of fluted pilasters and dentils — and Art Deco motifs abound: circles, diagonal lines, squares with radiating half-circles, and so on.

SOUTH CAROLINA

COLUMBIA

Atlantic Greyhound Bus Terminal

Blanding and Sumter Streets
1939

GEORGE D. BROWN

The bus depot as a Streamline Moderne transportation machine has a deep horizontal band of glass bricks leading around each of the street corners to a sheltered concourse. The horizontality of the box is slightly offset by the four piers that project through the entrance canopy. The front walls are sheathed in panels of bright blue Vitrolite trimmed in ivory. Originally a vertically oriented neon sign rose from the canopy over the entrance. The architect also designed several other Streamline Moderne bus stations in the Southeast for Greyhound. In 1990 this station was adapted for use by the Lexington National Bank. For its careful retention of the building's Streamline Moderne image the bank received a National Preservation Award from the National Trust for Historic Preservation.

Atlantic Greyhound Bus
Terminal, Columbia, South
Carolina. University
Lithoprinters

R.J. Reynolds Tobacco Company Building, Winston-Salem, North Carolina. *Inset*, R.J. Reynolds Tobacco Company Building (elevator lobby). R.J. Reynolds Tobacco Company.

TENNESSEE

CHATTANOOGA

America Lava Company Building

Cherokee Boulevard and
Manufacturer's Road
1926, 1936, 1941

The original 1926 warehouse was updated in the Streamline Moderne style in 1936 (some of the remodeling took place as late as 1941). The three-story building, as we now experience it, plays off deep horizontal bands of glass brick alternating with bands of red brick (whose edges are defined by thin lines of cast stone). Several of the building's corners are dramatically curved, while the entrance reverts to a late Art Deco verticality. The parapet of the slightly projecting entrance pavilion displays a stepped pattern exaggerated by the contrast between the light-colored cast stone and the red brick of the walls.

United States Post Office and Federal Courthouse (now the Joel Soloman Federal Building)

Georgia Avenue between 10th and
11th Streets
1933

R. H. HUNT COMPANY; SHREVE, LAMB &
HARMON

White Georgian marble adds a vigorous note of permanence and elegance to this five-story PWA Moderne building. The two entrances, one at either end of the long street facade, are sunk deeply into the building. Within these recesses a theme of verticality is asserted through a slightly curved bay of glass and aluminium. The retaining walls flanking the exterior stairways exhibit large-scale eagles. Wall grilles in stone occur beside the entrance pavilions. Above, a horizontal band extends around the entire building. The principal interior public spaces, realized in dark polished stone, metal, and wood, reveal a broad array of angled and curvilinear Art Deco patterns.

NORRIS

Norris Dam

Fourteen miles northeast of Norris
1936

ROLAND A. WANK; TENNESSEE VALLEY
AUTHORITY

Although Elizabeth Mock of New York's Museum of Modern Art advanced the Norris Dam as a purely modernist work, the structure contains many references to the Streamline Moderne. The horizontality of this 265-foot-high, 1,872-foot-long reinforced-concrete dam and its accompanying buildings is emphasized by the grouping of its windows and doors, and by banding inserted into the exposed concrete surfaces. Heavy block letters are situated within rectangular frames cast into the concrete, and although curved openings and surfaces do not dominate, they are present in sufficient quantity to remind one that this is a 1930s design. Hugh Ferriss, the great illustrator of the Moderne, was referring to this structure when he wrote, "The air age gives a new facade to architecture." As it turns out, this particular facade has at least as much to do with the Streamline Moderne as with the architecture we call "modern." Like many Art Deco and Streamline Moderne structures, the dam and its powerhouse assume their most futuristic image when illuminated at night.

Norris Dam, Norris, Tennessee. Tennessee Department of Parks & Recreation.

VIRGINIA

HIGHLAND SPRINGS

Henrico Theater

305 E. Nine Mile Road
1939

EDWARD F. SINNOTT

The architect of this suburban movie theater began with what is essentially an Art Deco massing and then brought it up to date with Streamline Moderne details. Two wings with curved corners contain recessed central panels of accordion grooves. Between these wings is the recessed taller section of the building. The name of the theater is inscribed into the concrete face; below "Henrico" is a small projecting panel with corner squares and a clock face. The general effect of this reinforced-concrete design is monumentality of the sort that one associates with public buildings of the mid- to late 1930s.

Henrico Theater, Highland Springs, Virginia. History & Preservation Program, Virginia Recreation and Parks.

LYNCHBURG

Allied Arts Building

725 Church Street
1930–31

STANHOPE S. JOHNSON AND RAY O.
BRANNAN

The "stripped vertical" theme of Howells and Hood's Daily News Building (1930) in New York City is echoed in the design of this 17-story Art Deco skyscraper. The upper shaft of the building, with its narrow vertical bands of wall surface alternating with recessed window-and-spandrel strips, is sheathed in yellow brick. In contrast, the three-story base, the spandrels, and the recessed top of the structure are clad in dark green polished stone. Wavy horizontal lines skim across the building's third floor. The spandrels between the third and fourth floors boast stylized fronds and lions' heads; plant-inspired ornament also occurs in the spandrels above the windows of the 15th and 17th stories. The parapet of the building's recessed attic story contains rectangularized plant forms that draw attention to a sculptured eagle. After passing under the patterned metal grille above the entrance doors, there are in the lobby metal elevator doors that present landscape scenes: ocean waves and fishes and, above, a mountain range with clouds and flying birds.

Allied Arts Building,
Lynchburg, Virginia.
Virginia State Library.

RICHMOND

Model Tobacco Building

1100 Jefferson Davis Highway
1938–40

SCHMIDT, GARDEN & ERICKSON

Here one experiences a building as a sign. The focus of the narrow entrance end of this six-story brick-sheathed structure is a series of elongated piers that rise to a pair of boxes framing the words "Model Tobacco." The overall impression is that of an enlarged cigarette package. The remainder of the building plays on the theme of horizontality; recessed bands containing metal-frame windows are set between bands of masonry whose edges are emphasized.

Model Tobacco Building, Richmond, Virginia. D.G. Pendleton, photographer; Virginia State Library.

MIDWEST

ILLINOIS

AURORA

Paramount Theater (now Paramount Arts Center)

23 E. Galena Boulevard
1929–31

C. W. RAPP & GEORGE L. RAPP

The interior of the Paramount Theater, designed by a leading American firm that was responsible for many theaters built in the 1910s and 1920s, is a rich example of the Art Deco. The lobby displays wine-and-gold pilasters, elaborate gold cornices, and painted ceilings. The capitals of the Ionic pilasters in the auditorium are of colored glass backed by lights. Above each capital a colored-glass flame spreads into the ceiling decoration. Murals occur between the pilasters, and a sumptuous light fixture is suspended from the blue ceiling. The theater was restored in 1976.

BATAVIA

Campana Factory

Fabyan Parkway at Route 31
1937

FRANK D. CHASE; CHILDS & SMITH

"Located in open country, this long white terra-cotta-tile and glass-block factory building has been advanta-

Campana Factory,
Batavia, Ilinois.
Architectural Forum
(1938).

geously placed on a main highway where its dramatic facade serves as an excellent advertisement for the beauty products made within," wrote the editors of *Architectural Forum* in 1938. The building consists of a central tower articulated by two narrow vertical bands of glass brick and, on either side of the tower, three floors of factory articulated by deep horizontal bands of glass brick that extend around the sides of the building. At night the vertical and horizontal bands are illuminated, as is the neon script at the top of the tower.

BELVIDERE

Municipal Auditorium

W. 1st Street
1929–39

RAYMOND A. ORPUT

This highly refined Art Deco building was designed at the beginning of the Depression. Its construction was delayed until 1938, when PWA funds became available. A few refinements were made to the initial plans, but for the most part the auditorium was built as originally designed. The building consists of a central pavilion dominated by a large parabolic arch; to either side are batterwall stair towers that read as separate volumes. The strictly decorative features of the building are kept to a minimum: cast ornament above the narrow windows on the stair towers and at the parapet of the central pavilion. Within the parabolic arch are glass blocks and a stained-glass window featuring a standing human figure against a backdrop of rainbow patterns. The windows and openings in the main lobby utilize a motif of circles and half-circles.

CHICAGO

Adler Planetarium

Achsah Bond Drive, South Island,
Grant Park
1929–30

ERNST GRUNSFELD, JR.

The planetarium is approached via a long Beaux-Arts axis defined by a pair of walkways separated by twelve cascading pools. The building is composed of four layered volumes: a large and a small dodecagonal base, a drum, and the domed viewing room. The building is sheathed in dark red granite; the dome is copper. Twelve bronze plaques by Alfonso Iannelli, corresponding to the signs of the zodiac, occur high on the exterior corners. On the interior, the nickel-silver dedication plaque set against dark-red marble walls was also designed by Iannelli.

Adler Planetarium (sculpture panel), Chicago, Illinois. *Architects DC.*

Chicago Board of Trade

Jackson Boulevard at La Salle Street
1929–30

HOLABIRD & ROOT

For many years the Chicago Board of Trade was the tallest building in Chicago. Its upward thrust is interrupted by various setbacks, and the

Chicago Board of Trade, Chicago, Illinois.
Architectural Forum (1930).

building finally terminates in a central tower with a hipped copper roof. At the peak of the roof is the cast-aluminum 31-foot-high figure of Ceres by the sculptor John Storrs. Art Deco ornament occurs throughout the building and is especially rich in the large Exchange Hall.

Chicago Daily News Building (now the Riverside Plaza Building)

400 W. Madison Street
1929

HOLABIRD & ROOT

The site of this Art Deco building overlooking the south branch of the Chicago River provided the architects with a number of opportunities unusual in most downtown urban sites. The architects pulled the building back from the river, thus creating a broad plaza with views across the water to the Civic Opera House. The entire structure, including the plaza, was built over a wide expanse of railroad tracks, and this was taken advantage of by letting this raised section serve as a podium for the complex. Especially from across the river, the 26-story structure reads as three distinct buildings: a projecting base (floors 1–7) articulated by piers and buttresses, the windowed rectangular shaft (floors 8–23), and a recessed buttressed crown. The two wings that project forward into the plaza are, in their monumentality, highly reminiscent of Bertram G. Goodhue's design for the Nebraska State Capitol. The building's exterior and interior ornament, realized in limestone, polished granite, marble, and white metal, reveals a broad array of Art Deco pat-

Chicago Daily News
Building, Chicago, Illinois.
Architectural Forum
(1930).

terns. At the center of the building, facing onto the plaza, is the Victor F. Lawson Memorial Fountain, which is flanked by griffins and relief sculpture by the New York artist Alvin W. Meyer. Meyer also provided relief panels on the projecting pylons, between pilasters, and on the major piers of the podium. The Chicago muralist John Norton covered the 180-foot-long barrel vault of the public concourse with an abstract Art Deco painting that depicts various activities of the Chicago Daily News.

Church of Saint Thomas Apostle

5472 S. Kimbark Avenue
1921–22

BARRY BYRNE

Depending on how one divides the cake, this early work by Byrne could be plunked into the pigeonhole of archi-tectural Expressionism or it could be singled out as an instance of the Art Deco sensibility predating the Paris exposition of 1925. Perhaps, in a way, it is both. It seems in any case related to Dutch and German Expressionism of the 1910s and to the later work of Bruce Goff. The architect has applied the Gothic theme of verticality to a series of brick volumes. The angled corners are vertically stepped; finials and upward-thrusting buttresses articulate the skyline; and the elongated windows and doors exhibit V-shaped headers.

Fisher Apartment Building

1209 N. State Street
1936–37

A. N. REBORI AND EDGAR MILLER

The machine imagery of the Streamline Moderne has here been employed in such a way that the building reads as an elegant brick-sheathed container. Above the curved entrance wall is a row of four projecting "vegas," carved in the form of a horse, a buffalo, a mountain lion, and a whale. Both sides of the four-story volume are quarter-circles. The right curve, partially contained within a brick frame on the first floor, is almost completely sheathed in glass brick. A brick pattern connects a set of three fourth-story windows to an extension of the glass brick wall. Behind the curved wall on the left side is an open stairway; its presence is registered in the pattern of ascending glass block slits. Beyond this staircase is a small garden court through which the ground-floor apartments are entered. The building's duplex apartments have a living space that is in part two stories high, lighted by a high glass-brick wall.

Kogen Miller Studio

155 W. Burton Place
1929

EDGAR MILLER AND SAUL KOGEN

The brick three- and four-story Kogen Miller Studio takes its place alongside the buildings of Barry Byrne and Bruce Goff as an example of Art Deco Expressionism. The street entrances are crowned by V-shaped openings realized by a pattern of stepped bricks, and vertical slit windows punctuate the brickwork of the facades. Played against these vertical elements are large horizontal studio windows. The ironwork and the leaded stained glass exhibit patterns that are recognizably Art Deco, yet at the same time appear to be derived from Central European folk art.

Madonna della Strada Chapel, Loyola University

6525 N. Sheridan Road
1938

ANDREW REBORI

The various elements of the Art Deco are here modified by the Streamline Moderne. Pleated walls curve over into the central tower. Clerestory walls of glass brick along the edges of these pleated walls light the interior altar area. A pair of miniaturized classical buildings (with strong Post-Modernist overtones) stand atop the fluted buttresses.

124th Field Artillery Building

Cottage Grove Avenue at 52nd Street,
   Washington Park
1930

C. HERRICK HAMMOND

Like many 19th-century railroad stations, this assembly hall, which has a hooped metal clear-span roof (the steel trusses span 220 feet and are 90 feet high at the center), is hidden behind a limestone masonry facade. On the north side, a pair of monumental towers house the primary entrances, and, to the east, facing Cottage Grove Avenue, an arched entrance has been placed between two low towers. Goodhue-esque figures of World War I soldiers and medieval warriors emerge from the masonry mass near the Cottage Grove Avenue entrance, and Indian figures set amid rows of stylized frontier block-houses are situated on top of the two northern towers. Around parts of the building is a deep entablature that contains stylized fluting and low-relief panels depicting abstracted eagles.

124th Field Artillery Building, Chicago, Illinois. *Architectural Record* (1931).

Palmolive Building

919 N. Michigan Avenue
1929–30

HOLABIRD & ROOT

The 37 floors of this Art Deco sky-scraper are arranged in the pattern characteristic of the style. In this instance, the limestone-sheathed volume is broken up by narrow projecting bays that rise 14 floors. The building culminates in a narrow aluminum tower that supports the famed Palmolive beacon.

333 N. Michigan Avenue Building

333 N. Michigan Avenue
1927

HOLABIRD & ROOT

This 435-foot-high tower anticipated by several years the slab-to-skyscraper design employed in New York City's Rockefeller Center. Like its New York counterpart, this building manages to seem at once soaring and monumental, capturing the spirit of some of Hugh Ferriss's drawings of skyscrapers. The uppermost section of the tower steps

back, and Goodhue-esque sculpture emerges at the four corners. The two-story bronze street entrance, set within dark Minnesota granite, displays a thin linear quality. The building's most outright commitment to the Art Deco was the Tavern Club on the 25th floor. This space, including its wall decoration and furniture, was designed by Winold Reis.

333 North Michigan Avenue, Chicago, Illinois. *The Book of the Boston Architectural Club for 1929.*

Union Carbide and Carbon Building

230 N. Michigan Avenue
1928–29

BURNHAM BROTHERS

The Union Carbide and Carbon Building is one of Chicago's most Art Deco structures. The exterior of this 40-story skyscraper is sheathed in bright terra-cotta. When completed, the building was said to be "the first all–terra-cotta skyscraper in color." Polished black granite with gold terra-cotta trim clothes the first three floors of the building. The pilasters and piers of the floors above, including the uppermost tower, are clad in green terra-cotta with detailing in brilliant gold and other colors. Although the ornament is identifiably Art Deco in its themes, much of it is arranged in a blocklike fashion reminiscent of pre-Columbian Mayan art. The walls of the two-story lobby are partly covered with black polished marble, and the railings, doors, and elevator doors are of patterned bronze.

CLEARING

Lady Esther Plant

7171 W. 65th Street at S. Harlem
  Avenue
1938

ALBERT KAHN, INC.

The office portion of the plant projects a classic Streamline Moderne image: a two-story lobby flanked by symmetrical single-story wings. The lobby is lighted by a two-story wall of glass brick; sections of the interior originally contained floor-to-ceiling mirrors. The central entrance pavilion with its stylized signage looks like an enlarged Lady Esther beauty package. The adjacent wings have continuous ribbon walls of glass that extend around the curved corners of the building.

DEKALB

Halsh Memorial Library

309 Oak Street
1930

WHITE & WEBER

The smooth surfaces of the exterior limestone are delicately patterned with classical and Art Deco motifs. Moldings create the impression of entablatures and cornices, and fluted pilasters are occasionally suggested, especially in the loggias on either side of the entrance. Two low-relief panels depicting medieval figures are situated over the doors. The main section of the library has a low-pitched aluminum-sheathed roof with a central skylight. A classical and Art Deco elegance is also evident within, where the walls are of pink Kasota stone and red Levanto

Lady Esther Plant, Clearing, Illinois. *Architectural Forum* (1938).

Haish Memorial Library, Dekalb, Illinois.
Architectural Forum (1932).

marble, and the hooped ceilings are painted green. The most outright Art Deco ornament is the exterior and interior metalwork.

FREEPORT

Krape Park Bridge

Krape Park, S. Park Boulevard and
   Demeter Drive
1934

MORGAN IPSEN, ENGINEER; R. K. EASTMAN,
   ARCHITECT

A graceful, slightly segmented curve joins the buttresses on either side of this 70-foot clear-span bridge. The buttresses are decorated with quarter-circles and extended wings, and the abutments are layered in characteristic Art Deco fashion. At each end of the bridge quarter-circle concrete parapets terminate the line of the steel railings and light standards.

LAWRENCEVILLE

Lawrenceville Armory

1522 Porter Avenue
1937

S. MILTON EICHBERG, SUPERVISING ARCHITECT

In the middle of the Depression, 11 small reinforced-concrete armories were built in Illinois with PWA funding and WPA labor. The armories were located at Carbondale, Champaign, Delavan, Dixon, Elgin, Lawrenceville, Mt. Vernon, Pontiac, Salem, Sycamore, and Urbana. Each of the buildings was designed under the supervision of S. Milton Eichberg. Each of them was Art Deco in style, with an occasional reference to the Streamline Moderne. The drill halls were covered with gable roofs, and the architect usually introduced decorative features to the principal gable above the entrance. At Lawrenceville the architect provided four piers that project above the roof and that seem almost to form a Gothic screen in front of the tall windows. The entrance block at Lawrenceville has four stout buttresses, and atop the two center ones are large-scale eagles. The eagles and the building's other cast decorative features were provided by the Federal Arts Project in Chicago.

PARK RIDGE

"The Modern Electric Home"

925 S. Cresent
1929

CHARLES RAWSON

This Art Deco model house, which was furnished and opened to the public, was sponsored by a local American

Krape Park Bridge, Freeport, Illinois. *Architectural Concrete* (1934).

Lawrenceville Armory (WPA precast eagles), Lawrenceville, Illinois. *Architectural Concrete* (1939).

Legion post. (The house was raffled off at the end of the tour period.) A pair of narrow layered pylons stands to each side of the arched doorway. The spring line of the entrance arch is continued in a horizontal band across the facade. A small entrance terrace is separated from the street by a low wall that is punctuated by piers with angled tops. Some of the windows are V-shaped, and others have triangular leading. Inside the house is a two-story stair hall with a skylight; the living room was originally domed and was lighted by a revolving, multicolored light fixture.

Pickwick Theater Building

Prospect Avenue at Northwest
   Highway
1928–29

R. Harold Zook and William F.
   McCaughey

The formal and monumental aspects of the Art Deco are here emphasized in a movie theater and its accompanying retail stores and offices. The presence of the theater, with its 1,500-seat auditorium, is announced by a stepped masonry-clad tower topped by an octagonal open-grille lantern (with interior lights). Each side of the tower has a slightly projecting gable pavilion with fluted pilasters, zigzag capitals, and a sunburst pattern that draws attention to the interior. On either side of the tower is a monumental pedestal supporting a large urn. The original interior contained a wealth of Art Deco ornament, including a colorful curtain in front of the stage. At the end of the foyer was a fountain with a female figure by the sculptor Alfonso Iannelli. Iannelli also designed other decorative features of the building, including the cast-iron marquee and the leaf-and-floral-patterned bronze radiator grilles in the lobby.

Pickwick Theater, Park Ridge, Illinois.
Architectural Forum (1932).

Urbana

The Elite Diner

Corner Cunningham and Elm Streets
1953

Fodero Company

Both before and after World War II prefabricated diners were manufactured by a number of companies. Many of these diners, including The Elite, beautifully mirrored the Streamline Moderne trains of the time. The Elite was manufactured by the Fodero Company of Massachusetts and shipped to Illinois, where it was first erected in Champaign. In 1976 it was removed from this site and eventually ended up in 1983 in nearby Urbana, where it was carefully restored with an accompanying new streamline kitchen area.

WESTERN SPRINGS

First Congregational Church

1106 Chestnut Street
1926–27

GEORGE GRANT ELMSLIE

Elmslie, along with his partner William Gray Purcell, was one of the principal exponents of the Prairie School during the first two decades of the century. Like many Prairie School practitioners, Elmslie shifted direction in the 1920s, when he began incorporating into his designs elements borrowed from European Expressionism and from the broad palette of the Art Deco. Although the cruciform plan of the First Congregational Church is tra-

ditional, its proportions and above all its details mingle the Prairie School style with the Art Deco mode of early Goodhue. Delight in the use of the triangle is apparent in the steeple, which assumes the form of a miniature pyramid above the crossing, in the four-gabled roof of the low bell tower, and in the triangular ornament at the gable end of the roof. Delicate linear designs emerge from the pilasters on either side of the entrance, in panels beside the doors to the Sunday school wing, and in four figures in the niches of the altar. These niches, plus the niche for the crucified Christ, are stepped in Art Deco fashion, and their stepped-back octagonal tops suggest the summit of an Art Deco skyscraper. Ornament carved in wood, some of it displaying a stylized pattern of musical clefts and notes, also conveys an Art Deco sensibility.

First Congregational Church, Western Springs, Illinois.

Acorn Knoll Estates (Ruth Page house). West Lake Forest, Illinois. *Architectural Record* (1934).

WEST LAKE FOREST

Acorn Knoll Estates

1936

GENERAL HOUSES, INC.

General Houses, Inc., designed and constructed five houses in Acorn Knoll Estates. These one-story prefabricated metal houses are all Moderne in style, with occasional hints of the Streamline Moderne. Prefabricated panels make up the walls and the combined flat-roof ceilings. Windows are treated as horizontal bands that often wrap around corners. On the exterior, each of the houses focuses attention on the automobile via a driveway and an attached garage.

WILMETTE

School of Saint Francis Xavier

808 Linden Avenue
1922–23

BARRY BYRNE

The School of Saint Francis Xavier is an early example of Barry Byrne's highly personal version of Expressionism, which often incorporated elements of the Art Deco. The school is a simple

two-story brick box whose walls are interrupted by brick piers. The piers support gabled recessed panels that contain the windows and brick spandrels. The edges of the piers are articulated with brick laid in an in-and-out pattern that creates a jagged edge. Much of the original ornament has been removed (the terra-cotta cornice and the exterior ironwork), but the principal entrance, with its recessed panel of zigzag terra-cotta, remains intact, as does the terra-cotta decoration along the vertical edges of the building.

School of Saint Francis Xavier (doorway), Wilmette, Illinois. *Architectural Record* (1930).

INDIANA

EVANSTON

Greyhound Bus Terminal

102 N.W. 3rd Street

1938

W. S. ARRASMITH (WISCHMEYER, ARRASMITH AND ELSWICK)

The design of this terminal centers on a curved corner pavilion, with a curved marquee below, glass bricks above, and then a neon-light vertical sign. This Streamline image bus terminal has paneled walls in green, red, and cream colors.

HAMMOND

Oliver P. Morton High School

7040 Marshall Avenue

1936–37

GEORGE GRANT ELMSLIE AND WILLIAM S. HUTTON

In the early 1930s George Grant Elmslie, one of the pre-eminent figures of the Prairie School movement, designed a number of Streamline Moderne houses (none of which was built) and several PWA Moderne buildings. The most impressive of the latter are several schools that he designed with William S. Hutton. While similar to some of Elmslie's work in the 1910s with William Gray Purcell, these schools exhibit a distinctly Moderne quality.

The Morton High School building, which was a PWA-funded project, is a U-shaped three-story structure clad in brick and polished marble, with decoration in cast stone.

Elmslie employed rows of piers that terminate below the parapet in terra-cotta ornament. Some of the piers, such as those on the auditorium, are layered in an Art Deco manner and have sculptured cast-stone tops. Elmslie created decorative patterns that are uniquely his own, but their placement on the facades reflects the Art Deco sensibility. Above the main entrance are two groups of figures and freestanding stone screens designed by Alfonso Iannelli. Adjacent to the entrance to the gymnasium, Iannelli's figures, which seem to grow out of the wall surface, owe an obvious debt to the work of Bertram G. Goodhue. Elmslie and Hutton also designed two other public schools in Hammond: the Edison School (7025 Madison Avenue) and the Irving School (4727 Pine Street). All three of these schools were constructed between 1936 and 1938. All display Art Deco elements of design.

INDIANAPOLIS

Blickman-Jones House

5601 N. Washington Boulevard

1938

EDWARD PIERRE

The Streamline Moderne elements of this house include curved walls and corner windows. The arched entrance is articulated by abstracted pilasters and voussoirs. Several of the windows are covered by the kind of masonry grilles associated with traditional Mediterranean architecture.

Coca-Cola Bottling Company Building (now the IPS Service Building)

801 N. Carrollton Avenue
1931,1940,1949

RUBUSH & HUNTER

This building is a delicate and quite formal version of the Art Deco. The structure is clad in white glazed terra-cotta tile. The ends of the building, which are treated as pavilions, exhibit fluted vertical panels that suggest pilasters. A stylized version of Ionic capitals occurs to the side (not on top) of these pilasters. Low-relief orna-ment — flowers, sunbursts, and styl-ized fountains — has been placed below the second-floor windows and above the entrance. A thin, decorated metal canopy exhibits the characteris-tic Art Deco pattern of receding planes leading to the door. The lobby has travertine walls and decorative metal grilles.

Livestock Judging Pavilion, Indiana State Fair

38th Street between Fall Creek Parkway and Winthrop Avenue
1939

RUSS & HARRISON

The style of this large brick-sheathed structure is primarily Art Deco, but many of the building's details are Streamline Moderne. The various pub-lic entrances are treated as slightly projecting screens that rise above the adjacent parapeted walls. Wide but-tresses between these entrances sug-gest engaged classical piers. Similar but smaller buttresses punctuate the glazed gabled ends of the building.

The large-scale windows, which butt up against the buttresses or entrance screens, are of Insulux glass brick.

WEST LAFAYETTE

Purdue Housing Research Project

Adjacent to the campus of Purdue University
1936–38

J. ANDRE FOUILHOUX; HOWARD T. FISHER & JOHN A. PRUYN; BURNHAM BROTHERS; HAMMOND INSULATED STEEL CONSTRUCTION COMPANY

Purdue University commissioned five experimental houses built of concrete and steel. All of the houses were Moderne in style, and all contained ele-ments of the Streamline Moderne. The houses were treated as one- or two-story flat-roofed stucco-sheathed boxes with occasional curved details in the roofs, decks, and railings. The earliest of the five houses, designed by the New York architect J. Andre Fouilhoux, employed a traditional wood frame that was covered by wire mesh and concrete stucco. Three later houses had steel frames covered with stucco. The walls, floors, and flat roof of House #3 were of reinforced concrete.

Purdue Housing Research Project, West Lafayette, Indiana. *Architectural Record* (1936).

IOWA

BURLINGTON

Schramm House

2690 S. Main Street
1938–39

HOLABIRD & ROOT

One of the very few houses designed by the Chicago firm of Holabird & Root, the Schramm House is a large two-story structure situated on a bluff overlooking the Mississippi River. The walls of the house are sheathed in white-painted brick that from a distance reads as concrete. Many of the hallmarks of the Streamline Moderne are present: horizontal bands of metal-frame casement windows, curved corners and bays, and glass brick. To the right of the deeply recessed entrance is a curved wall with a narrow glass-brick window. Behind this window is a staircase with a metal railings. The studio at the rear of the house has a wide glass-brick wall, and the screened porch off the dining room is treated as a continuation of the east wall of the adjoining studio.

Van Bennett House

1 The Oak Street
1941

DANE D. MORGAN

Three of America's most impressive Moderne houses are in Iowa: the Schramm House (see above) and the Van Bennett House in Burlington, and the Butler House (see page 119) in Des Moines. The Van Bennett House is the least well-known of the three houses, and it is in several ways the most unusual. The house plays a highly sophisticated dual game: there is much about the design that is Streamline Moderne, but there are also strong elements of the Art Deco; certain of the house's features are on the scale of a public building, but the design then opposes them with massing and details that are indisputably domestic. The house's parapeted flat-roofed volumes suggest both the domestic and the Streamline Moderne. Facing the road is an emphatically horizontal volume that contains the garages. A low flat-roofed loggia along one side of the garages leads to the entrance and adds another note of domestic scale. Offsetting this scale are the three vertically oriented windows to the left of the entrance. The narrow first- and second-floor windows are deeply recessed and separated by a metal spandrel panel. The panel itself is articulated with geometric Art Deco motifs. Another overly public note is the rustic limestone sheathing composed of large-scale blocks. Surprisingly, all of these seemingly disparate features come together in a handsome and coherent design.

War Memorial Auditorium

Front Street east of Jefferson Street
1938

ROBIN B. CARSWELL

This late PWA Moderne structure almost but not quite swings over into the Streamline Moderne. Its connected volumes are of reinforced concrete painted white. The Streamline Moderne elements of the design range from curved horizontal and vertical surfaces to glass-brick and porthole windows. The various facades are in their proportions treated in a balanced, classical fashion. The principal five-story block has at its center 10 narrow glass-block windows. To either side are small square openings covered by grilles. The doors and windows on the ground floor are arranged as deep-set, horizontally oriented openings that establish the base of the building. The plain walls of the tall tower are interrupted near the top by projecting roof drains.

CHARLES CITY

Charles Theater

N. Main Street south of Blunt Street
1935–36

WETHERELL & HARRISON

The street facade of this motion picture theater evokes the Streamline Moderne, but the terra-cotta ornament looks back to the Art Deco, with motifs ranging from abstracted flowers to elongated tassel-like forms. Most of the exterior surface of the building is a shimmering black-glazed terra-cotta, while the decorative elements are in brilliant golds, rusts, and blues.

COUNCIL BLUFFS

Lewis and Clark Monument

North end of Rainbow Road
1935

HARRY STINSON, SCULPTOR; GEORGE L.
    HORNER, ARCHITECT

The sculptor and the architect created an appropriately intimate yet expansive public space for a monument commemorating Lewis and Clark's meeting with members of the Otoe and Winnebago tribes. The gentle slope of a hill is interrupted by terraces on two levels; the terraces are contained by low rough limestone walls and curved stairs. The monument itself consists of a pair of quarter-circle slabs lined with low benches on one side. The slabs continue the gentle semicircle of the stairs that lead to the upper platform. The figures in low relief on both faces of the slabs occasionally project beyond their boxlike frames.

DES MOINES

Bankers Life Building

711 High Street
1939–40

TINSLEY, MCBROOM, HIGGINS, LIGHTER &
    LYONS

The Bankers Life Building could easily be mistaken for a government office building, carrying on the long tradition of banks, newspapers, and insurance companies wishing to associate themselves (at least symbolically) with the seats of power. This T-shaped seven-story building employs a late 1930s ver-

Bankers Life Building, Des Moine, Iowa. Iowa Historical Society.

sion of the American Vertical sky-scraper style. As with other late examples of this Art Deco style, the building's design is not so obviously based on classical precedent. The Bankers Life Building also incorporates various Streamline Moderne details: glass brick, curved and banded walls, metal ship's railings, and so on. The ground floor of the building is sheathed in an elegant polished rainbow granite; above this granite base the walls are covered with smooth, finely jointed pale yellow/tan limestone. The building is discreetly ornamented with low-relief sculpture and molded glass panels. The sculpture, whose themes are ostensibly Native American, seems influenced by pre-Columbian art of Mexico and Central America. The unusual molded-glass panels were designed and executed by Lowell Houser and Glenn Chamberlain.

Butler House (now the Kragie, Newell Advertising Agency)

2633 S. Fleur Drive
1935–37

GEORGE KRAETSCH (KRAETSCH & KRAETSCH)

The house's original owner, the engineer Earl Butler, asked the Des Moines architectural firm Kraetsch & Kraetsch to design for him "the most modern house in the world." The architect obviously looked intensely at examples of both the International Style and the Streamline Moderne. The result was a complex arrangement of one- to three-story volumes exhibiting curved facades, cantilevered roof decks, V-shaped bays, metal ship's railings, horizontal strip windows, and glass brick. Inside the house are metal staircases and an ascending ramp, as well as a

wide array of mechanical and electrical gadgets. The monumentality of the reinforced-concrete walls is emphasized by the deep reveals around the windows and doors. An embedded horizontal line extends around the upper walls of the house. The third-floor sunroom, with its cantilevered roof and terrace, conveys the sense of being on a ship's deck. The house was sensitively renovated and enlarged in 1988–89.

Fire Department Headquarters

Mulberry Street at 9th Street, northwest corner
1937–38

PROUDFOOT, RAWSON, BROOKS, & BORG

Although not as well known, the Des Moines Fire Department Headquarters building has many of the same features as the celebrated Pan Pacific Auditorium in Los Angeles. The firehouse's five bays are separated by curved fins that project above the parapeted roof. The corner of the building facing the intersection is curved, and the metal-frame windows set in horizontal bands reinforce the impression of rapid movement.

Valley National Bank Building

512 Walnut Street
1931–32

PROUDFOOT, RAWSON, SOUERS, & THOMAS

The Valley National Bank Building illustrates how the Art Deco swept, quickly and with great refinement, across the country in the late 1920s and early 1930s. The building was originally planned as a 16-story skyscraper, but because of the Depression it was cut back to five floors. The five floors are contained in a single block. A band of black marble envelops the ground-floor storefronts and the entrances to the bank. Across the four upper stories there is the characteristically Art Deco hint of fluted pilasters, as well as vertical bands of recessed windows and spandrels. In the lobby, a row of elevator doors presents a shimmering series of black marble and reflective metal surfaces. The decorative panels on the metal doors include husks of corn. The two-story banking room on the second floor is richly embellished with fluted stone pilasters, an elaborately painted ceiling, suspended metal-and-glass light fixtures, and even a hanging metal octagonal Art Deco clock. The building was carefully restored in 1979.

Valley National Bank Building, Des Moines, Iowa. Valley National Bank.

KANSAS

BELLEVILLE

Republic County Courthouse

Courthouse Square
1939

R. E. MANN AND A. R. MANN

This PWA Moderne courthouse is lighter in feeling than most mid- to late 1930s Moderne designs. The building is of reinforced concrete, with stone exterior surfaces and stone and metal ornament. Between the piers are recessed panels (containing windows and black granite spandrels) that read as voids. Various geometric patterns—circles, squares, and repeated vertical lines—were sandblasted into the polished black granite. The

parapet exhibits interwoven spirals in a narrow sculptured band. Behind the elongated horizontal opening in which the building's name appears are the windows to the third-floor jail.

Republic County Courthouse, Belleville, Kansas. *Architectural Concrete* (1939).

MICHIGAN

BLOOMFIELD HILLS

Kingswood School for Girls, Cranbrook Academy

Big Beaver Road west of Highway 10
1929–31

ELIEL SAARINEN

Any building designed by Eliel Saarinen does not fit comfortably into a set style. Still, his buildings for the girls' school at Cranbrook have a decided Art Deco quality about them, even if their essential design premise lies within the turn-of-the-century European Arts and Crafts tradition. The buildings' gate posts, light standards, and many of the loggia piers reveal a

highly abstracted floral motif, and the tall layered chimneys feature a pattern of inserted squares. The metalwork of the gates and of the exterior and interior light fixtures seems at one moment derived from northern European and medieval designs and at other times reminiscent of the Art Deco.

Other buildings at Cranbrook—among them the Cranbrook School for Boys (1914–30) and the Institute of Science (1931–33)—exhibit similar qualities. Eliel Saarinen's later Cranbrook Academy of Art (1932–42), particularly the museum with the Carl Milles sculpture in the forecourt, contains elements of the Streamline Moderne.

Kingswood School for Girls, Cranbrook Academy, Bloomfield Hills, Michigan. Museum of Cranbrook Academy.

DETROIT

Elwood Bar

2100 Woodward Avenue
1937

Located at the angled corner of Woodward Avenue and Elizabeth Street, this shimmering metal building easily dominates its urban setting. The exterior is sheathed in a light cream color, accented with deep, dark blue and red neon. At the junction of the two streets the building curves and projects upward to form a round tower; indented into the curve at ground level is the entrance. The Streamline Moderne's reference to automated speed, via the horizontal line, is expressed here by repetitive banding around the tower, by a projecting horizontal band over the windows, and by the single row of metal-and-neon lettering on both street facades.

Fisher Building

W. Grand Boulevard at 2nd Avenue, northwest corner
1927–28

ALBERT KAHN, INC.

The architecture of Albert Kahn is closely associated with the automobile industry of Detroit. In addition to designing many automobile production plants, Kahn's firm contributed substantially to Detroit's commercial downtown. One such contribution was the 26-story Fisher Building, which in fact comprises three structures: an office tower, a 2,800-seat theater, and an 11-story 1,000-car parking garage. The entire complex is rich both in imagery and in the variety of its costly materials. The tower employs the classic skyscraper setback scheme first made popular in New York (although it is used here for aesthetic effect, not in

Elwood Bar, Detroit, Michigan.

Fisher Building, Detroit, Michigan. *American Architect* (1929). *Inset,* Fisher Building. *The Book of the Boston Architectural Club for 1929.*

response to zoning requirements). The first 21 floors present a relatively conservative massing, but above that point the design turns to the French Chateauesque. Tall gabled dormers and upward-projecting buttresses provide the base for a steep pyramidal copper roof. Exterior floodlighting emphasizes the building's verticality while also illuminating its elaborate upper stories and roof. Stylistic borrowing occurs throughout the building. The numerous arched windows and the main entrance seem inspired partly by the Romanesque, partly by Beaux-Arts classicism. The interior of the theater was a close-to-impossible mixture of the Mayan and the Art Deco; regrettably, this dramatic exercise in Art Deco pre-Columbianism was destroyed when the theater was remodeled in the 1960s. The sculpture for the office tower and the theater was produced by Ricci and Zari, and Thomas Di Lorenzo; the numerous cast aluminum pieces were designed by the Edward F. Cauldwell Company. The Cauldwell firm also modeled much of the ornament within the arcade.

Ford Rotunda

Rotunda Drive (Dearborn)
1933

ALBERT KAHN, INC.

The 1941 *WPA Guide to Michigan* describes this circular building as "modernistic" and "resembling four different-sized gears, one above the other." The rotunda, which has accordion-pleated walls, was originally designed and built for the 1933 Century of Progress Exposition in Chicago; it was subsequently moved to this site to serve as a visitor's center for the Ford Motor Company. No windows puncture the exterior of the building (natural light enters via skylights), so that the vertical patterning of the four receding cylinders becomes its architectural statement.

Livingston Memorial Lighthouse

Lakeshore Drive (east end), Belle Island
1930

ALBERT KAHN, INC.

This is a lighthouse in the form of a highly abstract classical fluted column, constructed of Georgian white marble and surmounted by a bronze lantern. The base of the 58-foot shaft is centered by a bronze door with Art Deco motifs. Overhead a relief sculpture in marble depicts wind and water; it is anchored by a bronze relief portrait, by sculptor Geza Maroti, of William Livingston, a prominent figure in the development of shipping on the Great Lakes.

Radio Station WWJ Building

630 W. Lafayette Boulevard
1936

ALBERT KAHN, INC.

The high, narrow street facade of this radio station building resembles a Moderne box, or even a frosted-glass light fixture. The pale Indiana limestone is treated as a series of five slightly concave surfaces. At the base, near the entrance, are panels of artificial black stone into which two high-relief sculptures by Carl Milles are carved. The station's call letters appear over the entrance, carved into the dark stone, and also as freestanding metal letters arranged vertically and reaching to the uppermost parapet.

Shrine of the Little Flower

11 Mile Road at Woodland Avenue
(Royal Oaks)
1929–33

HENRY J. MCGILL AND TALBOT F. HAMLIN;
RENÉ PAUL CHAMBELLAN, SCULPTOR

McGill, with his early collaborator Talbot Hamlin, was one of the country's most interesting and exciting exponents of the Art Deco. His talents are evident in the Church of the Most Precious Blood (1931–32) in Queens, New York (see page 52), as well as in the Shrine of the Little Flower. Both buildings, especially the Detroit church, have a primitive, pre-Columbian feeling about them, and the tower is reminiscent of a temple in Tikal. The numerous figurative sculptures around the building and at the base of the tower emerge from the stone surfaces in a Goodhue-esque manner. One of the country's first "radio priests," and a highly controversial figure in the early 1930s, Father Charles E. Coughlin commissioned this avantgarde Art Deco church, which surprisingly did not draw much adverse comment.

Union Trust Building (now the Guardian Building)

500 Griswold Street
1927–28

WIRT C. ROWLAND (SMITH, HINCHMAN & GRYLLS)

Wirt Rowland, a designer in the Detroit firm of Smith Hinchman & Grylls, produced two of the city's major Art Deco monuments in the 1920s: the Union Trust Building and the Greater Penobscot Building. With its 47 floors, the Greater Penobscot Building

Guardian Building (Union Trust Building), Detroit, Michigan. *American Architect* (1929).

(1927–28), at 645 Griswold Street, is the taller of the two, but the Union Trust Building is the more exuberant. It is also one of the most colorful of America's Art Deco skyscrapers. The cragged form of this 535-foot-high building exhibits a pre-Columbian quality. The building's base is sheathed in multicolored granite and Mankato stone, and the higher floors have a skin of orange-tan brick. Mary Chase Stratton of the Pewabic Pottery in Detroit produced the glazed tile in green, buff, cream, orange-red, and blue; other tiles were provided by the Rockwood Pottery of Cincinnati, Ohio. The entrance hemicycle, with its stepped corbeled arches, exhibits a wonderful tiled half-dome. On either side, emerging out of the stone, is a male figure. Projecting above the keystone is a winged mask form that is supposedly Aztec. The stepped pre-Columbian motif occurs throughout the interior and is especially evident in the three-story vaulted lobby and in the elevator bays. Tiffany and Company of New York City provided the Favrill glass that was inserted in the elevator doors. The mosaic mural in the main lobby is the work of the New York artist Ezra Winter, who is also responsible for the large mural in the main banking room.

GRAND RAPIDS

Grand Rapids Airport, Administration Building

Madison Avenue, S.E. at Pennell Road
1939–40; demolished c. 1965

F. SPENCER WEBER

Writing in 1940, then manager of the Grand Rapids Airport, Thomas E. Walsh, boasted that "Spencer Weber, the Lansing engineer who designed our administration building, caught the spirit of modern flying in his design. And architectural concrete has caught his moving, fluid design and has frozen it in graceful lines and masses" (*Architectural Concrete* 6, no. 4 (1940): 9). This building was built by Works Project Administration laborers and is composed of four round-cornered concrete sections: a two-story center with the control tower overhead, and a wing

Cedar Water Conditioning Plant (Lansing Waterworks), Lansing, Michigan. *Architectural Concrete* (1938).

on either side. Horizontal window bands encircled the corners, and above the pairs of entrance doors was a small turretlike glass bay. Concrete wall grilles framed the entrance, and the building's name was cast in horizontal bands, facing both the street front and the runway boarding area.

George W. Welsh Civic Auditorium

227 Lyon Street N.W.
1932–33

ROBINSON AND CAMPAU; SMITH, HINCHMAN AND GRYLLS

This structure is an impressive example of the PWA Moderne (according to Kathryn Bishop Eckert in her 1993 *Buildings Of Michigan*, the building is one of the most impressive PWA Moderne buildings in Michigan). Monumental piers (reading both as wall and pier) provide the formal classical entrance. The sculptor Corrado Joseph Parducci provided the decorative relief sculpture depicting waves and sea shells, together with figures representing various sports, the arts, industry, and science. The building was restored in 1985.

LANSING

Lansing Waterworks (Cedar Water Conditioning Plant)

148 S. Cedar Street
1938–39

BLACK & BLACK; ALVORD, BURDICK & HOWSON, ENGINEERS

"Streamlining," it was noted in a 1940 article on the Lansing Waterworks, "is the keynote of the [building's] architectural design even to such small details as the handles of the operating tables." In truth, though, this building represents a combination of the Streamline Moderne and the earlier Art Deco. Many of the exterior walls exhibit fluted pilasters alternating with vertical bands of windows and square panels. Over the entrance is a 32-foot-high relief sculpture depicting a woman with small-scale children at her feet. Perhaps the strongest nod to the Streamline is the horizontal band containing air vents that begins on either side of the entrance and continues around the entire building. Almost all of the windows are of glass brick. The central two-story lobby space, which has a concrete gabled ceiling, is lighted by high glass-brick clerestory windows. The sculpture was a product of the Federal Arts Project, and the building itself was constructed by the WPA.

MINNESOTA

FARIBAULT

Rice County Courthouse

218 3rd Street N.E.

1932

NAIRNE W. FISHER

Here is a PWA Moderne building designed even before the establishment of the PWA. In contrast to most buildings in this style, the Rice County Courthouse has exterior walls in which heavy rustic limestone alternates with thin bands of smoothly worked stone. The traditional sculptural quality of masonry is enhanced by the deep recesses provided for the windows and doors. The entrance is framed by a pair of low towers, and the three floors of windows and their accompanying metal spandrels are arranged as deep slots within the walls. The windows and spandrels above the entrance are covered with Art Deco metalwork in a linear pattern. Recessed rectangular panels high on the facade contain low-relief sculpture.

GRAND MARAIS

Naniboujou Club

Fifteen miles northeast of Grand Marais on Highway 61

1928–29

HOLSTEAD & SULLIVAN

A year before the main lodge was built, the Brule Land and Outing Company purchased 3,000 acres that included a mile of Lake Superior shorefront. The Naniboujou Club was planned as a fashionable resort that would include public beach facilities as well as several hundred private cabins. With the coming of the Depression, these grandiose plans were abandoned. The only substantial part of the plan realized was the lodge. The exterior of this story-and-a-half shingle-clad structure seems appropriate for its North Woods setting, with the exception of such features as the V-shaped windows and the numerous pencil-like lightning rods rising from the ridges of the roof. The interior, however, is a different story, for it offers one of the few public examples of rustic Art Deco. The walls and tent-like ceiling of the main dining room, which features a stone fireplace, are covered in Art Deco and Native American motifs (based upon Cree Indian designs). The brilliant patterns of reds, oranges, blues, and greens that cover these surfaces were painted by the French-Canadian artist Antoine Gouffée. The lodge also boasts Art Deco lighting fixtures and leaded stained glass.

MINNEAPOLIS

Apartments

2805 and 2801 Xerxes Avenue S.
1935–36

PERRY CROSIER

This pair of boxy Moderne apartment buildings wanders back and forth between the late Art Deco and the Streamline Moderne. The buildings' white stucco walls, metal-frame corner windows, and ship's railings are Streamline elements to be sure, but they are offset by vertical banding and stepped patterns that occur near the entrance. The most unusual features of the design are the four small stepped volumes that house the interior stairway.

Farmers and Mechanics Bank Building (now the Marquette Bank Building)

88 6th Street S.
1941

MCENARY & KRAFFT

A warm Kasota stone forms the facade of this late, highly refined version of the

Art Deco. High-relief sculpture occurs alongside the entrance. To the left is the figure of a farmer, to the right a worker; the two figures were sculpted by Warren Mosman. On the interior, the two-story banking room has an elegant Streamline Moderne atmosphere, with gold palmettolike suspended light fixtures, panels in wood depicting aspects of Minnesota's economy, and numerous other details in chrome and polished bronze.

Foshay Tower

821 Marquette Avenue
1926–29

MAGNEY & TUSLER; HOOPER & JANUSCH

The client, who greatly admired the Washington Monument, prompted his architects to design a 32-story, 447-foot-high tower in the form of an obelisk. The tower rests on a two-story base, and below this are two subterranean levels

Foshay Tower, Minneapolis, Minnesota.

of parking. The entire building is sheathed in light gray limestone. While the obelisk itself is undecorated, the base exhibits, in a reticent fashion, recessed panels containing low-relief Art Deco ornament. Many Art Deco motifs are employed on the interior, including a stylized presentation of the Foshay Tower itself on the elevator doors.

Larson Monument

Lakewood Cemetery, 36th Street at
   Hennepin Avenue
1939

CLARENCE DUNN (BRAHAM MONUMENT
   COMPANY)

It is surprising how many cemetery monuments dating from the late 1920s and subsequent decades reflect the influence of the Art Deco. One would assume that the conservative nature of a funerary monument, plus the general sobriety of client, monument maker, and designer, would argue strongly for the continuation of traditional forms.

Larson Monument, Minneapolis, Minnesota.

But as the Larson Monument indicates, current fashions tend to infiltrate even monument design. Modest in size, the Larson Monument is organized in three distinct parts: a central stone, layered at its side and top edges, flanked by two highly stylized quarter-circular fanlike seashells. These three sections, slightly separated from one another, are placed on a horizontal slab that disappears into the surrounding turf. The monument's lettering and small decorated panel are Art Deco in feeling. The entire monument is realized in a soft orange-pink granite. Not far to the north is another, simpler Art Deco monument that dates from 1940 and was designed for the Magee family.

Minneapolis Armory

500 6th Street S.
1935–36

P. C. BETTENBURG, ARCHITECT; WALTER H.
   WHEELER, ENGINEER

The Minneapolis Armory is one of the country's most impressive PWA Moderne buildings. Two large towers frame the drill hall; with their semicircular ends, these towers can be interpreted either as abstracted medieval towers or as dramatic Streamline Moderne forms. Between the towers are the entrances. Centered and just below the top of the parapet over each entrance are dramatic, sharply angular eagles in high relief. Above the shiny metal doors, the limestone facade steps out and three narrow windows display a characteristic Art Deco pattern. Many Art Deco motifs are employed on the interior, and the Trophy Room contains two Federal Arts Project murals. One of these murals, by Lucia Wiley, presents the history of the Minnesota National Guard; the other, by Elsa Jemne, comments on the state's early history and its natural resources. The 85-foot-high drill hall, with its metal-truss hipped roof, is undeniably impressive.

Rand Tower (now the Dain Tower)

527–529 Marquette Avenue
1928–29

HOLABIRD & ROOT

The tall and narrow Rand Tower effectively sums up the late phase of the stripped American Vertical skyscraper style. Each of the facades contains dark vertical bands of windows and spandrels. The corners of the building are built out slightly to impart a sense of solidity. The building's upper reaches exhibit slight setbacks, enhancing the towerlike quality of the design. There is a restrained use of Art Deco ornament on the exterior, most notably the figures of an aviator and an airplane. The interior lobby employs rich materials and decoration, including a silver statue by Oskar J.W. Hansen entitled *Wings*.

United States Post Office Building

100 1st Street S.
1931–33

MAGNEY & TUSLER

This thick-walled, three- and four-story building combines a sense of modernity (the Art Deco in monumental mode) with the feeling of an ancient Babylonian (or is it pre-Columbian?) temple. The building has a base of black granite; the walls above the base are a warm cream-colored Shakopee dolomite.

Washburn Water Tower

Prospect Avenue at Overview Terrace
1931–32

FELLOWS & HUEY, ARCHITECTS; WILLIAM S. HEWITT, ENGINEER

The dome of this round reinforced-concrete water tower simply continues the wall plane up to its crown. The walls are articulated by pilasters that terminate in cast eagles. Emerging from

U.S. Post Office, Minneapolis, Minnesota.

Washburn Water Tower, Minneapolis, Minnesota.

the base of each pilaster is an over-scaled medieval warrior holding a sword. The swords' points echo the double-V motif that occurs below the eagles. The sculpture was executed by John K. Daniels.

White Spot Cafe

615 10th Street
1932

The 1920s and 1930s saw the proliferation throughout the country of small fast-food establishments, most of which specialized in hamburgers. This one presents a classic image: a towerlike structure housing the entrance and a generous, horizontally oriented window that not only provided light to the small counter-and-stool lunchroom but also, and perhaps even more importantly, served as an advertisement for the activity within. While such restaurants invariably had signs, the building itself served as the real sign (especially effective at night when intensely illuminated). The White Spot Cafe is sheathed in white glazed brick with decorative patterns in black glazed brick.

NEW ULM

Public Library and Historical Museum

27 Broadway N.
1936

ALBERT G. PLAGENS

The theme of fluting occurs across the facades of this small but vigorous PWA Moderne building: as spandrels below windows, as the curved tops of the pair of buttresses flanking the entrance, and elsewhere. Above the entrance, within a deeply recessed panel, is a relief sculpture of a prairie schooner.

SAINT PAUL

House

1775 Hillcrest Avenue
1939

A curved, two-story, glass-brick wall, stepped at its base, dominates this Streamline Moderne design. The off-center entrance exhibits a stepped parapet with curved ends. Below the parapet a thin horizontal band is inscribed. Porthole and corner windows interrupt the house's white-painted brick walls. A similar house was built at the same time in Kansas City.

Mickey's Diner

36 9th Street W. at Saint Peter Street
1937

MANUFACTURED BY THE JERRY O'MAHONY
COMPANY OF BAYONNE, NEW JERSEY

One of the country's classic Streamline Moderne diners, Mickey's has a porcelainized-metal facade that emphasizes movement via its continuous band of windows, which is accentuated by horizontal bands of color. A long, horizontally oriented roof sign with curved ends employs the typeface Broadway, which was commonly used in Moderne designs.

Saint Paul City Hall and Ramsey County Courthouse

15 Kellogg Boulevard W.
1931–32

HOLABIRD & ROOT; ELLERBE ARCHITECTS

Saint Paul City Hall and Ramsey County Courthouse, Saint Paul, Minnesota.

This civic building assumes the guise of an American Vertical–style Art Deco skyscraper. The designers employed the scheme of setbacks characteristic of the style, and the building eventually climbs to 265 feet, encompassing 19 stories. Verticality is emphasized via the recessed window-and-spandrel strips and by vertical grooving in the buff-colored limestone sheathing. Over the Kellogg Boulevard and the Fourth Street entrances are sculptures by Lee Lawrie. In the lobby the six elevator doors exhibit relief sculpture depicting the virtues of manual labor and of the machine. In the council chambers are murals by John Norton, an artist who worked with Frank Lloyd Wright and Purcell and Elmslie in the 1910s.

The centerpiece of the building, and without question one of the most impressive Art Deco spaces in the country, is the 45-foot-high concourse just inside the 4th Street entrance. The walls of this long hall with their projecting pilasters are lined with highly polished dark blue Belgian marble. The upper face of each pilaster is covered in bronze, and concealed lights carry the form up to the ceiling. The ceiling itself is mirrored; the floor is a light-colored marble. At the end of the concourse is Carl Milles's onyx sculpture of Peace (a standing figure of an Indian holding a peace pipe). Hidden lights cause the translucent onyx to glow, contrasting dramatically with the almost black surrounding space.

White Castle Hamburger Shop

Auditorium Street at 6th Street W.,
    southwest corner
c. 1941

Minnesota Museum of Art (Women's Club Building), Saint Paul, Minnesota.

Combining the Streamline Moderne with a child's image of a medieval castle might on the surface seem an impossible task, but the White Castle designers succeeded admirably. These little shops, with their large windows and simple hygienic white porcelain walls read as Moderne, but the delight of the little building is its image of a crenelated castle. As an added note the original five-cent hamburgers were placed in little white boxes in the form of the towered, crenelated hamburger shop.

Women's Club Building (now the Minnesota Museum of Art)

305 Saint Peter Street
1931

MAGNUS JAMNE

This building, sheathed in light yellow-buff Mankato travertine, manages to avoid reading as a monumental masonry structure. Its detailing and form look to the Art Deco, but there is a refined, almost linear quality about the building that is reminiscent of the English Regency style of the early 19th century. There is a strong hint as well of the Streamline Moderne in the use of angular bays and horizontal bands of metal-frame windows. The surfaces of pale travertine project forward slightly from the black marble base of the building. Motifs such as the stepped walls of the chimney and the corbeled steplike lintel over the entrance are recognizably Art Deco. Although the interior has been remodeled, it still retains many of its Art Deco details, including the fireplaces in the ground-floor reception hall and third-floor lounge. The three principal public spaces of the building—the first-floor auditorium, the second-floor dining room, and the third-floor lounge—all terminate in a curved window wall.

VIRGINIA

Maco Theater

Chestnut Street near 5th Street W.
c. 1940

LIEBENBERG & KAPLIN

In the 1920s and 1930s the Minneapolis firm Liebenberg & Kaplin designed several motion picture theaters in the Art Deco and Streamline Moderne styles. The Maco Theater is an exuber-ant Streamline Moderne example of their work. The street facade is beautifully summed up in the vertical sign that sprouts from the marquee. The marquee itself is stepped, with curved corners, and it springs from a wall with curved corners of glass brick. The brightly colored metal and other materials provide effective advertising during the day, but the theater reveals its real glory at night when its glass brick, neon bands, and rows of incandescent bulbs are all brightly lit.

MISSOURI

CLAYTON

Bath House, Municipal Swimming Pool

City Park
1936

HAL. LYNCH

The park, along with the facilities within it, was acquired by the city of Clayton with the help of WPA funding. Since the construction team consisted basically of unskilled WPA labor, the design was kept simple. The small bath house, despite a certain do-it-yourself quality, is nonetheless a vigorous example of the Art Deco. The entrance facade is enlivened by projecting pilasters that terminate below the cornice. Within the pilasters are vertical lines (flutes) that ascend to capitals composed of horizontal zigzags. Even while the pilasters hint at classicism, the wavy zigzag capitals suggest water, which can also be imagined as running down the flutes of the pilasters. Above the entrance is a recessed panel on which are depicted roaring waves that recall the curvilinear motifs of the turn-of-the-century Art Nouveau.

KANSAS CITY

Bixby House

6505 State Line
1936–37

EDWARD W. TANNER AND KEM WEBER

The Bixby House is one of a handful of dwellings built in the 1930s that was billed by its makers and perceived by the public as "modern." While the house displays many hallmarks of the International Style (stucco walls, ribbon windows, etc.), it also owes a great deal to the popular Streamline Moderne. A dramatic curve of the lower roof terminates the walled balcony over the principal garden terrace; a tripartite horizontal band races along

Bixby House, Kansas City, Missouri.

the parapet; and curved glass-brick walls abound.

Kem Weber, one of America's leading exponents of the Art Deco and the Streamline Moderne, designed the interiors. He also produced a wide array of metal, plastic, and plywood furniture and lighting fixtures for the house.

Fidelity Bank and Trust Company Building

911 Walnut Street
1931

HOIT, PRICE & BARNES

This 39-story skyscraper culminates in a pair of small rectangular towers crowned by recessed high-pitched hipped roofs. The lower floors of the building, which house the bank, are sheathed in Indiana limestone, while the upper floors play brick surfaces

against terra-cotta. The ornament, rendered in stone and terra-cotta, combines Beaux-Arts classicism with Art Deco motifs. The fluting of the numerous elongated pilasters is in fact composed of thin, narrow shafts that terminate abruptly in shallow horizontal bands rather than traditional capitals.

Fidelity Bank & Trust Company Building, Kansas City, Missouri.

Forest Hill Pantheon

6901 Trost Avenue

1921–22

SIDNEY LOVELL

Instead of abstracting from the Greco-Roman tradition, the architect of this building looked to ancient Egypt. On either side of the main entrance stands a squat form reminiscent of an Egyptian obelisk. The form is repeated in front of the adjoining walls of the building. The Art Deco quality of the design resides primarily in the bold play of masonry masses. Egyptian architecture and decoration were, of course, among the many sources of inspiration to Art Deco designers.

Kansas City Civic Center
Jackson County Courthouse

415 E. 12th Street

1934

WIGHT AND WIGHT; KEENE AND SIMPSON; FREDERICK C. GUNN; WARD F. NEILD

City Hall

414 E. 12th Street

1937

WIGHT AND WIGHT

Kansas City is one of the few American cities that came close to realizing an Art Deco Civic Center. The two key buildings of the group are the court-

Forest Hill Pantheon, Kansas City, Missouri.

Kansas City Civic Center and Jackson County Courthouse, Kansas City, Missouri. Short and Brown, *Public Buildings* (1939).

ried above the sixth story. The panels of this frieze on the west and east sides of the building were designed by Ulric Husen; those on the north are by Walker Hancock; and those on the south are by Paul Jennewin.

Kansas City Power and Light Company Building

1330 Baltimore Avenue
1930–31

HOIT, PRICE AND BARNES

For a number of decades the Kansas City Power and Light Company Building was the tallest structure in the state. The drama of its 469-foot height was enhanced by the building's narrowness, its layered setbacks, and its strong emphasis on vertical bands of windows and their adjoining pilasters. Befitting the offices of an electric

house and the city hall. Each building employs, albeit in an abbreviated fashion, the Goodhue-esque concept of a classical boxlike base surmounted by a tower. Each building is sheathed in limestone and has vertical panels of windows and spandrels. Each building has setback towers, and each exhibits recessed horizontal panels of sculpture and decoration at the parapet of its bases and again in the uppermost reaches of its tower. Charles L. Keck executed the sculptural panels over the entrance of the Courthouse, and Jorgen C. Dreyer provided the strong hexagonal bronze-and-white metal plaques over other doors. The history of the city is depicted in a frieze car-

Kansas City Power and Light Company Building, Kansas City, Missouri. Landmark Commission, City of Kansas City.

power company, floodlights emphasized the tower's various setbacks at
night. The overall building was lit by
moving multicolored lights, and prismatic glass was used to send beams of
light into the sky. Characteristic Art
Deco motifs: circles, seashells, V-shaped
configurations, and so on, adorn the
parapets. The building's crown is a
high central tower set on an octagonal
base. Sculptured rays of sunlight symbolize electricity, and a pattern of lightning bolts occurs within each of the
tower's tall windows.

Liberty Memorial

100 W. 26th Street
1923–26

H. VAN BUREN MAGONIGLE

The editors of the *Journal of the
American Institute of Architects* posed
the question as to whether two competitions held in the early 1920's—"the
Nebraska State Capitol and the Kansas
City Memorial—may at some not far distant date be scanned by the historians
of American architecture with something akin to the belief that they will
have to take rank as turning points or
landmarks." Both competitions attracted wide interest among architects. The
runners-up to Magonigle's winning

Liberty Memorial, Kansas City, Missouri.

Liberty Memorial were designs submitted by two of America's pre-eminent
architects of the era, Bertram G.
Goodhue and Paul P. Cret (associated
with Zantzinger, Borie and Medary).

Magonigle's scheme was based on
a grand Beaux-Arts plan. A high shaft-
like tower rises from a walled podium.
Abstracted temples—a memorial hall
on one side, a museum on the other—
flank the tower. Completing the south
forecourt of the complex are two
sphinxlike figures whose visages are
veiled by their wings.

Magonigle's original entry placed
the whole composition on a high
podium. The revised scheme, in which
the podium was reduced, deprived the
memorial of some of its intended
drama. The Art Deco atmosphere of the
project is apparent in its abstract
"cubistic" massing and in the manner
in which sculpture and ornament are
integrated into the composition. The
extensive sculptural frieze (148 feet
wide by 18 feet high) along the front of
the podium was planned by Edith
Magonigle, the architect's wife, and was
executed and completed in 1935 by
Edmund Amateius. The subject of the
frieze, according to the architect, was
". . . the restless march of the hosts of
mankind." The 217-foot-high tower was
conceived of as the memorial proper.
"Out of the huge cylinder," wrote the
architect, "are hewn a cluster of four
buttresses and four round piers which
soar aloft in unbroken lines to the Altar
of Sacrifice, surrounded by four colossal Guardian Spirits, forty feet high,
which carry the bowl of censer upon
the tips of their up-stretched wings".
These grand-scale figures by Robert
Aitken are centered on the censer, in
which a flame was simulated by steam
electrically colored. The shaft itself was
lighted from below, so that it and the

two adjacent temples appeared glow in the dark. Within the memorial hall are murals by Jules Guerin and Daniel MacMorris.

Municipal Auditorium

211 W. 13th Street
1933–34

GENTRY, VOSCAMP AND NEVILLE; HOIT, PRICE
& BARNES

This auditorium building, which takes the form of a somewhat squat masonry block, houses an exhibition space, an arena with a seating capacity of 14,000, a music hall, and a "little theater." Because of grade changes across the site, access to each of these facilities can be gained directly from one of the adjoining streets. Each of the street elevations is treated as a slightly projecting pavilion, with the corners of the building recessed. The building's mass and its limestone facing reinforce its monumental and public character. Large-scale medallions relating to historic and social themes adorn the exterior walls. A pair of horizontally banded metal marquees sprout Streamline Moderne metal bases for flagpoles that, in turn, echo the verticality of the adjacent pilasters. The orchestra promenade and lobby, with its curved walls and balcony and its rich materials and ornament, suggest the Regency Style as well as the Art Deco. Albert T. Stewart and H. F. Simons produced the exterior and interior medallions and relief sculpture, while Ross Braught, Walter Alexander Bailey, and Larry Richmond provided the interior murals.

Municipal Auditorium, Kansas City, Missouri.

Shank Building (Delmar and DeBaliviere Building), Saint Louis, Missouri.
Landmarks Association of Saint Louis.

Shank Building (doorway). *Architectural Record*
(1930).

SAINT LOUIS

Delmar and DeBaliviere Building (the Shank Building)

5654 Del Mar Boulevard
1928

BOWLING AND SHANK

This three-story brick–and–terra-cotta apartment building (with shops on the ground floor) could be interpereted either as an American imitation of European Expressionism or as an early version of the Art Deco. The red-and-black geometrically patterned terra-cotta panels point obviously to the contemporaneous work of Frank Lloyd Wright. But the geometric patterns created with the in and out of the black brick are more closely related to the 1920s designs of such Dutch architects as M. de Klerk. The building's recessed openings and its black cladding (with red trim) are typical Art Deco features.

Eden Publishing House (Evangelical Synod Building)

1716–20 Chouteau Avenue

1930–31

HOENER, BAUM & FROESE

Like several other Art Deco buildings in Saint Louis, this one owes a debt also to modern Dutch design of the late 1910s and 1920s. The structure comprises two buildings; the older, three-story sec-tion was remodeled when the five-story section was built. The exterior of both buildings is sheathed, according to its owners, in "warm toned brick in a full range of buff shades," while the recessed spandrels, exhibiting a pattern of inverted V's, were realized in terra-cotta. The narrow tower that projects from the five-story section is sur-mounted by a glass-and-metal lantern intended to "serve as a beacon visible at a great distance."

Eden Publishing House (Evangelical Synod Building), Saint Louis, Missouri. *Architectural Forum* (1932).

Neighborhood Gardens Apartments

Between 8th, Biddle, and O'Fallon
   Streets
1935

HOENER, BAUM AND FROESE

This is another of Saint Louis's Expressionist/Art Deco building complexes. Brick laid in patterns to create a variety of surface textures provides decoration around windows and doors and as terminal lines for sections of the wall surfaces. Bands of brick that extend out from either side of the windows establish a strong sense of horizontality. Patterned brick is also carried above windows to form stepped gables. The prime inspiration seems to have been Dutch Expressionist architecture of the 1920s, although the bands of decorated low-relief terra-cotta exhibit patterns similar to those designed by Frank Lloyd Wright for houses built in California between 1920 and 1925.

Person House

7 Warson Terrace
1936
WILLIAM P. M. MCMAHON & SONS

In the mid-1930s magazine advertisements for the glass block manufactured by the Owens-Illinois Glass Company were illustrated with images of the Person House. Glass brick was used in the house's two-story curved stair hall, for the curved walls of the breakfast room, and for various corner windows. The house's street facade is dominated by the curved form of the stairway. Although remodeled and altered in recent years, the Person House remains a major example of the Streamline Moderne domestic architecture.

Person House, Saint Louis, Missouri. *Architectural Forum* (1937).

Saint Mark's Episcopal Church

4712 Clifton Avenue

1939

FREDRICK DUNN AND CHARLES NAGEL

From the street the visitor sees a slightly raised forecourt leading to a tall rectangular block. At the top of the block is the slight hint of a gable. A band on the lower part of the facade incorporates a single round window. The entrance exhibits restrained classical details. To the left of the door is an over-scaled relief sculpture of Saint Mark by Sheila Burlingame. Inside the church one encounters an equally severe atmosphere; the stained-glass windows were designed by Robert Harmon.

Soldier's Memorial Building

Bounded by Market, Pine, 13th and 14th Streets

1938–39

MAURAN, RUSSELL AND CROWELL; PRESTON J. BRADSHAW

The classical peripteral temple is here reduced to essential cubic forms. Thirty-eight square fluted piers take the place of the columns. The attic story is a smooth plane inscribed with two thin horizontal bands suggesting dentils; between these are medallions. Four overscaled lanterns occur at the corners of the podium. On the interior, the horizontal banding of lights and of wall surfaces seems derived from the Streamline Moderne.

SAINT LOUIS AREA (MARLBOROUGH)

Coral Court Motel

7755 Watson Road

1941 (demolished)

ADOLPH L. STRUEBIG

This motel stood as an exuberant ode to the Streamline Moderne. Curved walls abounded, articulated by glass brick and glazed multicolored brick. The glass brick was arranged in stepped patterns on the rounded corners and as decorative inserts between bands of dark glazed brick. The machinelike, futuristic image of the motel contrasted sharply with the mature forest within which it was located.

Coral Court Motel, Marlborough, Missouri. Saint Louis History Center.

SPRINGFIELD

Bath House, Municipal Swimming Pool

City Park
1936
EARL HAWKINS

The pool side of this small, single-story, reinforced-concrete bath house is a segmented curve that mirrors the curved walls of the adjacent pool. The poured-concrete walls are inscribed with two parallel horizontal grooves halfway up their sides; at the top, forming the parapet, is a band of rectangles containing a zigzag pattern suggestive of waves and water. The central entrance is covered by a projection of this zigzag band. Over the windows on the two side facades are thin concrete canopies.

NEBRASKA

ARAPAHOE

Public Bath House and Swimming Pool(The Arapahoe Plunge)

Arapahoe City Park, Elm and
    7th Streets
1935–37

HUGH M. McCLURE (McCLURE & WALKER)

The bath house, a small single-story, reinforced-concrete structure, displays a repeated pattern of deep-set horizontal grooves. At the parapet edge, sets of vertical grooves help to define the terminus of the building. Three rows down from the parapet are recessd squares containing an abstracted sunflower motif. The most unusual feature of the

Public Bath House and Swimming Pool, Arapahoe, Nebraska. *Architectural Concrete* (1937).

design is the way in which the architects have carried over one of the horizontal bands so that it becomes a half-capital for the pairs of columns that define the entrances on the pool side of the building. The walls and their ornament were all cast in place.

KEARNY

Public Bath House and Swimming Pool

7th Avenue and 33rd Street

1936–37

HUGH M. MCCLURE (MCCLURE & WALKER)

The reinforced-concrete bath house sits upon a concrete base that contains a water-treatment plant. The bath house projects a classic Art Deco frontispiece: three deep-set openings separated by pierlike forms. Above each of the entrances is a cast-in-place ornament featuring stylized plants and angled and vertical lines. The corners of the building's central pavilion are curved, and the walls of the bath house and its base are inscribed with deep horizontal grooves.

Public "Sonortorium" Open-Air Theater

7th Avenue at 33rd Street

1937–38

HUGH M. MCCLURE (MCCLURE & WALKER)

The Art Deco is here employed for a folly set in a landscaped park. Two pylonlike forms define the left and right edges of the stage, whose curved front is articulated by cast concrete in a vertical zigzag pattern. The rear of the stage has a set of three rising vol-

umes, one to each side. Grooves in the walls of the structure and in the tall pylons create horizontal bands that are in turn offset by a central motif of vertical ribs. On either side of the stage complex is an open shelter. A park garage completes the composition.

LINCOLN

Nebraska State Capitol

15th Street at K Street

1919–32

BERTRAM G. GOODHUE

The New York architect Bertram G. Goodhue won a national design competition for the Nebraska State Capitol in 1919. His entry combined two building types: a skyscraper, and a low, classical, noncolumned structure. The marriage of these particular building types had been accomplished on previous occasions, such as in the Oakland City Hall (1911–14), but this was the first (and would not be the last) time that the combination was used for a state capitol. Goodhue obviously looked closely at the work of Eliel Saarinen and Lars Sonck before he designed the skyscraper portion of the building. As Goodhue continued to refine the design after 1920, he simplified the building, making it even more monumental but also more primitive: it began to take on resemblance to the ancient architecture of Mesopotamia. By the time construction began in 1922, Goodhue had produced what has become one of the most admired American buildings of the 1920s. The capitol is Art Deco not so much in its specific details or ornament, but, rather, in the manner in which it employs both ornament and abstraction.

Nebraska State Capitol, Lincoln, Nebraska. Art Museum, University of California, Santa Barbara.

The program for the building's ornament was drawn up by Hartley B. Alexander, a professor of philosophy at the University of Nebraska. The stated themes ranged from the political and social milestones of Mediterranean and European history to the Native American cultures of the Great Plains, from 19th-century pioneer life in Nebraska to the state's flora and fauna. The sculpture was executed by Lee Lawrie, who often collaborated with Goodhue; the murals, the metalwork, and the mosaics are by Hildreth Meiere and August Tack. At the top of the great buttresses, which flank the building's four entrances, are heroic figures that seem virtually to grow out of the masonry. Lawrie also provided the wonderful relief carvings of buffalo that appear on the balustrades along either side of the entrance stairs. The motifs were derived from local subjects—corn, cattle, and so on—and were transformed into Art Deco patterns by Lawrie. The sculptor also designed bronze grilles featuring stylized Indians and animals native to the region. On the interior, two high points (although not Art Deco in style) are Meiere's tooled leather doors for the House Chamber and Lawrie's carved wood doors for the Senate Chamber. One has only to experience the Art Deco and PWA Moderne buildings of succeeding years to understand this building's immense influence.

OMAHA

Joslyn Memorial Art Museum

2200 Dodge Street
1928–31

JOHN AND ALAN MCDONALD

Long, wide, impressive stone stairs lead up to an equally impressive monumental Art Deco building. The seeming coldness and aloofness of the design are countered by the warm pink color of the marble walls. A pair of pierlike forms project from the central section of the building. Between them is a deep-set portico defined by four fluted columns. The columns are abstracted versions of the Ionic order, with the capitals modified to contain the Plains Indian thunderbird motif. The front walls of the wings to either side of the entrance contain inset panels of relief sculpture by John David Borcin. The theme of these sculptures, as well as of the round plaques above the north and south entrances, is the Indians and the early pioneers. Other Classical relief ornament, with a slight Art Nouveau tinge, occurs in the interior and in the courtyard.

Joslyn Memorial Art Museum, Omaha, Nebraska. Lynn Meyer, photographer.

Union Pacific Railroad Station (Western Heritage Museum, Omaha, Nebraska. Landmark Heritage Preservation Commission, City of Omaha.

Union Pacific Railroad Station (Union Passenger Terminal, now Western Heritage Museum)

801 S. 10th Street at Marx Street
1929–31

GILBERT STANLEY UNDERWOOD

This near-perfect example of the Art Deco style reveals several of the style's sources: the buildings in Finland designed by Eliel Saarinen in the first decade of the 20th century and the designs in the 1910s and early 1920s of Bertram G. Goodhue. Although Underwood's sculptured figures tend to be more abbreviated than Saarinen's or Goodhue's, they emerge from the stone sheathing of the building in a similar fashion. Seashells and other Art Deco motifs occur on the exterior, accompanied by references to Native American art. Murals on the interior depict the history of tranportation. The building's exterior sheathing of cream-colored glazed terra-cotta is a Moderne touch that removes this railroad station from the realm of the traditionally monumental.

NORTH DAKOTA

BISMARCK

North Dakota State Capitol

Between 5th and 7th Streets north of the Boulevard

1932–34

JOSEPH BELL DEREMER; W. K. KURKE; HOLABIRD & ROOT

The North Dakota state capitol was the most radical of the state capitols designed in the 1920s and 1930s in the form of skyscrapers. Instead of setting a towerlike office building atop a base, the architects here placed the tower to one side and connected it via a memorial hall to a separate building housing the legislative chambers. The scheme is in many ways reminiscent of the so-called International Style designs of Le Corbusier and Walter Gropius and of the post–World War II design of the United Nations Building in New York City. The 18-story tower also recalls many of Holabird & Root's office buildings in Chicago. Slightly projecting pilasters, rising from the ground to the parapet, alternate with vertical bands of windows and spandrels. The frontispiece of the building is a wide flight of stairs leading to a plaza. Facing onto the plaza is a row of two-story windows flanked by smaller-scale doors. The semicircular form of the two legislative chambers is apparent in projecting bays that are articulated by wide fluted pilasters. The

North Dakota State Capitol, Bismarck, North Dakota.

public and monumental nature of the complex is established by the elegant black granite, which provides a striking contrast to the pale tan Indiana limestone walls above. Edgar M. Miller supplied the touches of bronze sculpture above the entrance doors and at key points on the interior. The various high-relief sculptures relate to episodes in the history of the state, while the low-relief panels on the elevator doors depict pioneers of the Northwest Territory.

MINOT

Ward County Courthouse

315 S.E. 3rd Street
1928–29

TOLTZ, KING AND DAY

A cascade of terraces, stairs, and balustrades creates a classical base for this three-story Art Deco building. A sense of the monumental has been created by playing a game of alternate projection and recession along the surface of the stone walls. Art Deco ornamental patterns occur near the top of the buttresses and piers and again in the stone- and metalwork above and below the windows. Over the entrance a pair of stylized eagles flank a large medallion. R. W. Sexton, in his 1929 volume *The Logic of Modern Architecture*, referred to this building when he wrote, "Yet it is logical that in designing a building today to be constructed of stone the details be of such a character that the building will bear little or no resemblance to a stone building designed three or four centuries ago" (p.61).

Ward County Courthouse, Minot, North Dakota. State Historic Society of North Dakota.

OHIO

CINCINNATI

Cincinnati Bell Telephone Company Building

Bounded by Elm, 7th & Plum Streets
1930–31

HAKE & KUCK

This is one of many impressive telephone company buildings that were constructed across the country in the 1920s and 1930s. The design is typical: a classical sculptured base surmounted by an office tower exhibiting a pattern of buttresses alternating with recessed window-and-spandrel panels. Wonderful relief sculpture depicts subjects ranging from stylized telephones to the human figure. The Art Deco ornament by Oscar Bach constitutes some of the most successful Art Deco metalwork to be found in the United States.

Cincinnati Bell Telephone Company Building, Cincinnati, Ohio.

Coca-Cola Bottling Company (now F and W Publications)

1507 Dana Avenue
1937

JOHN HENRI DEEKEN

The often repeated formula of a vertical centerpiece, countered by a pair of horizontal wings, is here realized in smooth (machine-like) surface of limestone. The low central circular tower has pleated walls suggesting the flutes of a classical column. The tower is topped by a metal lighthouse. The horizontality of the two-story wings are strongly emphasized by bands of glass and glass brick. The building was sensitively restored and remodeled in 1987.

Netherlands Plaza Building (now the Carew Tower & Omni Netherlands Plaza Hotel)

Bounded by 5th, Vine and Race
    Streets
1929–30

WALTER AHLSCHLAGER; DELANO & ALDRICH;
    GEORGE UNGER, INTERIOR DESIGNER

An unusual mix of uses for the late 1920s: a 48-story (574-foot-high) office and hotel tower, a shopping center, and an accompanying parking garage. In style, the building is exuberant Art Deco, with, on the exterior, only a touch of the delicate classical revivalism associated with much of the work of the New York firm Delano & Aldrich. The architect and the interior designer obviously looked very closely at specific French versions of the Art Deco for the luxurious decoration of the interior. The most impressive public spaces are the connected hotel's foyer, lobby, and staircase, and, above all, the luxurious Palm Court. The upper walls of the Palm Court exhibit murals on the theme of recreation, while the detailing looks to Egypt, to Mesopotamia, and to the France of Louis XV. The central fountain with its seahorses was produced by the famed Rockwood Pottery of Cincinnati. The entire building, including the ground-level shopping mall, was restored in 1982–83.

Union Railroad Terminal (now the Greater Cindinnati Museum Center)

Ezzard Charles Drive
1929–30

ROLAND A. WANK (FELLHEIMER & WAGNER);
    PAUL P. CRET

The Cincinnati Terminal was part of the final wave of large-scale railroad station construction in the United States

Union Railroad Terminal (Greater Cincinnati Museum Center), Cincinnati, Ohio.

in the late 1920s and 1930s. In style, the terminal matches many of the buildings erected at the 1933 Century of Progress Exposition in Chicago. The overall design was predominantly Art Deco, but many of the details reached into the Streamline Moderne. The building might well be thought of as an ode to aluminum, which at the time was just coming into its own as a decorative material. In the great rotunda shiny aluminum detailing contrasted with red Verona marble, a ceiling that was originally brightly colored, and the large murals by Winold Reis and Pierre Bourdelle (which have been moved to the Cincinnati Airport Terminal). Other parts of the interior play fine veneered woods against aluminum doors and doorframes, light fixtures, signage, and railings. The building has been adapted for use as a museum.

CLEVELAND

Epworth Euclid Methodist Church

E. 107th Street
1919, 1924–28

BERTRAM G. GOODHUE (GOODHUE
    ASSOCIATES); WALKER & WEEKS

This church was one of the last designs from the hands of Goodhue. The building was modeled on the famous medieval Gothic church at Mont St. Michel in France. Although there is a primitive sculptural quality to the building, it reads more as thin skin accentuated by vertical details. Goodhue's design is Art Deco primarily in its abstraction of details and forms; there are only a few specific motifs of the style in evidence in the building.

Greyhound Bus Terminal

1465 Chester Avenue
1948

WILLIAM S. ARRASMITH (WISCHMEYER,
    ARRASMITH & ELSWICK)

A perfect and complete Streamline Moderne design—which, of course, should have been built before World War II. Three horizontally oriented volumes terminate in an L-shaped vertical sign and in a thin canopy over the entrance. A leaping greyhound, lighted by neon at night, tops the pylonlike projecting sign. Horizontality is emphasized by three metal bands that run in front of the glass-brick windows and by a thin band just above the ground that accentuates the dark terra-cotta wainscot.

Lorain-Carnegie Bridge

Carnegie Avenue southwest of 9th
    Street, spanning the Cuyahoga River
1931–32

FRANK WALKER (WALKER & WEEKS),
    ARCHITECT; WILBUR WATSON, ENGINEER

The steel-truss frame of this 4,490-foot-long bridge projects from four monumental limestone pylons. The sides of the pylons facing the river carry the suggestion of a row of pilasters. The ends of the pylons facing the lanes of traffic contain colossal winged figures whose sharp rectilinear forms echo the lines of the pylons. Each of the four figures holds a tray bearing a transportation machine. The figures are the work of the New York sculptor Henry Herring.

Lorain-Carnegie
Bridge, Cuyahoga
River, Cleveland, Ohio.

United States Coast Guard Station

Whiskey Island, north end of River
  Road
1939–40

J. MILTON DYER

This station effectively poses as a Streamline Moderne coast guard cutter that has been docked at Government Pier. The high round lookout tower, with a chimney attached at the rear, resembles the enclosed bridge of a ship. The Streamline theme is carried on behind the one- and two-story station building in the boat house, where walls with curved and tapered ends enclose a launching dock. Large horizontally oriented windows with half-circle ends occur in the mess room and again at the lookout tower. Thin canopies appear on the boat house and at the entrance to the station itself. Upon entering the building, any sense of being on land is lost, for the atmosphere is entirely that of a ship. The architect commented that the building was designed "to give the impression of wind and wave resistance." By using the nautical Streamline Moderne, he succeeded admirably.

COLUMBUS

American Education Press Building

Front Street between Fulton and Engler
  Streets
1936

RICHARDS, MCCARTY & BULFORD

The surface of this three-story building consists of alternating horizontal bands of stucco and glass brick. These bands are carried around the curved corners of the building, creating the impression of a garment hung lightly over an internal frame. A pair of curved walls articulated by brightly polished metal bands draws one into the building's entrances.

General Electric Company & T. W. Frech Experimental House

Nela Park, off Noble Road at Euclid
  Avenue
1935

HAYS & SIMPSON

In the doldrums of the Depression, the construction of model houses was sponsored by national, regional and

U.S. Coast Guard Station, Cleveland, Ohio. *Architectural Concrete* (1940).

local businesses in the hope that such houses might spur the building industry. This (mildly Streamline Moderne) house was built by the General Electric Company adjacent to Nela Park, the site of the company's local operations. The house was built of Haydite concrete wall units and was sheathed in white stucco. The Streamline theme was most strongly asserted in the high curved canopy that shelters the front entrance and that also terminates the high metal-framed bay window of the living room. The design was intended to be flexible: a basic unit (living room, dining room and kitchen) to which various configurations of bedrooms could be added.

MIDDLETOWN

Research Laboratory for American Rolling Mill Company

701–703 Curtis Street

1937

AUSTIN COMPANY; HAROLD GOETZ,
   CONSULTING ARCHITECT

The building poses as a gleaming white porcelainized-metal container. The exterior cladding, composed of Steelox panels and shiny metal horizontal metal bands, swishes around the building, similar to a 1937 streamlined automobile. The machinelike Streamline Moderne quality is enhanced by a

American Rolling Mill Company, Research Laboratory, Middletown, Ohio.
Architectural Forum (1937).

deep band of glass brick (occasionally interrupted by metal-frame windows) that extends around all four sides of the building. The principal entrance returns to the classically balanced verticality of the Art Deco, with walls articulated by shiny vertical fins that curve in toward the entrance doors.

NEWARK

Research Building, Owens-Illinois Glass Company

Case Avenue near Shields Street
1936–37

FOSTER ENGINEERING COMPANY

As befits the research laboratory of an industrial manufacturer of glass building products, this two-story structure is banded in glass brick. A play of vertical volumes occurs at the entrance: a glazed tower is overlaid by a narrow block that, in turn, exhibits one corner of glass brick. Metal lettering running down one side of the small masonry block forms a visual link between the two volumes. The walls are of cream-colored glazed brick accented by narrow horizontal bands of darker glazed brick. Like many other glass-brick buildings, this one is most impressive at night when the translucence of the glass-brick walls becomes aggressively apparent.

TOLEDO

Ohio Bank Building (now the Owens-Illinois Building)

405 Madison Avenue
1929–30

MILLS, RHINES, BELLMAN & NORDHOFF

This 30-story, 368-foot-high setback skyscraper might have come straight from the drawings of Hugh Ferriss. The arched windows of the first four floors convey a Romanesque-Byzantine quality that is reinforced by the impression of mass created by the limestone facing. At the street level, a band of black Wisconsin granite unifies the bronze-trimmed shop windows and the entrances. The arched, recessed, two-story entrance on Madison Avenue, with its pair of overscaled Goodhue-esque figures and central eagle, provides an impressive Art Deco prelude to the interior. The low, richly decorated lobby leads up through a central staircase to an arcaded three-story banking room. Although there are occasional Art Deco motifs in the lobby and the banking room, the general flavor of these spaces is classical.

Toledo Public Library

325 Michigan Avenue
1939–40

HAHN & HAYES

The PWA Moderne is here realized in a rectangular masonry-sheathed box. At the center of the balanced facade is a recessed entrance formed by a series of layered walls that enclose the doors. To either side of the entrance are three fluted piers separated by recessed window-and-spandrel panels. Above the piers a delicate horizontal pattern of chevron and sunflower motifs suggests a cornice. A decorative band of vertical lines occurs just below the recessed top of the parapet. In typical PWA Moderne fashion, the building's corners are indented, creating the impression that each of the surfaces is thought of as separate and that each is in fact a very thin masonry skin cast over the building's frame. The core of the interior is a two-story central hall with Vitrolite-sheathed piers and a mural painted on Vitrolite that acts as a spandrel between the open loggia at ground level and the windows above. A set of murals painted on green Vitrolite is located in the children's reading room.

TROY

Hobart Brother's All-Steel Model House

23 Hobart Drive

1935

WILLIAM G. WARD

This tiny cubelike cottage contains elements of both the Streamline Moderne and the Regency Revival. The house has a symmetrical street facade and is surmounted by a hipped roof with a chimney at the top. Vertical bands extending up from the windows on the front of the house echo the vertical bands on the chimney face. The roof of the vestibule projects forward in a gentle curve, and below it is a horizontal decorative metal band of repeated X's. The house was constructed of 4-by-9–foot prefabricated metal panels. The end panels are joined to form a Moderne curved corner. The final coat of white paint, sprayed on after assembly, contained white sand to suggest that the surface was really stucco and, therefore, Regency in style.

SOUTH DAKOTA

BROOKINGS

College Theater (now Movies to Go)

Main Street

1941

FRANK MCCARTHY

The curves and insistent horizontality of the Streamline Moderne character-ize this theater and its adjoining shops. The marquee gives the impression of projecting even though it doesn't, because the ticket booth and the doors to the theater are recessed into the building. The horizontally banded walls of the storefronts curve and lead toward the theater entrance. The upper facade is composed of horizontal bands of glass brick and a projecting

College Theater (Movies to Go), Brookings, South Dakota. *Architectural Concrete* (1941).

curved surface bearing the theater's name. The display windows of the shops terminate in half-circles and seem to point toward the theater entrance.

SIOUX FALLS

Municipal Building

9th Street and Dakota Avenue
1936

HAROLD SPITZNAGLE

Sioux Fall's Municipal Building is a restrained example of 1930s PWA Moderne. The three-story structure rests on a low base of dark polished granite, and this granite facing extends up and around the slightly projecting entrance. The exterior is quite reserved in its decoration. Over the entrance is a low-relief figure in granite by Mrs. Hugh Seavers, and twenty abstract panels by Palmer Eide occur over the first-floor windows. On the interior, three frescoes by Edwin Boyd can be found in the Commissioners' Room. Other spaces within the building are relatively plain; the most telling Moderne elements as the star-shaped ceiling lights of the main lobby and some of the suspended circular light fixtures in the offices.

Municipal Building, Sioux Falls, South Dakota. *Architectural Forum* (1937).

YANKTON

Dakota Theater

328 Walnut Street

1941

D. W. RODGERS, BUILDER

The Streamline Moderne facade of this theater is the result of a remodeling in 1941 of an opera house built near the turn of the century. The facade has been reduced to a single plane covered with yellow, red, blue, and white Vitrolite tiles in a pattern that contains references to the Art Deco but that primarily suggests a Navaho rug. The V-shaped marquee is indented at its apex, and within this recess is an abstract vertical element that might be perceived as the model of a skyscraper.

Dakota Theater, Yankton, South Dakota. South Dakota State Historical Preservation Center.

WISCONSIN

MILWAUKEE

Model House, 1933 Home Show Winner

3840 N. 55th Street

1933

HENRY PHILLIP PLUNKETT

Like many Moderne houses of the early to mid-1930s, this two-story dwelling contains elements of both the Art Deco and the Streamline Moderne. The basic cube of the house leans toward the Streamline, with corner windows, ship's railings around the roof terrace, and porcelainized-metal panels as cladding. The Art Deco asserts itself primarily in the narrow three-story stair tower. The tower's 45-degree cut corners are decorated with fluting, and the stair window is exaggerated in its vertical dimension.

Northwest Hanna Fuel Company Offices

2150 N. Prospect Avenue

1934

HERBERT W. TULLGREN (MARTIN TULLGREN & SONS)

This small gem of an Art Deco building is highly colorful in its pink brick and orange terra-cotta garb. The facades center on a row of projecting cylindrical pilasters. The intervening spandrels display wonderful terra-cotta relief sculpture depicting coal-mining activities. The entrances, which are located on the outside edges of the street facade, are covered by thin semicircular canopies; above these canopies are narrow semicircular metal-frame bay windows.

1260 North Prospect Avenue Apartments

1260 N. Prospect Avenue

1937

HERBERT W. TULLGREN

Five-sided vertical bays, corner windows, and curved canopies place this nine-story apartment building comfortably within the Streamline Moderne. The theme of the curve is repeated in the vestibule and in the hall around the staircase. The building contains 32 five-room duplex apartments and 2 six-room units. On the first floor of each apartment the bay is part of a circular dining room; on the upper level the bay becomes a sunroom between two bedrooms.

Temple of Music

N. 40th Street at W. Vliet and W. Lloyd Streets, Washington Park

1938

FITZHUGH SCOTT, ARCHITECT; CHARLES S. WHITNEY, ENGINEER

An essentially Art Deco composition has been infused with elements of the Streamline Moderne. This concrete band shell is composed of a series of receding semicircles that decrease in size as they recede. Two low-relief panels on the pylons exhibit an abstract version of music. Two concrete "sound columns" rising from the sides of the stage contain T-shaped decorated metal grilles facing the audience. Behind these patterned grilles are amplifier-speakers.

Town of Lake Water Tower and Municipal Building

4001 S. 6th St.

1938–39

WILLIAM D. DARBY, ENGINEER

In the 19th century architects from time to time came up with the notion of combining an office building and a water tower. The idea was that the water tank, posing as a medieval tower, would lend visual substance to the building at its base. This was the approach taken by Darby in his Art Deco design for a concrete water tower–cum–municipal building in what was, at the time, the independent community of Lake, Wisconsin. The structure consists of a domed nine-story octagonal water

Temple of Music, Milwaukee, Wisconsin. *Architectural Concrete* (1939).

Town of Lake Water Tower and Municipal Building, Milwaukee, Wisconsin. *Architectural Concrete* (1940).

tower rising above a one- and two-story building. The faces of the octagon are articulated in such a way that they suggest pilasters and, in so doing, emphasize the vertical mass of the tower. Similar pilasters occur near the entrance, and three-tiered pilasters intervene between the windows on the single-story portions of the building. Above the entrance is a metal grille with an Art Deco pattern of intertwined V's and circles. Inside the complex are a central rotunda, council chambers and offices.

RACINE

Church of Saint Patrick

Erie Street at Prospect Street

1924

BARRY BYRNE (BYRNE& RYAN)

Byrne designed this building shortly after he had completed his first church, Saint Thomas the Apostle of Chicago. The body of the Church of Saint Patrick is a centralized sanctuary accentuated on its east elevation by two low corner towers. The narrow buttresses that terminate in finials in the upper reaches of the towers are an abstraction of the Gothic, as are the windows, which rise to inverted V's rather than to rounded or pointed arches. The church's detailing and decoration recall the linear verticality of the American Vertical style, which was often used in the design of skyscrapers in the 1920s. Byrne employed a similarly Gothic-inspired version of the art Deco in his design of two other Racine buildings: Saint Mary's High School (1923–24), now demolished, and Saint Catherine's High School (1923–24).

Johnson Wax Company Administrative Building

1012 16th Street

1936

FRANK LLOYD WRIGHT

The curve—as a circle or, more often, as a arc of a circle—began to appear with increased frequency in Wright's work in the mid- to late 1930s. Wright's use of the curve was often abstract; but in a number of instances it was a direct reference and response to the ideals of the machine—and thus might reasonably be characterized as Streamline Moderne. Wright in fact produced three of America's great monuments of the Streamline Moderne: the Johnson Wax Company Administrative Building, the Guggenheim Museum (1942–59) in New York City, and the Marin County, California, Civic Center (1957–72).

In contrast to most Streamline Moderne designs, the Johnson Wax Company Building is not an instance of overscaled aerodynamic packaging; rather, it is an abstract homage to the ideal of the machine and its products. It is as if Wright looked intensely at the illustrations of Buck Rogers's rocket ship in the comics of the mid–1930s and transformed these symbols of speed and contemporaneity into a refined art object. Even though most of the walls are sheathed in brick, a highly traditional material, the building still manages to give the impression that it might be a colony on Mars. All of the exterior surfaces exhibit curved corners, the most dramatic being the curved parapets of parallel glass tubes.

On the interior, Wright's commitment to the curve is most evident in his famous inverted mushroom columns with their circular banding. One enters the building via the automobile (never on foot). The glass entrance wall is the only transparent wall in the building—and what does it look out on? The "mushroom"-infested parking garage and America's (and Wright's) most beloved machine, the automobile. The atmosphere of a city on another planet —one of the major themes of science fiction during these years—is evoked in the insistent horizontality, in the curves of the building's surfaces, in the furniture that Wright designed for the offices, and in the almost unearthly light provided by the glass-tube clerstories and skylights.

If one were arranging a methodical tour of the Streamline Moderne, the Johnson Wax Company Building should be left to the end. One could then see how in the right hands this style could be elevated to the realm of very serious high art.

Racine County Court House

Southwest corner of 7th Street and
    Wisconsin Street
1931

HOLABIRD & ROOT

The theme of public building as sky-scraper is here pursued by the Chicago

Racine County Courthouse, Racine, Wisconsin. *Architectural Record* (1932).

firm that specialized in commercial high-rise buildings. Although at 10 stories the structure is reasonably tall, its width and mass are so emphasized that the building appears to be an only slightly elongated version of a typical PWA Moderne public building. The plan takes the form of a stepped H, with stone terraces inserted between the projecting arms. Both the exterior, which is sheathed in pale granite, and the interior convey a sense of reserve and reticence. The parapets at various levels exhibit delicate horizontal bands of low-relief decoration (inverted V's and curvilinear motifs). The courtrooms, paneled in a wood veneer, contain occasional suggestions of fluted pilasters. The lobby has walls of dark- and light-colored polished marble and a dark coffered ceiling. The most pronounced Art Deco elements on the interior are metal light fixtures on the walls and ceiling. The projecting entrance on the west facade features low-relief sculptures by Carl Milles.

WAUWATOSA

Annunciation Greek Orthodox Church

N. 92nd Street and W. Congress Street
1956

FRANK LLOYD WRIGHT

Space ships, or even whole cities, were frequently depicted as flying saucers in science fiction stories of the late 1930s (and, needless to say, later as well). Wright posed his saucerlike auditorium on pierlike forms that bear ornament in the fashion of the Art Deco. The overall theme of the church is that of the Streamline Moderne, though, as is always the case with Wright, his version ends up being a highly personal version of the style.

SOUTHWEST

ARIZONA

BISBEE

Cochise County Courthouse
Quality Hill
1930–31
ROY PLACE

The courthouse is situated at the base of a high hill and in its ascending forms seems to mirror the surrounding landscape. The building's hill-like quality is further emphasized by its three-tiered base. The central portion of the courthouse projects up to a full five floors. A gable on the front parapet heightens the sense of verticality. Upward-thrusting buttresses are stepped at their tops. The building's sculpture, executed by Lew Place, the architect's son, employs many typical Art Deco motifs, including seashells, chevrons, and stylized plant forms. The bronze entrance doors contain two blind figures of Justice against a backdrop of radiating lines. A regional theme is evoked in panels over the entrance depicting stylized native cacti and a pair of kneeling miners.

CASA GRANDE

Southern Pacific Railroad Passenger Station
Main Street and Sacaton Street
1939–40

J. H. CHRISTIE AND WILLIAM F. MEANEY

The building's stepped massing calls to mind the Indian pueblos of the Southwest. The principal entrance to the waiting room suggests the entrance to a Mayan temple, and the thick primitive columns of the outdoor waiting room recall similar columns at the pre-Columbian site of Mitla in Mexico. The geometric ornament in low-relief painted patterns is derived from the designs of the Indians of the Southwest, especially the Navaho. The architects were most likely influenced by the famous adjoining pre-Columbian ruins of Casa Grande. Still, the station's overall atmosphere, its massing, and its fenestration are Art Deco.

PHOENIX

Arizona Biltmore Hotel

24th Avenue at Missouri Street
1927–29

ALBERT CHASE MCARTHUR; FRANK LLOYD
    WRIGHT, CONSULTANT

If one thinks of the Art Deco strictly as the style associated with the 1925 Paris Exposition of Decorative Arts, then the Phoenix Biltmore Hotel would not be Art Deco. But as numerous American buildings of the 1920s and 1930s indicate, America's version of the Art Deco also drew inspiration from a wide variety of non-French sources: the pre-Columbian buildings of Mexico and Central America, indigenous architecture of the American Southwest, Viennese design predating World War I, the turn-of-the-century work of Prairie School practitioners in the American Middle West, and European Expressionist architecture of the 1910s and 1920s. While there is clearly much about the Biltmore for which precedent can be found in Frank Lloyd Wright's concrete-block houses of the 1920s, the hotel's essential sensibility and ornament are directly related to the Art Deco. The plan—a Beaux-Arts affair of principal and minor axes—is complicated by off-center passages, unexpected alignments, and diagonal projections. The building's massing registers the influence of Southwestern pueblo architecture, but the motif of piers and vertical fenestration seems pure Art Deco. The ornament, designed by McArthur and modeled by Emry Kopta, incorporates chevron motifs, swirling waves, and highly stylized plants.

Arizona Biltmore Hotel, Phoenix, Arizona. *Architectural Record* (1929).

General Motors Testing Laboratory

2001 E. Roosevelt Street
1937

AUSTIN COMPANY

This testing facility for late-1930s GM automobiles (and, later, for World War II tanks) might have been streamlined in emulation of the company's products, which range from automobiles to refrigerators. The building is treated as a series of volumes with curved corners, and many of the surfaces are sheathed in glass brick. A single narrow horizontal band connects the headers of all the windows and doors. Under the entrance canopy, just beside the door, is one of the hallmarks of the Streamline Moderne: a large metal-framed porthole window.

Josephine Goldwater House

2932 N. Manor Drive
1938

MALCOLM SEASHORE

A Streamline Moderne design set within the green grass of suburbia.

Horizontal bands of white stucco with intervening bands of glass pull one's eye across the surfaces of this dwelling. Curved corners, thin cantilevered canopies, and parapeted roof decks contribute to the house's shiplike aura.

Luhrs Tower

45 W. Jackson Street
1929–30

HENRY C. TROST (TROST & TROST)

This miniaturized skyscraper rises 14 stories and has setbacks at the 9th and 12th floors. Since it is a freestanding structure, all of the facades are articulated with corner buttresses. The massing consists of a central tower; two lower volumes that project forward and read as secondary towers; and, finally, a narrow block on either side. The building's ornament offers evidence of both Art Deco and Spanish influence. Near the top of the building, conquistadors of green terra-cotta emerge from the building in a Goodhue-esque fashion. The arched entrance has a Spanish flavor, but its sensibility and even some of its decorative motifs are Art Deco.

General Motors Testing Laboratory, Phoenix, Arizona. General Motors Desert Proving Grounds.

Maricopa County Courthouse and Phoenix City Hall

125 Washington Street
1928

EDWARD NEILD; LESCHER & MAHONEY

This was an unusual project in many ways, with the county engaging one architect (Edward Neild) and the city another (Lescher & Mahoney). The overall scheme for the building was a Beaux-Arts H-shaped plan with a pair of four-story wings flanking a taller, recessed centerpiece. A nod to the Southwest occurs in the hipped tile roof of the central six-story section. The exterior and interior ornament in stone, terracotta, and metal expresses the Art Deco. Regional notes include the use of the thunderbird motif atop the suspended exterior light fixtures and the colored plant forms around the third-floor windows. The projecting scrolls at the top of each pilaster and the impressive phoenixes on either side of the entrance to the city hall constitute the building's most assertive ornamentation.

Maricopa County Courthouse and Phoenix City Hall, Phoenix, Arizona.

NEW MEXICO

ALBUQUERQUE

Albuquerque Indian Hospital

801 Vassar Drive N.E.
1934

HANS STAMM

The classical Beaux-Arts origin of the Albuquerque Indian Hospital are evident in the building's symmetrical plan, its massing, and its elevations. The central portion of the building is four stories high, surmounted by a central tower and a tall chimney that plays the role of a traditional lantern. The wings on either side step down a story and are flanked by still lower two-story sleeping porches. The building's facades are interrupted by projecting piers that rise above the parapets and terminate in a stepped-pyramidal motif. One enters the hospital under a stepped corbeled overhang.

The building reveals its "Pueblo Deco" nature primarily through its painted and stenciled interior decoration, whose motifs range from arrows and arrowheads to thunderbirds, zigzags, and diamonds. The palette is confined to muted shades of brown, orange, red, and blue.

Albuquerque Indian Hospital, Albuquerque, New Mexico.

KiMo Theater

Central Avenue N.W. at 5th Street,
  northeast corner
1926–27

CARL BOLLER AND ROBERT BOLLER

The goal of the owner, Oreste Bache-chi, was to build a theater that would reflect each of the three distinct cultures of the American Southwest: the Indian, the Hispanic, and the Anglo. The overall massing of the building suggests an early New Mexican adobe church (although the structure is in fact brick, supplemented with concrete and steel). The richly painted and sculptured ornament both inside and outside the theater combines Pueblo and Art Deco motifs. The theater seems a perfect embodiment of what Marcus Whiffen and Carla Breeze have called "Pueblo Deco," for it is an Art Deco

KiMo Theater, Albuquerque, New Mexico.

work that utilizes many design devices inspired by the pottery, weaving, and other arts of the Pueblo Indians. (See Marcus Whiffen and Carla Breeze's *Pueblo Deco: The Art Deco Architecture of the Southwest*, 1984, and Carla Breeze's *Pueblo Deco*, 1990.)

The front facade is divided into three parts, with the theater and its marquee occupying the center and shops on either side. The architect employed a typical Art Deco pattern of fenestration: three sets of three windows interrupted by pierlike elements. The piers terminate in a band of brightly colored terra-cotta shields. The interior of the theater, much of which was designed by the artist Inez B. Westlake, continues the use of terra-cotta and includes stylized buffalo skulls atop the piers. Accompanying Westlake's work are murals by Carl Von Hassler that illustrate the Spanish myth of the "Seven Cities of Cibola." In the manner characteristic of Art Deco murals, the colors of Von Hassler's work are earthy and muted, providing a quiet backdrop for the exuberantly colored terra-cotta and painted structural members.

SANTA FE

Wheelwright Museum of the American Indian

704 Camino Lejo
1927–37

WILLIAM PENHALLOW HENDERSON

The House of Navaho Religion, as it was originally called, was the brainchild of Mary Cabot Wheelwright. The museum was built to house her collection of Navaho religious artifacts (primarily sand paintings), and its design was based upon the Navaho "hogan" (house). Wheelwright engaged the

Santa Fe painter William Penhallow Henderson, who had a close knowledge of the architecture of the American Southwest. Henderson's approach was to retain the octagonal form of the traditional "hogan" but to transform it into something more abstract, monumental, and modern. The form he created was an elongated octagon with a truncated pyramidal roof. For the museum's structure Henderson employed reinforced concrete, and for its modernist image he looked to the Art Deco. The design retains the tunnel-like entryway found in the Navaho "hogan," and the interior features a truncated ceiling of cribbed logs. The interior is lighted by a single skylight (reminiscent of the traditional smoke hole) through which light falls dramatically to a raised altar. The form of the original entrance, with a stairway that led down into the building and then up to the principal exhibition space, has been altered.

Wheelwright Museum of the American Indian, Santa Fe, New Mexico. Wheelwright Museum.

OKLAHOMA

ENID

Garfield County Courthouse

Public Square, bounded by Broadway
   and Independence, Randolph, and
   Grand Streets
1934–35

HAWK & PARR

The massing of this PWA Moderne
building applies the Beaux-Arts formula of descending and receding
sculptural volumes. At the center of
the building is a raised, recessed, two-
story section that gives the impression
of waiting to acquire additional stories
so that it can become a skyscraper. The
entrance frontispiece consists of two
wide buttresslike forms and, between
them, a pair of fluted piers. The building's exterior surfaces and its minimal
decoration are rendered in smooth
limestone.

OKLAHOMA CITY

Oklahoma City Courthouse and Jail

200 N. Walker Street
1936–37

LAYTON AND FORSYTH

Occupying an entire city block, the
Oklahoma City Courthouse and Jail
represents the larger type of PWA-
funded public buildings constructed
during the Depression. Although the
building presents the usual PWA
Moderne theme of a base and tower,
the tower is in this case so broad and
low that mass, rather than height, is
emphasized. The building's Art Deco
features include recessed vertical window-and-spandrel panels as well as a
wide array of ornament realized in
stone and metal. Above the principal
entrance is a recessed panel of relief
sculpture depicting Indians, cowboys,
and others; long narrow panels flanking this panel portray George
Washington and Abraham Lincoln.

TULSA

Boston Avenue Methodist Church

1301 S. Boston Avenue
1926–29

BRUCE GOFF (RUSH, EDACOTT & RUSH);
   ADAH M. ROBINSON

That building type so favored by Art
Deco architects—the skyscraper—
was here adapted for a 255-foot-high
church tower. Like Barry Byrne's
nearby Christ the King Church, Goff's
design transmutes Gothic verticality
into Expressionist Art Deco verticality.
The church itself, which has a semicircular auditorium, is a low-lying, horizontally oriented structure. Yet Goff has
manipulated his composition to read
as a narrow and soaring building. Like
Byrne, Goff looked for inspiration to
the Expressionist architecture of
Holland, Denmark, and Germany. He
was also certainly aware of the
California work of the two Wrights and
the concurrent church designs of
Henry J. McGill and Talbot F. Hamlin.
Goff's approach to sculpture—with the
figures emerging from the stone of the
building—draws on earlier work by
Eliel Saarinen and Bertram G.

Boston Avenue Methodist Church, Tulsa, Oklahoma.

Goodhue. While these many, varied sources would have been known to Goff primarily through published drawings and photographs (Byrne's work being the local, notable exception), he managed to distill ideas from these sources and to produce one of the most brilliant examples of the Art Deco in the country. The familiar Art Deco patterns of triangles, diamonds, circles, and so on, abound, but Goff tends to treat them here in a highly individual manner. The culmination of the design is the tower's summit, whose highly angular, shimmering surfaces of copper, steel, and glass dramatically reflect light in a prismatic fashion.

Christ the King Roman Catholic Church

1530 S. Rockford Avenue
1926

BARRY BYRNE (BYRNE AND RYAN)

Christ the King Church could justifiably be classified as an American example of Expressionist architecture rather than as an Art Deco building. Its design looks to work built in the 1910s and 1920s in Holland and Denmark as well as to the contemporaneous work of Frank Lloyd Wright and Lloyd Wright. Jagged linear forms played off against a smooth brick background characterize the design. While some terra-cotta ornament was employed, most of the angular decoration was realized via patterns of projecting and receding brick. The verticality associated with the Gothic is evoked in the narrow windows with triangulated ends, in the grouping of slender piers, and in the pinnacles projecting from the buttresses. The statues of St. Joseph and the Blessed Virgin were executed by the Chicago sculptor Alfonso Iannelli, who also designed the sparse terra-cotta ornament on the exterior of the church.

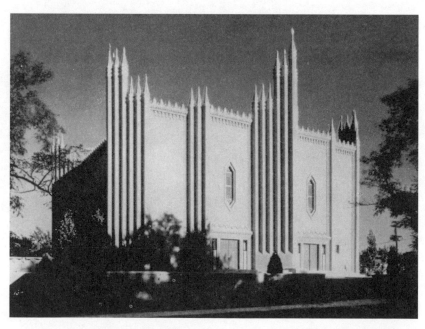

Christ the King Roman Catholic Church, Tulsa, Oklahoma. *American Architect* (1930).

John Duncan Forsyth House

2827 Birmingham Place
1937

JOHN DUNCAN FORSYTH

For his own house the architect John Duncan Forsyth made a full commitment to the Streamline Moderne. The structure is reinforced concrete and steel. On the house's once light pink (now white) exterior surface are indented horizontal bands that connect the tops and the bottoms of the windows. At one end of the street facade, a large glass-brick window in a curved wall lights a staircase. The garden facade exhibits a cantilevered canopy and expanses of glass brick. A low concrete wall between the house and the street contains small horizontal openings filled with metal grilles whose decorative pattern consists of a single cross intersecting receding squares.

Gillette-Tyrrell Building

423 S. Boulder Avenue
1929–30

EDWARD W. SAUNDERS

The Gillette-Tyrrell Building was originally planned as a 3-story office building with a setback 10-story hotel tower. The tower was to have terminated in a recessed ballroom with a curved mansard roof. The Depression intervened, however, and only the three-story office portion of the project was built. It survives today as a vigorous example of multicolored terra-cotta and tile employed to realize the Art Deco. The crisp and angular motifs of the exterior terra-cotta— all zigzags, triangles, diamonds, and circles—approach the Art Deco Expressionism of Bruce Goff and Barry Byrne, both of whose work was very prominent in Tulsa. The floor, walls, and ceiling of the L-shaped lobby dis-

Gillette-Tyrrell Building, Tulsa, Oklahoma.

play patterns derived from Native American art. The interior tilework is primarily green and blue against a background of burnt sienna, while the exterior terra-cotta juxtaposes blues and greens with a light cream color.

Theodore N. Law House

1841 E. 27th Street
1935

WILLIAM H. WOLAVER

This two-story white-painted brick house embodies most of the primary characteristics of the Streamline Moderne. The structure is parapeted and flat-roofed; there are curved bays, ribbon windows, and glass brick; metal-framed windows extend around corners; and large and small round openings impart a distinctly nautical flavor. A horizontal canopy above the first-floor windows is carried around the semicircular bay and becomes a covering for the doorway. Receding vertical bands of brick announce the entrance; to one side of the door is a circular wall fixture comprising three vertical lights.

Riverside Studio

1381 Riverside Drive
1929

BRUCE GOFF

Designed as a combined residence and recital hall for the musician Patti Adams Schriner, the Riverside Studio presents itself as two discrete stucco boxes. The most striking feature of the building is the facade facing the river. Here a large round window is recessed into the surface, and to either side a stepped pattern of vertically oriented windows and small rectangles leads one's eyes up to the corners of the parapet. Like certain other works of Expressionist architecture (and much of Goff's own later work), the building has a Surrealist air about it. A cubist sculpture by Alfonso Iannelli and interior murals by Olinka Hardy, which were centerpieces of the original design, have been removed.

Security Federal Building

129 W. 4th Street
1937

HARRY H. MAHLER

Given the economic climate of the 1930s, minimal remodeling frequently took the place of new construction or more extensive renovation. Many buildings were modernized by having their street fronts refaced with Vitrolite or Carrara glass panels. In this instance, the architect selected black Vitrolite and alternated polished and flat panels in checkerboard fashion. Redesign of the entrance focused on vertical elements that step up and back to a low-pitched gable. Decorative features included a centrally placed clock face etched into the Vitrolite, a similarly realized Greek key pattern, and a stainless-steel canopy over the entrance. Stylisti-cally, the building hovers between the late Art Deco and the Streamline Moderne.

Theodore N. Law House, Tulsa, Oklahoma.

Riverside Studio, Tulsa, Oklahoma.

Tulsa Fire Alarm Building

1010 E. 8th Street
1930–31

FREDERICK V. KERSHNER (SMITH & SENTER)

Compared with the Tulsa Union Depot (see below), the Fire Alarm Building is a smaller and more delicate version of the PWA Moderne. The building is symmetrical and sits on a high stone base; its main floor is sheathed in tan brick and cream-colored terra-cotta. Over the entrance is a broad terra-cotta panel depicting a male nude with Gamewell alarm tapes passing through his hands. On either side is a helmeted firefighter set against a complex pattern of hoses, nozzles, firefighting axes, and lightning bolts. Some of the motifs employed in the horizontal bands above the windows draw inspiration from the pre-Columbian art of Mexico and Central America.

Tulsa Union Depot

3 S. Boston Avenue
1929–31

R. C. STEPHENS

Although this monumental railroad station predates the New Deal, it could well fit into the stylistic cubbyhole that we have come to call the PWA Moderne. The building's form is that of a low, somewhat Goodhue-esque structure that has been brought up to date via bold simplification of massing and surfaces and by the incorporation of Art Deco ornament. Stephens, who was the chief architect of the Frisco Railroad, introduced the Greek key pattern in a horizontal band and then modified it with eagles, winged wheels, and motifs derived from Native American art. But the decorative program is entirely subordinated to the building's solid monumental volumes, which are sheathed in variegated Bedford limestone.

Warehouse Market

925 S. Elgin Avenue
1929

B. GAYLORD NOFTSGER

An Oklahoma City architect designed this single-story farmers' market. To attract attention to his low building the architect placed a tall tower at its center. The tower, with a setback summit, resembles some of the buildings at the 1925 Paris exposition, but its exuberant, brilliantly colored terra-cotta decoration sets it far apart from the generally more subdued European models. Patterns of intertwined flowers and leaves in low relief contrast with circles, triangles, projecting rays, and chevrons. The ornament on the tower, around the entrance to the market, and along the top of the parapet is realized in brilliant red, blue, green, cream, and gold glazed terra-cotta. Beside the entrance are two large terra-cotta medallions: on one of them a goddess holds a sheaf of wheat and a cornucopia; the other shows a winged, helmeted god holding in his hands a train engine and an oil derrick. The building's ornament was probably inspired by a catalog of the Northwest Terra Cotta Company that contained illustrations of a Chicago building designed by B. Leo Steif, with terra-cotta designed by Eduard Chassaing.

Westhope, the Richard Lloyd Jones House

3704 S. Birmingham Avenue
1929

FRANK LLOYD WRIGHT

Before it became surrounded by trees and shrubs and the neighborhood developed as an upper-middle-class suburb, Westhope posed as a vertically articulated factory on the prairie. The walls, composed of vertical concrete piers and recessed glass panels, offered no indication of scale, and from a distance one had no way of establishing whether this building was a factory or a private residence. Although the house is in fact quite domestic in scale, its lack of traditional points of references makes it difficult to comprehend its actual size. The patterning of the concrete block, though similar to Wright's work in Los Angeles, here seems more Art Deco than pre-Columbian. Some of the built-in furnishings and light fixtures contain suggestions of the Streamline Moderne.

Tulsa Union Depot, Tulsa, Oklahoma.

Warehouse Market (entrance), Tulsa, Oklahoma.

TEXAS

AMARILLO

Potter County Courthouse

511 S. Taylor Street
1930–32

TOWNES, LIGHTFOOT & FUNK

This eight-story setback tower employs the typical Art Deco scheme of wall surfaces articulated by alternating pilasters and recessed window-and-spandrel panels. The exterior sheathing is cream-colored terra-cotta that poses as cast stone. High on the tower are two heroic-scaled low-relief figures in terracotta: a frontiersman and an Indian. Other regional motifs include stylized prickly-pear cacti in terra-cotta and the cast-aluminum head of a longhorn steer above the lintel of the principal entrances.

AUSTIN

Herbert Bohn House

1301 W. 29th Street
1938

ROY L. THOMAS

Like many Moderne houses built in the late 1930s, the Bohn House balances the staid monumentality of the Art Deco with the fleeting forms and surfaces of the Streamline Moderne. Above the classically framed door of the two-story entrance pavilion is a vertically articulated panel containing a pair of narrow windows. The Streamline Moderne nautical theme is asserted by portholes on either side of the entrance and by a canopy with rounded corners that extends along the entire facade. Other Streamline elements include the metal-framed corner windows, the curved form to the left of the entrance that recalls the bridge of a ship, and a metal railing that curves down to the ground.

Sewage Treatment Plant

Colorado River
1937

LOUIS C. PAGE AND G. S. MOORE

Adjacent to the settling tanks are three handsome reinforced-concrete Streamline Moderne boxes that house laboratories and offices. The small laboratory building near the road has a curved facade, and the two ends of its parapeted roof curve dramatically inward. The treatment building, which is larger, exhibits a similar curved parapet at one end; the glass-enclosed opposite end recalls the bridge of a 1930s ocean liner. Like many such facilities, this Austin plant was financed by the PWA.

DALLAS

Texas Centennial Exposition Buildings

Fair Park at Parry Avenue
1935–36

GEORGE L. DAHL

The Harvard-trained architect George Dahl carried into the mid-1930s many of the design themes that emerged at the 1933 Century of Progress Exposition in Chicago. The site plan and the architecture of the Dallas exposition grounds fall within the realm of the classicized Art Deco. Unlike many exposition facilities, the Dallas buildings were conceived as permanent structures and are therefore still with us.

A long axial esplanade terminates at the concave entrance screen of the Hall of State Building (Donald Barthelme and Adams & Adams). Between the tall fluted piers of the entrance is a bronze sculpture of a Tejas Indian by Allie Tennant. While the exterior of the Hall of State Building is impressive, the building's crowning glory is the 94-by-68-foot Great Hall, with its rows of fluted piers and its murals by Eugene Savage, Buck Winn, and Reveau Bassett. Additional decorative art within the building was executed by Tom Lea, Olin Travis, and Lynn Ford.

The exposition's other notable Art Deco buildings include the Maintenance Building (George Dahl), which has a raised pool centering on an arched opening with a female figure standing on top of a cactus (by Raoul Josset); the Centennial Building (George Dahl, with sculpture by Lawrence Tenney Stevens); and the Tower Building (Donald S. Nelson). Smaller Art Deco structures on the grounds include the Dallas Museum of Natural History (Mark Lemmon and Clyde Griesenbeck), the Dallas Museum of Fine Arts (Paul P. Cret, Roscoe Dewitt, and Ralph Bryan), and the Aquarium (Fooshee & Cheek, Flint

Texas Centennial Exposition Buildings, Fair Park, Dallas, Texas. Dallas Historical Society.

& Board, H. B. Thompson). The exposition's most significant Streamline Moderne building was the Magnolia Lounge (the Margo Jones Theater) (William Lescaze), which projected the image of an ocean liner.

The exposition grounds and several of the buildings were restored in 1986 for the Texas Sesquicentennial.

Basset Tower, El Paso, Texas. El Paso Historical Society.

EL PASO

Bassett Tower

E. Texas Avenue at S. Stanton Street, northeast corner
1929–30

HENRY TROST (TROST & TROST)

Three stepped-back walls provide the transition to the tower of this 13-story Art Deco skyscraper. The tower is sur-

mounted by a high-pitched metal roof reminiscent of the French Chateau-esque style, and its fenestration is almost Gothic. The exterior walls are of tan brick; the vertical slots for the windows and spandrels are deeply recessed, emphasizing the solidity of the corners. The ornament varies considerably, from the recognizably Art Deco (spirals, triangles, chevrons, and stylized plant motifs) to forms reminiscent of those produced by the Viennese Secessionists at the turn of the century. The decoration is realized in patterned brick, inlaid marble, cast bronze, and, above all, brightly colored terra-cotta.

FORT WORTH

"Aparthome" House

3240 Waits Street
1935

ZOE AND C. M. DAVIS

This daughter-and-father team of architects produced several small reinforced-concrete houses that they labeled "aparthomes," that is, apartment-sized houses. This one is pure Streamline Moderne, with a thin curved roof over the front porch, strong dark horizontal banding, and metal-framed corner windows.

Martin E. Robin House

3817 White Settlement Road
1941

FRED W. MURPHREE

The Art Deco design of this single-story concrete-sheathed house is enriched by occasional reference to the Streamline Moderne and to the indigenous architecture of the Southwest. Buttresslike piers with fluting project slightly above the parapet. The parapet edges have three-tiered setbacks, as does the round tower adjacent to the garage.

Will Rogers Memorial Auditorium, Colosseum, and Tower

3301 W. Lancaster Avenue
1934–36

WYATT C. HEDRICK AND ELMER G. WITHERS

The 208-foot-high Pioneer Tower—which, as Judith Singer Cohen has pointed out in her book *Cowtown Moderne* (1988) is the preeminent example of the Art Deco in Fort Worth —is flanked by a colosseum on one side and an auditorium on the other. With its solid corner blocks projecting upward and embracing a narrow central piece topped by aluminum cladding, the tower looks back to the early 1920s work of Bertram G. Goodhue, and also to several of the pavilions at the 1925 Exposition of Decorative Arts in Paris. With the possible exception of the vertical bands of glass brick, the tower's ornament is entirely Art Deco. Inside the tower is a small high rotunda decorated with sparse Art Deco ornament.

The convex street facades of the colosseum and the auditorium are dominated by massive piers; fluting on the front of each pier suggests a pair of pilasters. Behind and above the flat-roofed porticos is a low-pitched gable roof, subtly suggesting a classical temple front. The entablatures of the colosseum and the auditorium display brightly colored mosaic friezes. Each of the friezes (accomplished by Kenneth Dale and Byron Shrider, under the direction of Herman P. Koeppe) is

200 feet wide and takes as its subject the history of Texas.

Other exterior decoration includes the metal grilles covering vents and wonderful stylized relief panels depicting Will Rogers astride a horse. Although the auditorium's interior is reasonably plain, the colosseum contains a rich array of Art Deco ornament, wall and ceiling paintings, and inserted plaques. With the exception of Electra Waggoner Biggs's life-size equestrian statue of Will Rogers and some of the colosseum's painted interiors by Seymore Stone, the decorative designs are by Herman P. Koeppe.

Texas & Pacific Passenger Terminal and Warehouse Building

Lancaster Street between Main Street
   and Jennings Avenue
1930–31

HERMAN P. KOEPPE (WYATT C. HEDRICK)

A 13-story terminal adjoins a 7-story warehouse structure. Narrow towers that frame the terminal building exhibit the characteristically Art Deco pattern of piers and recessed window-and-spandrel panels. The building's monumental base belongs to the PWA Moderne, while the upper 10 floors are almost Gothic in feeling. A wide band of terra-cotta ornament terminates the central portion of the design. Eagles rendered in high relief occur above the principal entrance and again at the top of the parapet. The building's exterior and its foyer, lobby, and three-story waiting room display abundant decoration in a variety of styles: Art Deco, Gothic, classical, and so on.

The 611-foot-long warehouse has been divided into four units via changes in the facade patterning. As in the terminal, towers at each end frame the building; the remainder of the facade is dominated by three vertical panels. Projecting piers suggest that the building is an office skyscraper, but the intervening strips do not contain the typical Art Deco window-and-spandrel panels. Most of the warehouse's exterior ornament is realized in patterned brick accented by brightly colored mosaic tile.

HOUSTON

Clarke and Courts Building

1210 W. Clay Avenue
1936

JOSEPH FINGER

The architect provided his clients with the best of two worlds: the staid Art Deco in a central tower and the Streamline Moderne as a wrapping for the rest of this reinforced-concrete structure. Below the parapet are three projecting strips of molding that accentuate the horizontal orientation of the metal-frame windows. Especially effective—and appropriate since the building was designed for a printing establishment—is the integration of the lettering. Near the top of the tower, at the base of a setback, the word "Clarke" projects forward; in the center of the four recessed surfaces of the tower the word "Courts" is arranged vertically. Other cast-concrete lettering appears on the sides of the building. Above the entrance a projecting metal panel contains four rows of text.

Gulf Building (now the Texas Commerce Bank Building)

712 Main Street
1929

ALFRED C. FINN, KENNETH FRANZHEIM, AND J. E. R. CARPENTER

New York-based architects provided Houston with this classic 36-story, 450-foot-high Art Deco skyscraper. The vertically articulated upper reaches of the building look back to Eliel Saarinen's 1922 entry in the Chicago Tribune Tower competition. The building's first six floors, which originally housed a retail store, are sheathed in limestone; the soaring tower section is clad in light-brown brick. The Main Street lobby exhibits a variety of typical Art Deco motifs; the interior also boasts murals by Vincent Maragliatti.

Heights Theater

341 W. 19th Avenue
1934

Two narrow pylonlike elements, studded with rows of incandescent bulbs, curve upward and over the parapet of this white stucco Streamline Moderne box. The projecting metal sign plays with a vertical step design that is tempered by curved horizontal and vertical lines. Below the projecting marquee glass-brick windows step down at each end; above the marquee three large porthole windows call to mind a 1930s ocean liner.

Texas Commerce Bank Building (Gulf Building), Houston, Texas. National Trust for Historic
Preservation.

Harvey R. Houck, Jr., House

3780 Grammercy Boulevard
1947

HARRY B. GROGAN

A perfect domestic example of 1930s Streamline Moderne—only in this case it materialized after World War II. The two-story sections of this white stucco house have dramatically curved corners; the curve is repeated in the thin canopy over the entrance.

Houston City Hall

901 Bagby Street
1929–39

JOSEPH FINGER

The original architects of this building —James Ruskin Baily, Alfred C. Finn, and Hedrick & Gottlieb—proposed first a Spanish Colonial Revival design and then, in 1929, an Art Deco tower similar in spirit to the Los Angeles City Hall (1926–28) and to several of the buildings designed in the late 1920s by the Chicago firm Holabird & Root. The Depression prevented the project from moving forward, and when PWA funds eventually became available a new architect, Joseph Finger, was engaged. His design consisted of a 10-story tower held solidly in place by flanking 4-story blocks. Recessed panels of relief sculpture occur over the principal entrance and above each of the window-and-spandrel recesses. The interior seems committed to the Streamline Moderne, with curved metal light fixtures and railings. The lobby contains murals by Daniel MacMorris.

Houston City Hall, Houston, Texas.

Houston Municipal Airport Terminal and Hangar (now the William B. Hobby Airport)

8401 Travelaire Road
1940

JOSEPH FINGER

From the mid-1930s to the end of the decade the PWA sponsored the design and construction of several new airport terminals throughout the country. Befitting their commitment to the airplane, most of these terminals and hangars were Moderne in design, and most of them adopted a Streamline Moderne image. With rare exception, these terminals were superseded by larger facilities in the years after World War II. One of the few that have survived is this Houston airport, which remains primarily because a new municipal airport was built in an entirely different location.

The centerpiece of the terminal is a tiered tower surmounted by a hipped roof; the metal-sheathed control tower at the apex suggests a classic cupola. The sides of the tower are curved, while the upper tier's corners are angled. Above the entrances are recessed decorative panels, and vertical piers articulate the single-story section to the left of the automobile entrance.

Restored in 1988, this terminal offers a rare glimpse of what a late 1930s airport was like.

Houston Municipal Aiport Terminal and Hangar, Houston, Texas.

Petroleum Building

1314 Texas Avenue

1926–27

ALFRED C. BOSSOM

The British-born and -educated New York architect Alfred C. Bossom advocated an "American style of architecture" based upon the pre-Columbian art of the Mayans. Bossom's approach was to integrate Mayan design principles and motifs with an Art Deco sensibility. The 22-story Petroleum Building is not as out-and-out Mayan as some of the architect's projects, but its terraced setbacks do subtly suggest Mayan temples. Mayan motifs occur in the spandrel panels and in decoration on the upper setbacks, and Mayan glyphs appear on the ceiling of the adjoining two-story garage.

Petroleum Building, Houston, Texas.

San Jacinto Monument

3800 Park Road
1935–38

ALFRED C. FINN

In a sense, the purest building is a monument, for its only function is to commemorate a person or an event. The PWA-sponsored San Jacinto Monument commemorates a battle on April 21, 1836, between Sam Houston's Anglo Texans and the Mexican army, led by the country's president, Lopez de Santa Ana. When the 570-foot-high tower was completed, it was proudly pointed out that the structure rises 12 feet higher than the Washington Monument. Built of reinforced concrete, the San Jacinto Monument is sheathed in golden buff Texas limestone. The shaft tapers inward, and its sides are articulated in characteristic Art Deco fashion, with the suggestion of thin vertical piers. Atop the upper recessed section is a single stylized star. The shaft projects up from a two-level terrace, and the base houses a foyer, an elevator lobby, and three small museum rooms. The relief sculpture at the base of the shaft, the star at the top of the monument, and the decorative work in metal were executed by William M. McVey. The San Jacinto Monument gives the overall impression of being an elongated and miniaturized version of Bertram G. Goodhue's Nebraska State Capitol.

SAN ANTONIO

Joske's Department Store

100 Alamo Plaza
1939; 1952

BARTLETT COCKE, JOHN GRAHAM COMPANY

This five-story department store employs the Art Deco to convey a sense of urbane sophistication. The smooth limestone walls are interrupted on one facade by slightly projecting pavilions whose finials and vertical patterns of ornament look to the Spanish Colonial Revival. Between these pavilions are fluted piers that spring from metal balconies and terminate in a highly decorated entablature and cornice. At the corner the building curves and meets a facade composed of fluted piers interspersed with vertical grillework. While the building's overall design is Art Deco, much of its detailing refers to the city's Hispanic heritage.

Kress Building

315 E. Houston Street
1938

EDWARD F. SIBBERT

In the 1930s the Kress Company's in-house architect, Edward F. Sibbert, designed small and large Kress stores for cities across the country. All of these are sophisticated designs, and some, like the store in San Antonio, are outstanding examples of the popular Moderne. In general, Sibbert's designs tend toward a delicate, linear version of the Art Deco. Most of his buildings are sheathed in cream-colored terra-cotta, with bright accents of green, yellow, pink, copper, and white. For the San Antonio store Sibbert treated the center of the building as a group of wide fluted piers. Vertical fins project above the parapet, and ornamented towers rise on either side. At street level the cantilevered canopy and the original Kress sign are still in place.

WACO

Coca-Cola Bottling Company Building

Between Austin and 12th Streets
1939

ROBERT V. DERRAH

The Los Angeles architect Robert V. Derrah, who designed Coca-Cola's famous Streamline Moderne concrete ship in his home community, also pursued a Streamline theme for this Waco building. Wide plate-glass windows on the ground floor provide the pub-

lic with a view of the bottling operations. The second floor contains corner windows and a pair of enlarged portholes. Behind the slightly stepped-back parapet is a low-pitched gable with a central projecting cylinder that holds a flag pole. The only Art Deco feature of the design is the entrance, which carries the suggestion of Ionic pilasters.

Thomas Jefferson High School

723 Donaldson Avenue
1932

ADAMS & ADAMS

Like Joske's Department Store (see page 189) in San Antonio, this concrete-and-brick-veneered high school plays a visual game between the monumental Art Deco (à la Bertram G. Goodhue) and the Spanish Colonial Revival. Art Deco features include the building's massing, which focuses on a central drum and dome, and the pattern of vertical buttressing. The cast-stone ornament employs Spanish as well as Art Deco motifs. Some of the ornament, such as the band around the parapet, conveys a pre-Columbian feeling.

Coca-Cola Bottling Company Building, Waco, Texas. *Architectural Concrete* (1939).

WEST

CALIFORNIA

BAKERSFIELD

Retail store and office building

Chester Street at 18th Street, northwest
corner
1940

ERNEST KUMP (FRANKLIN & KUMP)

Kump, who designed many of
California's modern school buildings
in the years just before and after World
War II, also designed a number of
Moderne buildings in the 1930s and on
into the early 1940s. He experimented
with the entire spectrum of styles, from
the Art Deco to the PWA Moderne to
the Streamline Moderne. This example
of his work is one of America's outstanding Streamline Moderne buildings. Like Frank Lloyd Wright's
Johnson Wax Company Building, the
design transcends the merely popular
and approaches the realm of art.
Three horizontal bands of brick race
along the front of the building and
around the corner, then continue along
the building's shorter street facade. The
ground-floor stores and the entrance to
the office building are deeply recessed
beneath the first of these projecting
brick bands. The windows of the upper
two floors of offices are set still further
back, creating a dark band that contrasts with the bands of brick above
and below.

BARD (WINTERHAVEN)

All-American Canal

18 miles northeast of Bard on the west
bank of the Colorado River, Imperial
Dam
1935–38

U.S. BUREAU OF RECLAMATION, DENVER
OFFICE

The All-American Canal was built during the Depression to provide water for
the Imperial and Coachella valleys.
The great metal roller gates and their
control towers are supposedly a direct
response to utilitarian needs. Far from
ordinary, however, they look as if they
were lifted from the cover of a late
1930s science fiction magazine or from
a drawing by Hugh Ferriss. The circu-

lar metal gates seem to plunge through the reinforced-concrete towers. The towers themselves exhibit an angled front, and, together with the horizontal metal-frame windows, they suggest the bridge of a ship.

BERKELEY

Berkeley High School

Grove Street between Allston Way and
  Bancroft Way
1938, 1940

GUTTERSON & CORLETT

The Streamline Moderne is captured here in exposed reinforced concrete. The building's corners are curved, and its facades exhibit the style's characteristic horizontal speed lines. The windows on the second floor are set deep within the walls, which become curved fluted surfaces on either side of the windows. Several of the windows on the first floor contain glass brick. The building's most dramatic moment is the cast-concrete relief sculpture by Jacques Schnier. This large panel features a leaping horse and rider set against a radiating sun, patches of clouds, and thunderbolts. The bottom left corner of the panel carries a text whose lines are separated by horizontal zigzags.

BURBANK

Burbank City Hall

Olive Avenue at Third Street, southwest corner
1941

WILLIAM ALLEN AND GEORGE LUTZI

One might expect this handsome early 1940s public building to exemplify the PWA Moderne or the Streamline Moderne, but in fact its design owes more to the earlier Art Deco. If it exhibits an additional affinity, it would be to the English Regency mode, which was also popular at the time. Although built of exposed reinforced concrete, the Burbank City Hall does not read as a heavy sculptural mass; rather, it is delicate and refined, with windows, doors, and detailing kept close to the plane of the adjoining surfaces. The building is rich in decorative and sculptural detail: large cast-concrete screens bearing Art Deco patterns, elegant relief eagles on the balustrades to either side of the entrance stairs, and bold relief by Bartolo B. Mako on the Third Street facade.

CATALINA ISLAND

Avalon Casino

1 Casino Way
1928–29

SUMNER SPAULDING (WEBBER & SPAULDING)

From the outside this great casino— which houses, among other spaces, a grand ballroom and a motion picture theater—appears to be of Byzantine/ Moorish design. The building becomes openly Art Deco only on the interior, particularly in the wall and ceiling patterns, the light fixtures, and the details of doors and windows. The Art Deco high points of the casino are the stenciling and paintings by John Gabriel Beckman. Many of these evoke themes relating to the sea and marine life. Beckman's art is in many cases combined with or framed by Art Deco patterns of zigzags, diamonds, and wavy lines.

While in Avalon also see another monument, the William Wrigley, Jr.,

Berkeley High School, Berkeley, California.

Burbank City Hall, Burbank,
California.

mausoleum (Bennett, Parsons, and Frost, 1924). This monument plays off the Art Deco against the Spanish Colonial Revival. The Wrigley monument is located high on the hillside at the west end of Avalon Canyon Road.

EMERYVILLE

Cook Stove Oil Company Building (now the Balaam Brothers Building)

1350 Powell Street

1940

This small office building—in the form of a rectangular box with rounded corners and a slightly stepped-back parapet—looks like a Streamline Moderne pillbox that has been grandly enlarged. Metal-frame windows with semicircular ends wrap around the corners, and at the center of the street facade is a large circular window. The principal mullions of the windows are vertical, while the secondary mullions form delicate horizontal and curved lines. The building is a classic of the Streamline Moderne style.

EUREKA

Apartment building

2400 H Street

1940

SAMUEL BURRE

A splendid example of Streamline Moderne packaging. The building's projecting frontispiece curves back toward the entrances on either side. This projection has corners of glass brick, and its surface is decorated with horizontal lines. At the center are a large round window and, beneath the

window, an urnlike console. Curved stairs lead up to the entrance at the right; each of the entrances is covered with a metal-banded curved roof. Another example of Burre's talent as a Moderne designer can be seen in a small single-family house located at 2505 G Street; this house, built in 1938, boasts a large round window.

Eureka Theater

612 F Street

1937

R. C. YOUNGER

Displaying the Streamline Moderne in a somewhat monumental mood, this building encompasses the theater proper and stores on either side. The two-story-high theater is surmounted by a series of volumes that step upward and back. The windows on the second floor are contained within dark horizontal bands. As with many movie theaters, especially those of the 1930s, the sign is the center of attention. It rises vertically against the building and culminates in a semicircular top. Below the sign is a projecting marquee with a curved fascia. The whole building comes to life at night when lit with incandescent bulbs and bright neon tubes.

FRESNO

Mayfair Shopping Center

McKinley Street at 1st Street, northeast corner

1945

A post–World War II continuation of the Streamline Moderne, this shopping plaza's crowning glory is the small

Balaam Brothers Building (Cook Stove Company), Emeryville, California.

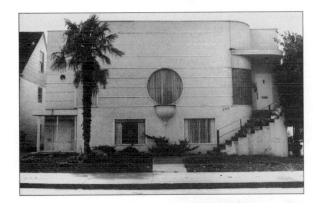

Apartment Building, Eureka, California.

Eureka Theater, Eureka, California.

building at its center that looks like a Streamline Moderne coffee pot. The building comprises a series of concentric drums that decrease in size as they rise. At the top is a small round domed knob with a projecting flagpole. The coffee pot's pouring lip and its handle are abstractly represented, reduced to simple rectangular volumes.

HUNTINGTON PARK

Lane-Wells Company Building (now the Winnie & Sutch Company and W.W. Henry Company buildings)

5608–10 S. Soto Street
1938–39
WILLIAM E. MYER

The complex consists of two separate buildings. The main building, a four-story office structure of reinforced concrete, is a vertical composition of boxes with rounded corners that step in as they ascend. Each of the boxes exhibits continuous bands of glass. At the entrance, pylons that curve and weave up three of the boxes offset the emphatic horizontality of the design. The architect himself noted that "the design is modern, conforming in spirit with the products manufactured"—in this case, equipment used in the drilling and production of oil. This building and its companion to the north (now the W. W. Henry Company) are impressive examples of the Streamline Moderne.

Lane-Wells Company Building (now the W. W. Henry Company), Huntington Park, California.

KING CITY

Auditorium, Union High School

One block north of old Highway 101
1939

ROBERT STANTON

Three volumes are joined together to form the building. At the entrance front is a high volume with a curved facade. Behind is the auditorium, whose sides curve in toward the third form, the stage house. On the exterior the two side walls of the auditorium are set back with three tall narrow pilasters placed in front of the wall. Vertical grooves give the wall a tactile quality. Near the top of the wall are decorative grilles covering vents. The piers themselves bear the suggestion of capitals. The commanding element of the design is the entrance, where two elon-

Union High School Auditorium, King City, California.

gated columns are topped by sculptured masks: comedy and tragedy. Between these columns and to either side is a low-relief perforated panel; the subject of these three sculptured panels is the history of the theater. The masks and the panels are the work of the sculptor Jo Mora.

LONG BEACH

Buffums' Autoport

1st Street between Pine and Pacific
 Avenues
1941

J. H. DAVIS, ENGINEER

The very name of this four-story concrete parking garage—"Autoport" —conveys the Streamline Moderne's fascination with the airplane. The name runs across the front of the building in uppercase boldface letters contained between two projecting horizontal bands. Offsetting the building's commitment to the horizontal is a vertical plane to the left of the entrance. Within this plane are three narrow windows, stacked one on top of another, each of which is covered by a curved concrete canopy. Originally, gasoline pumps were located to the left of the garage entrance.

Pacific Auto Works

1910 Long Beach Boulevard
1928

SCHILLING & SCHILLING

This two-story Art Deco building calls to mind the grille of a 1920s automobile. A large wingspread eagle dominates the center of the principal facade. To either side is a pair of

Buffums' Autoport, Long Beach, California.

Pacific Auto Works, Long Beach, California.

pilasters, and between these are cast-concrete ornament, including seashell forms and a vertical V motif. The upper corners of the three entrances exhibit convex forms that are carried up into the building's cast-stone ornament.

LOS ANGELES

Bullock's Wilshire Department Store

3050 Wilshire Boulevard

1928

JOHN AND DONALD PARKINSON; FEIL & PARADICE; JOCK D. PETERS

From the moment it was completed, Bullock's Wilshire Department Store has been acknowledged as a paragon of the Art Deco style. The form of the building is composed of several intersecting stepped volumes, all of which are vertically articulated. The entire store is sheathed in tan terra-cotta and trimmed with copper. The element that most immediately attracts attention is the 12-plus-story tower, whose richly decorated lantern resembles the top of a perfume bottle. The store's entrance is not actually on Wilshire Boulevard but at the rear of the building, where a large parking lot was created. Metal gates—which bear an Art Deco pattern entitled "Times Fly"—mark the entrance to the parking lot. On the ceiling of the porte cochere is a colorful mural by Herman Sachs. The store's interior features relief sculpture by Gjura Stojano in the Sports Shop, as well as murals and decorative art by Mayer Krieg, David Collins, George De Winter, and John Weaver. Referring to the store's three floors designed by Jock D. Peters, one contemporary critic wrote, "Every room flows into the next by the way of design transition in form and color. . . . The old box architecture is over."

Bullock's Wilshire Department Store, Los Angeles, California.

Coca-Cola Bottling Company Building

1334 S. Central Avenue
1936–37

ROBERT V. DERRAH

The Los Angeles offices and bottling plant of the Coca-Cola Company constitute one of the sacred icons of the Streamline Moderne. Here is a stream-lined ship straight out of a drawing by Norman Bel Geddes, only in this case the ship is fixed solidly on land and built of reinforced concrete. The Coca-Cola "ship" is equipped with a bridge, decks and railings, and portholes. The interior, which over the years has been remodeled, was originally as nautical as the exterior. "The effect throughout the interior," wrote one commentator, "is that of gleaming white enamel, enhanced by cobalt blue, port-holes, polished brass fittings, and mahogany trim."

Crossroads of the World

6671 Hollywood Boulevard
1936

ROBERT V. DERRAH

This small shopping center features a variety of worldwide architectural styles. Its centerpiece is a two-story streamline Moderne ship, sailing out onto Hollywood Boulevard. The curved bridge of the ship is capped by a tall tower upon which is placed a lighted globe of the world (bearing, of course, the name "Crossroads of the World"). This complex was designed by the same architect who produced the concrete Streamline ship for the Coca-Cola Bottling Company.

Darkroom Photographic Shop

5370 Wilshire Boulevard
1938

MARCUS P. MILLER

Among Los Angeles's architectural treasures are her many "programmatic" buildings—structures in the form of objects that suggest or symbolize the buildings' use. A few buildings of this type looked (indirectly, to be sure) to the Streamline Moderne. The Darkroom managed beautifully to advertise its products and services while at the same time giving the appearance of being very up-to-date. The street facade is a Streamline Moderne camera, with a round lens, a shutter mechanism, and viewfinders. The lens and the pair of viewfinders refer not only to the image of the camera but also to porthole windows characteristic of the Streamline Moderne. The camera body is of black Vitrolite, while thin bands of white Vitrolite simulate the metal banding of the camera.

Eastern Columbia Building

849 S. Broadway
1929

CLAUDE BEELMAN

Buildings that resemble nothing so much as oversize perfume bottles constitute a distinct subset of the Art Deco. By a similar token, the upper tower of the Eastern Columbia Building looks like nothing so much as an enlarged Art Deco clock. At the top of the building is an immense rectangular block with a clock face on each of its sides. The neon-lighted clock faces are contained by pilasters to the sides and

Coca-Cola Bottling Company Building, Los Angeles, California.

Darkroom Photographic Shop, Los Angeles, California.

Eastern Columbia Building, Los Angeles, California.

below. Over the faces is a horizontal band of ornament above which the word "Eastern" appears. At the very top, in the place of a carrying handle or the bell on an alarm clock, is an exposed metal truss.

The sides of this 12-story-plus-penthouse, 264-foot-high building are designed in characteristic Art Deco fashion, with slightly projecting fluted pilasters alternating with vertical bands of windows and spandrels. What catches the eye of the observer right away is the bright blue-green and gold glazed terra-cotta tile. A recurring motif in the decoration is the V-shaped chevron, set amidst circles, half-circles, and plant forms.

Thomas Jefferson High School

1319 E. 41st Street
1936–37

STILES O. CLEMENTS

This two-story reinforced-concrete high school complex enthusiastically employs the characteristic elements of the Streamline Moderne. The visitor is greeted by a concave entrance wall that, at second-floor level, announces the name of the school. The two rows of metal letters are set between three horizontal metal bands that extend around all three sides of the entrance pavilion. The wings to either side exhibit bands articulated by projecting horizontal fins; the bands contain the windows and dark-painted stucco. Pylonlike forms occur where the entrance walls meet the building and at the ends of the school's various wings.

Leimert Park Theater

33 W. 43rd Place
1931–32

MORGAN, WALLS & CLEMENTS

This building and the Warner Brothers Western Theater (see page 212) are two of the finest remaining Art Deco theaters in Los Angeles. Both buildings were designed by Morgan, Walls & Clements, as was the famed Richfield Building, which has not survived. Of the two theaters, the Leimert Park is the more correct interpretation of the French mode of the Art Deco. Like many suburban motion picture theaters, the Leimert Park is the focus of a small shopping plaza, with parking in front and retail stores on either side.

The structure and its rich ornamentation are of concrete. Originally the building was painted a light gray-green and the ornament a pale cream. The centerpiece of the building's exterior is the narrow decorated tower topped by a tall metal sign. The interior, which has been modified, formerly contained murals by Andre Durenceau in the lobby and auditorium.

Los Angeles City Hall

S. Spring Street at W. Temple Street,
   southeast corner
1926–28

JOHN C. AUSTIN, JOHN AND DONALD PARKINSON, ALBERT C. MARTIN, AND AUSTIN WHITTLESEY

The Los Angeles City Hall represents one of the most successful marriages of the time-honored classical building

Thomas Jefferson High School, Los Angeles, California.

Leimert Park Theater, Los Angeles, California.

and that paramount symbol of the pre-eminence of commerce in American life, the skyscraper. At the time of its construction the city hall was the only structure in Los Angeles allowed to rise above 150 feet, and it deliberately "cut the skyline" as the city's dominant landmark. The base of the 28-story, 452-foot-high steel-frame building is sheathed in granite, while the tower is covered in semiglazed terra-cotta that matches the light gray of the granite.

Although the building's architectural style has been described as "Italian classic," it in fact borrows freely from a variety of sources. The tower itself resembles an Egyptian obelisk, and its top recreates the Mausoleum of Halicarnassus. Spanish as well as Italian Renaissance influences are also evident. The spirit of the design, however, is Art Deco—in its approach to abstracting traditional forms; in its integration of ornament, sculpture, murals, and mosaics; and in its use of color on the interior. Hartley B. Alexander, who provided the inscriptions for the building, did not lay down a theme for the building's decoration. As a result, the themes expressed in the sculpture and paintings pursue a number of different directions. In the entrance colonnade, patterns of tiles depict the economic and industrial bases of Los Angeles: the motion picture, manufacturing, automobiles, oil, construction, shipping, airplanes, and printing. In the rotunda, on the other hand, are figures "symbolizing the various attributes of the municipal government." Much of the art was executed by Austin Whittlesey, Herman Sachs, and Anthony B. Heinsbergen.

Los Angeles City Hall, Los Angeles, California.

Los Angeles Public Library

S. Flower Street at W. 5th Street, south-west corner

1922–26

BERTRAM G. GOODHUE AND CARLETON M. WINSLOW

Like his Nebraska State Capitol, Goodhue's central Los Angeles Public Library exerted a significant influence on the design of later Art Deco and PWA Moderne buildings. Goodhue's sources for the library are complex and varied. The general atmosphere of the building and its garden calls to mind the sketches that Goodhue made during a visit to Persia, but borrowings from Rome, Egypt, and Byzantium are also identifiable. The walls of the building's three-story base are governed by heavy buttresses that rise in low-relief fashion until they curve into the parapet. Certainly one of the most powerful features of the design is the low square tower topped by a recessed tower that is in turn surmounted by a brightly tiled pyramidal roof; this tower was often imitated by other architects in the late 1920s and the 1930s.

The approach to the principal entrance on the west facade is bifurcated by a series of stepped "Persian" pools. Above the arched entrance are two pilasterlike forms that provide niches for a pair of standing figures. Directly above the entrance is a boxlike projecting balcony with its own sculptural panel. Relief sculpture occurs throughout the building, the richest group being on the south elevation. As in the Nebraska State Capitol, the ideological program for the sculpture was drawn up by Hartley B. Alexander, and the sculpture itself was designed and executed by Lee Lawrie. According to one contemporary source, "The theme of the sculptural decoration and inscriptions which adorn the building is the illuminated book, symbolized by the torch of knowledge which is handed down from one age to another by the great literary figures of all ages."

The interior is decorated with murals by Dean Cornwall, Albert Herter, Julian Garnsey, and A. W. Parsons. Of the greatest architectural interest are the twelve murals by Dean Cornwall in the rotunda, which relate the history of California.

Los Angeles Public Library, Los Angeles, California.

Los Angeles Times Building (now the Times-Mirror Building)

S. Spring Street at W. 7th Street, southwest corner
1931–35

GORDON B. KAUFMANN

In the same way that the offices of other leading newspapers across the country seek to associate themselves with seats of power, the Times Building, which stands directly across from the Los Angeles Civic Center, poses as a government building. The building's design is essentially late Art Deco—that is, PWA Moderne—with an occasional Streamline Moderne flourish. At street level, bronze-framed display windows penetrate the polished black granite base. The exterior is clad in pink granite to the top of the second floor; higher walls are clad in cream-colored limestone. Vertical piers alternate with inset double windows and metal spandrels. The manner in which sculpture and decoration are integrated into the edifice is Goodhue-esque, although the sculpture and detailing are more delicate and linear than those in Goodhue's work. Eagles, a typical Art Deco motif, appear below the clock face and again in panels near the entrance. The rotunda just inside the entrance contains a mural by Hugo Ballin.

May Company Department Store

Wilshire Boulevard at Fairfax Avenue,
northeast corner
1938–40

ALBERT C. MARTIN & SAMUEL A. MARX

At the time of its construction the May Company Department Store on Wilshire Boulevard was referred to as "the store of tomorrow." The five-story rectangular block of the building is essentially a backdrop for the impressive corner sign. The sign consists of a concave surface of highly polished black granite that recedes into the building. From this concave surface a convex surface of reflective gold mosaic tile projects forward. The name of the store runs down the polished black granite on either side of the gold centerpiece. At night this corner is brilliantly lit, as are the ground-floor display windows; the rest of the building simply disappears. Like the earlier Bullock's Wilshire, the May Company Department Store devotes the entirety of its two street facades to the advertisement of its merchandise. The store is entered via its extensive parking lot at the rear.

Oviatt Building

617 S. Olive Street
1927–28

WALKER & EISEN

The exterior of the 13-story Oviatt Building employs the Italian Romanesque, a style that was especially popular in Southern California in the 1910s and 1920s. The upper reaches of the building display arched corbeling, arched windows, tile roofs, and a campanilelike tower with a clock face on each side. The most Moderne feature of the exterior is the vertical pattern created by pilasters interspersed with recessed window-and-spandrel panels on the main body of the facade. Under the suspended marquee (which spans the entire front of the building) one enters the world of refined French Art Deco.

Los Angeles Times Building, Los Angeles, California.

May Company Department Store, Los Angeles, California.

A luminous Art Deco ceiling of Lalique glass occurs under the marquee. Doors containing Lalique glass lead into a lobby that might best be described as a very European interpretation of the Moderne. The elevator doors, also of Lalique glass, depict stylized California fruits. Almost all of the interior light fixtures, the wall and ceiling coverings, and the abundant Lalique glass were manufactured in France and shipped to Los Angeles. At the top of the building is James Oviatt's own penthouse "bungalow." These quarters, along with the interior of Bullock's Wilshire Department Store, represent the pinnacle of the Art Deco in California.

Samuel-Navarro House

5609 Valley Oak Drive
1926–28

LLOYD WRIGHT

In the 1920s, many of Lloyd Wright's houses incorporated elements or motifs that reflected the popular architectural styles of the day. The Samuel-Navarro House (its recent unfortunate remodeling notwithstanding) is a highly personal interpretation of the Art Deco. The dwelling is situated on a steep slope in the Hollywood hills. Projecting out from the stucco street facade is decorated pressed metal in a cruciform pattern; the metal is painted a dark color to contrast with the white stucco. The windows are set within a band of metal that extends from one end of the house to the other. The entrance is at a level below the street, alongside the garage. The main living area of the house extends out of doors to encompass a sheltered garden (hid-den from the street by a wall) with a swimming pool.

Other Lloyd Wright houses of the 1920s also express a strong sense of the Art Deco. Among these would be his own house in Hollywood (1928) at 858 North Dohney Drive; and the Derby House (1926) at 2535 Chevy Chase Drive, Glendale.

Selig Retail Store Building

Western Avenue at W. 3rd Street,
    northwest corner
1931

ARTHUR E. HARVEY

In this small single-story building one can begin to imagine the effect of the Richfield Building (1928) in Los Angeles, which was clad with similar black-and-gold glazed tiles and which unfortunately has been demolished. The Selig Building's two street fronts are sheathed in highly reflective terracotta, and all of the decorative details are in gold glazed tile (actual gold was used for the color). The facades are interrupted by fluted piers crowned by capitals containing an Art Deco pattern. These capitals melt into a horizontal band of zigzags and into the cornice itself, which is composed of stylized pointed arches surmounted by small gables.

Smith House

191 S. Hudson Avenue
1929–30

C. J. SMALE

The Smith House poses as a fragment of a monumental PWA Moderne build-

Samuel-Navarro House, Los Angeles, California.

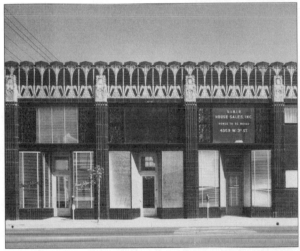

Selig Retail Store Building, Los Angeles, California.

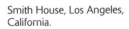

Smith House, Los Angeles, California.

ing. The house gives the impression of having been constructed of reinforced concrete, but in fact it is a wood frame covered with cement stucco. The house's exterior walls are divided by broad pilasters, its roof is parapeted and flat, and its entrances and windows are deeply recessed. Cast-concrete zigzag ornament occurs between the pilasters, and several windows contain colored leaded-glass in angular Art Deco patterns.

Storer House

8161 Hollywood Boulevard
1923

FRANK LLOYD WRIGHT

Wright's work is always so strong that it is difficult to characterize any of his designs as belonging to a particular style. But, in truth, his buildings often distill the essence of a popular architectural style while at the same time maintaining their great individuality.

His concrete-block houses of the 1920s in Los Angeles gather together several divergent trends; for example, they reflect the intense interest in developing new techniques for using concrete in domestic architecture, and they also express the era's preoccupation with period revivalism. The Storer House, which draws from pre-Columbian sources, contains many elements of the Art Deco.

In the facade that looks down toward Hollywood Boulevard, strongly accentuated piers alternate with deeply recessed windows and spandrels. Also characteristic of the Art Deco was Wright's use of decorative concrete block, both in terms of its disposition in the design and in its linear, angular patterns. The north facade, which faces a hillside, invokes (in miniature to be sure) the American Vertical style. Extensive restoration of the house took place in the 1980s and early 1990s. The Storer House is in many ways in better condition today than when it was built.

Storer House, Los Angeles, California.

All of Frank Lloyd Wright's Los Angeles houses of the late 1910s and 1920s exhibit an Art Deco atmosphere. Other of these houses are the Barnsdall "Hollyhock" House (1919–20) at Hollywood Boulevard and Vermont Avenue, Los Angeles; the Millard "La Miniatura" (1923) at 645 Prospect Crescent, Pasadena; the Ennis House (1924) at 2607 Glendower Avenue, Los Angeles; and the Freeman House (1924) at 1962 Glencore Way, Hollywood.

Sunset Towers

18358 Sunset Boulevard
1929–31

LELAND A. BRYANT

The 16-story Sunset Towers apartment building is, without question, one of the great monuments of the Moderne mode. It begins at ground level as a variation on the American Vertical skyscraper style; by the time the top is reached the imagery has shifted over to the Streamline Moderne. On the rear and side facades occur vertical bands of splayed bay windows; there are also windows that wrap around the building's curved corners. The upper sections of the building step back, and each of the parapets is elaborately decorated with typical Art Deco motifs. On the Sunset Boulevard facade, at the level of the ninth floor, is an elongated stepped console upon which stands a nude female figure. Within the cast-concrete decoration are the stylized forms of many plants and animals. At the rear of the building, cast-stone representations of automobile radiator grilles suggest the proximity of the garage.

Ulm House

3606 Amesbury Road
1937

MILTON J. BLACK

The Los Angeles area is the site of many small and large single-family Streamline Moderne houses. The Ulm

Sunset Towers, Los Angeles, California.

House is one of the most distinguished of these. Its dominant note is the projecting curved staircase bay, which is encased largely in glass brick. To the right of this bay, on the second floor, is a nautical-appearing deck with metal-pipe railings. The volumes of the house are horizontally banded, and the windows are contained between the bands. Corner windows abound, as do glass doors leading out to decks at various levels.

Val D'Armour Apartments

854 S. Oxford Avenue
1928

G. W. POWERS

The entrance to the Val D'Armour Apartments stands as one of the grand pieces of Art Deco architecture in the United States. A wide projecting lintel with a V-shaped opening seems almost to have sunk into the ground. The keystone of the opening (is it perhaps Mayan?) emerges as a sunburst. On either side of the keystone are rich patterns of curves and spirals suggesting the forms of plants encountered at the bottom of the sea. The oversize lintel rests on the shoulders of a pair of crouching nude male figures. The exterior walls of the five-story building are articulated with tubelike pilasters. Decorative patterns occur in the spandrels and again in the unusual open work of the parapet.

Warner Brothers Western Theater and the Pellissier Building (now the Wiltern Theater Building)

Wilshire Boulevard at Western Avenue, southeast corner
1930–31

MORGAN, WALLS & CLEMENTS

This complex, comprising a theater, retail stores, and an office tower, is unusual in several regards. First, the tower, which is recessed but centered on the theater entrance, is laid out at a 45-degree angle to the street corner.

Ulm House, Los Angeles, California.

Secondly, the tower poses as an American Vertical–style skyscraper when in fact it is quite small (only 12 stories). The narrowness of the pilasters and the window-and-spandrel bands makes it difficult to discern the scale and size of the building. The terra-cotta cladding on the exterior was provided by Gladding, McBean; its blue-green is a color characteristic of the Art Deco. The theater was designed by G. Albert Lansburgh, and the interiors were planned and executed by Anthony B. Heinsbergen.

Hollywood Bowl, Entrance Monuments, Pools, and Fountains

2301 N. Highland Avenue
1939–40

ALLIED ARCHITECTS; GEORGE STANLEY, SCULPTOR

Smooth sculptured figures seemingly grow out of a Streamline Moderne mountain, at the base of which are fountains and pools suggesting a river or per-

haps the sea. These entry monuments are best seen at night, when they are bathed in colored light. The early shells for the Hollywood Bowl, designed by Lloyd Wright, were first Deco (1924) and then Streamline (1928).

NEVADA CITY

Nevada City Hall

317 Broad Street
1937

GEORGE C. SELLON

Here is a late 1930s public building that asserts its presence on the street through signage. The two-story concrete structure becomes a mere backdrop for a sign that announces "City Hall" in squat uppercase Moderne letters. The words rests on a horizontal shelf that terminates on the right in an abstract pattern of lines, circles, and half-circles. On the first floor there are two deeply recessed entrances: one for people, the other for fire trucks. The walls adjacent to the entrances are horizontally banded and curve in toward the doors.

Nevada City Hall, Nevada City, California.

Nevada County Courthouse

North side of Church Street
1936–37

GEORGE C. SELLON

Within this Moderne (predominantly Streamline Moderne) structure is a late 19th-century courthouse, updated and remodeled in the fashion of the mid-1930s. Facing the steep hillside is a six-plus-story facade articulated by thin pilasters that rise four stories. As in the Nevada City Hall, the architect here provided a shelf for lettering; this shelf functions also as a cornice. The single-story wings to each side have curved corners and windows placed between thin horizontal strips.

OAKLAND

Alameda County Courthouse and Hall of Records

13th Street at Fallon Street
1935–36

W. G. CORLETT, J. W. PLACHEK, H. A. MINTON, W. E. SCHIRMER, AND CARL WERNER

The architects designed a low classical-inspired building and then at its center placed a massive tower that terminates in a hipped metal roof and a lantern. With the exception of the granite-encased base, the exterior walls are of exposed concrete. Most of the building's windows are contained, along with their spandrels, within recessed vertical bands; fluted pilasters occur at the Fallon Street entrance. The building's exterior and interior ornament is reserved, generally employing such classical motifs as the Greek key pattern. Certain individual features—the metal elevator doors, for example—are recognizably Art Deco. Other elements —such as the metal railings of the balconies overlooking the three-story space of the law library—move over into the Streamline Moderne. Within the Fallon Street lobby are two marble mosaics by Marion Simpson. The courthouse was partially funded by a PWA grant.

John Breuner Company Building

22nd Street at Broadway
1931

ALBERT F. ROLLER

The Gladding, McBean Company provided the sea-green glazed terra-cotta cladding for this eight-story structure, which housed a company that manufactured furniture. The upper reaches are vertically articulated in the typical Art Deco fashion, with recessed strips of windows and spandrels separated by pilasters of various width. Gold glazed terra-cotta ornament occurs at the parapet level, above the entrances, and within the spandrels. The best of the ornament is above the two entrances, where stylized representations of furniture occur amidst Art Deco spirals, zigzags, and sunbursts.

I. Magnin & Company Department Store

20th Street at Broadway
1931

WEEKS & DAY

The image of the I. Magnin & Company Department Store as an upper-middle-class establishment is well maintained in this elegant building.

John Breuner Company Building, Oakland, California.

I. Magnin & Company Department Store, Oakland, California.

The structure is clothed in vertical panels of shimmering aquamarine terra-cotta. Subtle, unobtrusive low-relief panels featuring a zigzag pattern occur here and there.

Income Security Building

364 14th Street
1928

FRED H. REIMER

Four buttresslike vertical elements terminate in stylized eagles below the parapet of this five-story building. Similarly winged images appear in the spandrels below the windows. Three large relief panels depicting male nudes occur above the openings on the ground floor. The themes addressed in these panels, which were designed by the Bay Area sculptor John Stoll, range from commerce to justice to "the progressive spirit of art."

Mormon Temple (Church of Jesus Christ of Latter-day Saints)

4770 Lincoln Avenue
1964

HAROLD BURTON

The architect looked back to the world of fantasy of German Expressionism of the 1920s, coupled with the accentuated verticalism associated with the Art Deco. The central pyramided tower is surrounded by four smaller towers placed at each corner of the building. The result, especially when lighted at night, has the science fiction quality of a cover illustration from *Astonishing Tales*, or of a scene from the Wizard of Oz.

Oakland Floral Depot

1900 Telegraph Avenue
1931

ALBERT J. EVERS

The gleaming blue-black terra-cotta tile (provided by Gladding, McBean), together with the highly contrasting silver ornament, brings a prominence to this petite Art Deco commercial structure. The brilliant light-reflecting silver ornament occurs across the top of the

Oakland Floral Depot, Oakland, California.

parapet and also on the sides of the low, two-story tower. The roof of the tower exhibits inverted triangles and a cascading pyramid at its summit.

Paramount Theater

2025 Broadway
1930–31

MILLER & PFLUEGER

As one observer noted of the Paramount Theater shortly after it was completed, "This narrow frontage has just two things to do: admit and discharge the audience and advertise the house." The architects solved the advertising problem very well. They provided a 120-foot-high double-face sign, and then placed a large (20-by-100-foot) colorful terra-cotta mural on either side of the sign. Each of the murals, which were designed by Gerald Fitzgerald, features a single elongated human form as well as four bands containing small figures engaged in activities ranging from sports to music to dance. Both by day and by night the front of the theater emerges as a gigantic billboard. On the interior, the grand lobby and its staircase, the mezzanine, the foyers, the lounges, and the auditorium abound with vibrant colors and rich Art Deco ornament. The lobby, for example, contains etched glass doors, elaborate light fixtures, and black lacquer walls accentuated with silver bands. The sculptured walls of the auditorium were decorated in metal leaf by the sculptor Robert Boardman Howard. The theater was restored in the early 1970s; it is now the home of the Oakland Symphony.

Paramount Theater, Oakland, California.

PASADENA

T. W. Warner Building

481 E. Colorado Boulevard
1927

JESS STANTON (MARSTON & MAYBURY)

The single-story Warner Building was designed to house seven retail stores. The central portion of the building, which rises slightly higher than the wings to the left and right, is defined on each side by projecting pilasters. The entire facade is divided horizontally into three zones: the display windows and doors at the base, a perforated band of decorative tile, and then an expanse of stucco that proceeds up to the decorative terra-cotta tile at the cornice. What distinguishes the building (and earned it an award from the Los Angeles chapter of the American Institute of Architects in 1930) is the decorative tile. Elizabeth St. John wrote in 1928, "Most striking among the stores on Colorado Street is the group occupying the T. W. Warner Building which sparkles in the California sunlight reflected from green tile glazed to the consistency of green jade.... The design is especially charming and happy. Intricate and amazing, as a pattern for tile, it still presents an untroubled picture and cheers and brightens the whole street as far as can be seen."

REDDING

Redding Fire House

Shasta Street between Market and Pine
  Streets
1939

MASTEN & HURD

This is a suave, very assured rendition of the Streamline Moderne. The design consists of a Moderne frontispiece on an otherwise undistinguished building, in this case a simple two-story stucco-covered box. At ground level the curved wall of the projecting entrance bay is broken by three doors for the fire engines. Above this is a curved window that runs across the entire bay and then moves around to meet the front walls of the stucco box. The window is divided in thirds vertically by two prominent horizontal mullions; it is also divided in thirds by two vertical strips of glass brick. Above the window is a projecting cornice. The flat roof is bordered by a ship's railing, implying a deck, but this detail is entirely symbolic since there is no access to the roof. Above the doors the building's name appears in a sophisticated Moderne typeface.

SACRAMENTO

Tower Theater

1518 Broadway
1940

WILLIAM DAVID

The architect took full advantage of this triangular site at the junction of two major streets. The theater itself, with its rounded five-story tower, is at the apex of the triangle. Single-story retail shops project out on either side. The tower is composed of several layers: first, a series of drums; then a taller, ribbed drum; finally, four vertical buttresses supporting the name of the theater. The horizontal lines on the face of the curved marquee are repeated on the entrance and lobby walls.

SALINAS

Monterey County Courthouse

W. Alisal Street at Church Street, northwest corner
1937

ROBERT STANTON

This building is PWA Moderne, with stronger than usual classical overtones. The reinforced-concrete structure was built around a late 19th-century courthouse that was demolished, leaving a central courtyard, when the new building was completed. One enters the courtyard, which has a rectangular pool at its center, through one of two piered loggias. The entrance to the three-story main section of the courthouse is through a portico whose fluted piers have capitals containing stylized eagles. Most of the building's windows are arranged within recessed

Monterey County Courthouse, Salinas, California.

vertical bands. The major exception, a pair of continuous metal window boxes which occur at the top of two of the courthouse's wings, are the strongest Streamline Moderne features of the design. Busts in bold relief, designed by the sculptor Jo Mora, occur within the spandrels.

SAN DIEGO

Ford Building, California Pacific International Exposition (now Aero-Space Museum)

Balboa Park

1935

WALTER DORWIN TEAGUE AND RICHARD S. REQUA

The 1935 San Diego exposition made use of the surviving Spanish Colonial Revival buildings that Bertram G. Goodhue had designed for an exposition in 1915. It also became the occa-sion for several new buildings, most of them designed under the direction of the San Diego architect Richard S. Requa, employing a variety of architectural styles: Spanish Colonial, pre-Columbian, and Moderne.

The Ford Exhibition Building terminated a long axis of the exhibition grounds and was surrounded by many of the new 1935 buildings; it was without question the major new building constructed for the 1935 exposition. The New York–based industrial designer Walter Dorwin Teague had also designed the Ford Motor Company's exhibition hall for the 1933 Century of Progress Exhibition in Chicago. Like the Chicago building, this one is circular. It consists of a large

Aero-Space Museum (Ford Exhibition Building, California Pacific International Exposition), San Diego, California. *Architectural Forum* (1935).

drum with an interior courtyard and a smaller drum that serves as the entrance.

Teague's Chicago building had merely approached the Streamline Moderne, but the San Diego hall was fully committed to the style. The 88-foot-high principal drum, which housed the Court of Nations, is clothed in concave ribs that pose almost as fluting. The edges of the flutes are strips of metal painted a deep blue. Above the fluting is a drum that repeats the name "Ford" four times. The facade of the lower drum features widely spaced pilasters; the surfaces between these pilasters exhibit a pattern of horizontal louvers near the top. Although the Ford Building was intended as a temporary structure, it remains, and was in fact restored in the early 1990s.

Gustafsons Furniture Store

2930 El Cajon Avenue

1938

The central section of this building's three-story white stucco Streamline Moderne facade is recessed and dominated by a two-story glass-brick window. Above this window, in the typeface Broadway, is the single letter "G." The nonrecessed portions of the facade are plain except for two horizontal bands of glass-brick windows. These surfaces curve in as they approach the recessed center, and curved glass-brick windows with horizontal fins continue the bands of glass brick from either side. The base of the building is shaded by cantilevered metal canopies (the center canopy is higher than those to its

Gustafsons Furniture Store, San Diego, California.

left and right). The sum effect is of an undulating two-story volume suspended above the street.

Mormon Temple (Church of Jesus Christ of Latter-Day Saints)

Highway I-5, La Jolla Boulevard
1993

DENNIS HYNDMAN AND SHELLY HYNDMAN
(DEEMS, LEWIS, AND MCKINLEY)

This recent church building illustrates that the science fiction world of the Art Deco/Streamline Moderne is still very much with us. In fact this church structure, with its 190-foot spires, together with a 14-foot-tall gold-leaf statue of the angel Moroni, is one of the most spectacular Art Deco buildings in the entire

country. During the day this vertical city of brillant white spires looms out and greets the freeway traveler, and at night it surpasses any science fiction scene one might see on television.

United States Post Office

E Street between 8th and 9th Streets
1936

WILLIAM TEMPLETON JOHNSON

The three public facades of this reinforced-concrete building employ fluted piers that have neither bases nor capitals. At each end of the primary facade are projecting pavilions treated in a cubist fashion. The walls of the lower rear section of the building are articulated by pilasters that rise to the

U.S. Post Office, San Diego, California.

top of the parapets. The decoration is as reserved as the building itself. Quotations incised in gold leaf occur in a horizontal band just below the cornice. Above the three-story window-and-spandrel recesses on the main facade are wonderful terra-cotta panels entitled *Speed of Transportation;* these panels were designed by the sculptor Archibald Garner.

SAN FRANCISCO

Apartment house (for J. S. Malloch and J. R. Malloch)

1360 Montgomery Street
1937

IRVING GOLDSTEIN; W. H. ELLISON, ENGINEER

From the street only four floors are visible, but to the rear this stucco-sheathed building cascades down the steep hillside (a garage occupies the building's lower regions). The design sways between the Streamline Moderne and high art of the International Style, and the delicate sensibilities of English Regency. Horizontal windows and balconies, glass brick, and rounded corners characterize the design. Above the recessed entrance is a two-story bay containing a remarkable etched-glass

mural by Alfred Dupont, depicting an abstracted view of the San Francisco Bay.

Coit Tower

Top of Telegraph Hill, approached via Lombard Street
1933–34

HENRY T. HOWARD (ARTHUR BROWN, JR.)

Like many Art Deco monuments, the Coit Tower evokes the theme of a classical column's fluted shaft. In this case, the capital takes the form of a ring of arches; above each arch are three smaller arched openings; still higher, where the diameter of the cylinder has diminished, are arches flanked by rectangular buttresses. The tower's 32-foot-high base consists of intersecting rectangular forms; from this platform rises the 180-foot-high reinforced-concrete tower. The tower houses a museum exhibiting works produced by the Federal Arts program. The mural paintings by Ray Boyton, Edward Terada, Edith Hamilton, and Ben F. Cunningham are the most Art Deco in feeling. These interior paintings were restored in 1989–92.

Malloch Apartment House, San Francisco, California.

Coit Tower, San Francisco, California. *Architectural Concrete* (1933).

Henry Doelger Real Estate Building

320 Judah Street
1932 and 1940

CHARLES O. CLAUSEN (CLAUSEN STUDIOS)

Small real estate sales offices were built across the country in the 1920s and 1930s. The Doelger office is unusual in that it poses more as a staid bank or even a governmental building. The builder Henry Doelger entered the arena of speculative housing in the San Francisco Bay area in 1926. From the late 1920s through the 1960s he built several thousand spec row houses in the Sunset district of San Francisco and elsewhere. Most of these would loosely fall within one or another of the Period Revival images of these years, but a few were mildly Art Deco or Streamline Moderne. The 1932 section of Doelger's own office building (to the right) presents a deeply cut vertical space that houses the entrance within a two-story glass wall. The entrance, which appears to be part of the 1940 remodeling, has a polished metal cornice, and the metal doors have the classic one-third curved glass lights. As one would expect, the 1940 section (to the left) is nautical Streamline Moderne, including a round clock that projects out as if it were a built-in ship's search light. At the ground level a curved wall of horizontal bricks leads into the automobile entrance.

450 Sutter Street Building

450 Sutter Street
1928

TIMOTHY PFLUEGER (MILLER AND PFLUEGER)

This 26-story medical/dental office building illustrates how idiosyncratic a design could be yet still fall within the Art Deco–inspired vertical American Skyscraper style. Instead of the usual vertical pattern of pilasters and recessed windows and spandrels, 450 Sutter Street Building employs V-

Howard House, San Francisco, California.

shaped bay windows. When the building opened in 1930, one critic noted that its decorative program was atypical of the Art Deco. "The new building derives its inspiration . . . from the New World, from Central America." (B.J.S. Cahill, "Four-Fifty Sutter Street," *Architect and Engineer* 101 [April 1930]: 35). Indeed, the ornamental terra-cotta, cast iron, and aluminum were inspired by the pre-Columbian designs of the Mayans. Richly decorated panels and screens greet the visitor as one enters the building. Within, the lobby shows more Mayan-inspired ornament, including wonderful elevator doors. The overall design is remarkable, with eight floors of ramped parking backing up against the medical suites.

Howard House

2944 Jackson Street
1939
HENRY T. HOWARD

This Streamline Moderne house both stands out and fits in with the traditional houses in its Pacific Heights neighborhood. Its theme is the moving horizontal band expressed in white stuccoed surfaces and deep, dark voids. The garage/entrance wall and the cantilevered balcony above are rectangular, whereas the second-floor balcony reflects the curve of its large bay window. On the third floor the stuccoed parapet mirrors the half-circle bay below. The window mullions emphasize the horizontal, as do the metal ship's railing of the second- and third-floor balconies. The architect, who in this case was his own client,

also designed Coit Tower (when he was working in the office of Arthur Brown, Jr.).

International Order of Foresters (now the Baha'i Center)

170 Valencia Street
1932
HAROLD STONER

An elegant Art Deco perfume bottle has been enlarged into a full-scale building. The street facade presents one of the country's most elegant Art Deco designs.

Lakeside Medical Building

2501 Ocean Avenue
1940–41
HAROLD STONER

The architect of this building not only produced several of San Francisco's most distinguished Art Deco buildings, but also a number of designs clothed in the Medieval English and Spanish Colonial Revival images. The focus of the design of the Lakeside Medical Building is a tall round shaft that projects above the stucco and glass brick tower. This thin needlelike spire, accentuated by horizontal neon disks, has a real Buck Rogers flair to it. The stucco building itself introduced both Art Deco and Streamline Moderne elements: fluted piers, horizontal banded windows, and even a hipped roof, which seems to have more to do with the woodsy Second Bay tradition of San Francisco than with the Moderne.

Lakeside Medical Center, San Francisco, California.

Leib House

815 Miramar Street
1932

G. A. BERGER

The Leib House represents a highly fanciful use of the Art Deco for a single-family residence. Here the stepped arches characteristic of the style are treated as slightly curved surfaces. The corners of both the first floor and the setback second floor are cut at a 45-degree angle. Occurring at these corners and at intervals across the facade are vertical moldings and grooves that suggest pilasters. Running along the top of the parapets are cartouchelike terra-cotta ornaments. The central motif of these cartouches is a partial sunburst, with a winglike form projecting to either side.

San Francisco Maritime Museum (now the National Maritime Museum)

680 Beach Street
1939

WILLIAM MOOSER, JR. (WILLIAM MOOSER, SR. AND JR.)

Los Angeles is the home of several Streamline Moderne "ships," most notably the Coca-Cola Bottling Company Building and the Crossroads of the World. This building is San Francisco's answer to the Southland, and, as one might expect, San Francisco's response is more refined and delicate than its Los Angeles counterparts. It also has the decided advantage of being situated right on the water, and having its use (a maritime museum) directly related to its image. The 1939 interior murals are by Hilaire Hiler, while the sculpture is by Sargent Johnson.

(and for many years the architect of the University of California at Berkeley and Los Angeles). In the late 1920s Kelham turned to the Art Deco. This 20-story building, which steps back at its upper levels, exemplifies the Art Deco–derived American Vertical style. The building is sheathed in a creamy tan terra-cotta. For the wealth of Art Deco ornament, in which the motif of the spiral shell occurs repeatedly, both terra-cotta and cast metals were employed.

Shell Oil Company Building
100 Bush Street
1929–30
GEORGE W. KELHAM

The architect was one of the major Beaux-Arts practitioners in California

Taravellier House
99 Ord Street
1931
FABRE & HILDEBRAND

A small two-story stucco box has been transformed into an Art Deco state-

San Francisco Maritime Museum, San Francisco, California.

Shell Oil Company Building, San Francisco, California.

Union Oil Company Building, San Francisco, California.

ment by means of ornament. On one facade two bay windows project upward and contain a complex sunburst pattern. The entrance on another facade features variations on Art Deco motifs. On the ground level the garage door opening presents a stepped gable design. Atop the house the chimney wall facing the street exhibits a pattern of inverted V's. The parapet top and the chimney display a double zigzag band.

Union Oil Company Building

425 1st Street
1940

LEWIS P. HOBART

This Streamline Moderne building is essentially all sign. The building consists of one- and three-story stucco-covered rectangular volumes. The facades of these boxes contain horizontal bands of windows, including abundant glass brick. But what dominates the building, both close up and from afar, is its great rectangular pylon announcing "Union" (as well as the time of day). At night the pylon is brilliantly lit and poses as a small skyscraper.

SANTA BARBARA

Boldt Mausoleum

Channel Drive, Santa Barbara Cemetery
1929

REGINALD D. JOHNSON

Situated at the edge of a cliff, overlooking the ocean, this marble-sheathed mausoleum asserts its presence through simple surfaces and refined lines. The building is octagonal, with four principal faces that are significantly wider than the four corner

Boldt Mausoleum, Santa Barbara, California.

faces. Like the shaft of a classical column, the mausoleum rests on a stepped plinth. The structure has finely carved base moldings; from these moldings the uninterrupted walls ascend to a carefully detailed cornice. Above the cornice the roof gently steps back via three planes. The bronze door, with its central angel, is exuberantly Art Deco.

SANTA MONICA

John Entenza House

475 Mesa Road
1937

HARWELL H. HARRIS

The client, the editor and publisher of the magazine *Arts and Architecture,* requested of his young architect a house that would immediately read as modern. Harris—whose work is usually associated with a woodsy, organic

Entenza House, Santa Monica, California.

approach—provided in this case a Streamline Moderne design. From the street one experiences a projecting curved wall, together with a projecting roof. Behind this are the carport and the entrance. Beside the entrance is a metal staircase that leads to the roof terrace. The master bedroom at the rear is also semicircular, only in this instance the entire wall, floor to ceiling, is glass.

SANTA VENETIA, SAN RAPHAEL (MARIN COUNTY)

Marin County Civic Center

San Pedro Road, off of Highway 101
1957–72

FRANK LLOYD WRIGHT, AARON GREEN, AND
    WILLIAM WESLEY PETERS (TALIESIN
    ASSOCIATES)

From the freeway (especially at night), the main Civic Center building has the appearence of a science fiction city on Mars. The main building bridges over between two hills, and the long facades are articulated by rows of arched openings. The building is termi-

nated at its far end by a low layered dome and a razor-sharp thin metal tower. Equally breathing the air of science fiction are the narrow balconied interior courts, which are lighted by skylights. As with the earlier Johnson Wax Company building in Racine, and the Guggenheim Museum in New York, the Marin County Civic Center illustrates how creatively Wright was able to express the romance of the Streamline Moderne.

VENTURA

First Baptist Church

Santa Clara Street at Laurel Street,
    southwest corner
1928–31

ROBERT B. STACY-JUDD

In a 1933 newspaper interview Stacy-Judd observed, "I am convinced that the approach to a clearly defined American architecture is in the story of that lost race [the Mayans]. If we can understand the reasoning behind the motives of this marvelous people and apply it to our own practice, I believe we can construct motifs under modern American conditions and secure a lasting American style that will harmonize with our present scheme of living." The architect's First Baptist Church in Ventura was one of the largest buildings in which he attempted to carry out his ideal of mingling the art of the ancient Mayans with modern architecture.

By "modern" Stacy-Judd in fact meant Art Deco. The church's stepped central tower, with its vertically accented walls, resembles an enlarged church organ (and is remarkably similar to the tower of P. V. Jensen Klint's Grundvig Church [1913, 1921–26] in Copenhagen, Denmark). At the base of the entrance tower is a Mayan corbeled arch. Mayan openings occur also at other points around the building. In addition to the often repeated motif of the stepped parapet, Stacy-Judd used an abstraction of the Mayan temple form to cap two of the building's wings. On the interior (now somewhat altered) the architect devised a variation on the Mayan sacrificial altar for the lectern. Although these pre-Columbian images are readily legible, the spirit of the design is undeniably Art Deco.

Mayfair Theater

Santa Clara Street at Ash Street, northwest corner
1941

S. CHARLES LEE

Lee designed an impressive number of theaters in California, Mexico, and elsewhere. His earliest designs were Spanish Colonial Revival; later he employed the Art Deco mode; and from the mid-1930s through the late 1940s he tended to favor the Streamline Moderne. In the Mayfair Theater, the Streamline image becomes even more eye-catching than usual. Lee tilted the curved roof above the entrance, extended the roof

First Baptist Church, Ventura, California.

Mayfair Theater, Ventura, California.

U.S. Post Office, Visalia, California.

beyond the facade, and then pierced the overhang with three large circles. The marquee, which cantilevers out from the curved stucco-covered wall, rests in part on the small round ticket booth, whose roof seems to be like the stylized foliage of a tree.

VISALIA

United States Post Office

Locust Street at Encina Street, southeast corner

1932

JAMES WITMORE AND W. D. COATES, JR.

The Visalia post office indicates that the PWA Moderne, so commonly associated with the era of the New Deal, was already firmly established as a style in the late days of the Hoover administration. This building is particularly successful in its proportions, its sensitive detailing, and its subtle use of color. The designer, W. D. Coates, converted the pilasters characteristic of the style into partial cylinders of varying height. The cylinders at the center and at the outside edges of the principal facade are relatively short; each of the two intermediate cylinders rises higher and is surmounted by an eagle. The tall windows are set within stepped recessed frames. Art Deco ornament occurs above the entrance and along the parapet. The brick is a warm orange-red, and all of the decorative trim is in terra-cotta of a similar color.

COLORADO

BOULDER

Boulder County Courthouse

1325 Pearl Street
1934

GLEN H. HUNTINGTON

Much of the public architecture in this university community (including the university's own facility) is sheathed in stone, mirroring the rock outcrops of the surrounding Rocky Mountain foothills. In the case of the Boulder County Courthouse, the cladding is a smoothly cut variegated stone. Buttresses supplemented by layered and stepped walls dominate the design. A narrow five-story tower rises at the center of the building; near the top of the tower's walls are inset panels that exhibit clock faces. A sculptural panel with a historic theme occurs above the main entrance.

Boulder High School

1604 Arapahoe Avenue
1935–37

FRANK W. FREWEN, EARL C. MORRIS,
AND GLEN H. HUNTINGTON

The rough random-ashlar surfaces of this two- and three-story building match the exterior surfaces of the nearby University of Colorado buildings. The massing and details encompass elements of both the Art Deco and the Streamline Moderne. Most of the windows are arranged in horizontal bands, but those above the entrance and those lighting the auditorium are placed between vertical pilasters. A curved wall to the left of the entrance contains one of the auditorium staircases. The building's four-story tower mildly suggests a ship's bridge. At one corner, the building is topped by horizontal layered fins. Two high-relief

Boulder County Courthouse, Boulder, Colorado. Boulder Historical Society.

sculptured panels are situated over the entrance. Within these panels are two nude female figures called Strength and Wisdom; the panels were designed by the Denver sculptor Marvin Martin.

DENVER

Bromfield House

4975 S. University Boulevard
1936

BURNHAM HOYT

Like many modern houses built in the 1930s, the Bromfield House straddles the line separating the Streamline Moderne from International Style modernism. The design hinges on a circular dining room whose walls are articulated as horizontal bands via the windows and the wooden railings. Other curved walls also occur, as do glass-brick windows. Over the years remodeling has altered the original design, the most dramatic changes being the replacement of the flat parapeted roof with gable and hipped roofs and the enclosure of the circular second-floor dining terrace.

Ana Evans Mountain House

Upper Bear Creek, Mount Evans, northwest of Denver
1927

BURNHAM HOYT

One suspects that there were not many Art Deco log cabins built in the United States. The idea of combining the imagery of the rustic backwoods with the urbane sophistication of the smart new style of the late 1920s would rarely have occurred either to client or to architect. But here it is, a cabin that is informal and rustic yet at the same time classical and monumental. The Evans Mountain House has exterior walls of vertical logs (hinting at rows of engaged piers). Smooth-board gable ends are separated from the walls below by the suggestion of an intermediate cornice. The roof is composed of flat stones laid in a mortar base. Within each gable end is a grille of overlapping pieces of wood containing Art Deco motifs: zigzags, triangles, lightning bolts, stars, and segments of paired circles.

Ana Evans Mountain House, nr. Denver, Colorado. *Architectural Record* (1928).

House, Denver, Colorado.

House

150 S. Bellaire Street
1937

RAYMOND H. ERVIN

An unusual house that plays a variety of late 1930s visual games. The house's white-painted brick walls, columned porch, and other details point to the then-popular Regency style. Countering these stylistic features are a two-story vertical panel and window with V-shaped mullions and a decorative relief panel that exhibits motifs associated with the Art Deco of the late 1920s. Certain other details, such as horizontal banding and curved surfaces, speak of the Streamline Moderne. Although the images that the house presents are diverse, the architect has molded them into a remarkably coherent whole.

Mayan Theater

110 Broadway
1930

MONTANA FALLIS

Early 20th-century buildings that incorporated pre-Columbian imagery were generally meant to be perceived as reviving a distant and romantic past; such buildings often ended up strongly reflecting the Art Deco. The composition of this theater's facade is Art Deco, but the details play back and forth between the Art Deco and motifs derived from Mayan and Aztec art. The tall central window rises to an inverted V, recalling the openings in many Mayan buildings. Above this window is supposedly an Aztec goddess in brightly colored terra-cotta.

Wahlgreen Mausoleum
Fairmount Cemetery

430 S. Quebec Street

c. 1932

This light pink granite monument conveys a magical effect of a large Art Deco bank building that by the touch of a wand has been reduced to the size of a dollhouse. Classical Art Deco relief ornament surrounds the entrance and occurs at the cornice.

Mayan Theater, Denver, Colorado.

IDAHO

BOISE

Capitol Boulevard Memorial Bridge

Capitol Boulevard spanning the Boise River

1930–31

CHARLES A. KYLE, ENGINEER

A reinforced-concrete bridge entirely in the Art Deco spirit. Tall concrete piers terminate the balustrades of the bridge. The tallest of the concrete pylons seems almost to be a dollhouse version of Bertram G. Goodhue's Nebraska State Capitol. Battered walls lead up to a stepped-back section with buttresslike corner elements. At the top is an open drum and a dome that houses the lights. Set into the faces of the piers are tile panels that depict scenes relating to the history of the Oregon Trail.

JEROME

Heiss House

400 E. Avenue A

1940

BOISE-PAYETTE LUMBER COMPANY

This two-story flat-roofed Streamline Moderne house was constructed using plans provided by Boise-Payette Lumber Company. The one-story section of the house is sheathed in white-painted brick; the two-story portion is sheathed in white stucco. The signature elements of the Streamline Moderne are all here, including metal-frame casement windows that wrap around corners, glass brick, ship's railings, and a curved metal canopy over the entrance. Across the street, at 401 E. Avenue A, is an earlier (1936) Moderne house.

PRESTON

Franklin County Courthouse

Oneida Street at 1st Street W.

1938–39

HYRUM C. POPE AND W. F. THOMAS

On the surface this would seem to be a typical late 1930s PWA Moderne courthouse. The building, consisting of a raised basement plus three stories, is of reinforced concrete painted white. The principal facade exhibits a row of strongly projecting pilasters with their front faces fluted. The ends of the two-story portion of the building are treated as solids, with the windows placed behind pierced-concrete screens. The building's unusual features, which enliven it considerably, include the seemingly random pattern of the windows between the pilasters, the maze of concrete walls and steps leading to the main entrance, and the small octagonal windows of the recessed third floor (from a distance these windows read as enlarged portholes).

Capitol Boulevard Memorial
Bridge, Boise River, Boise, Idaho.
Idaho State Historical Society.

Heiss House, Jerome, Idaho.
Idaho State Historical Society.

RUPERT

Minidoka Stake Tabernacle (Church of Jesus Christ of Latter-Day Saints)

8th Street at G Street
1936–37

LORENZO S. YOUNG

A low octagonal tower has been fitted between the building's two wings. The tower has tall narrow windows that terminate at the metal-sheathed entablature. The tower's copper roof is layered (almost in the fashion of Frank Lloyd Wright) and culminates in a small metal lantern. The wings of the building are sheathed in brick, their surfaces broken by flat pilasters. Indented rows of brick tie the horizontally oriented metal-frame windows together. The entrance is sheathed in white brick.

Minidoka Stake Tabernacle (Church of Jesus Christ of Latter-Day Saints), Rupert, Idaho.
Minidoka Stake Tabernacle.

MONTANA

BILLINGS

Union Bus Terminal

26th Street at 1st Avenue

c. 1939

This bus station and the bus station in Great Falls are full-fledged examples of the Streamline Moderne. Both buildings are sheathed in Vitrolite panels, and both have large horizontally oriented windows with semicircular ends. Metal canopies that read as horizontal bands reinforce the theme of rapid movement.

BOZEMAN

Griffin Apartments

Highway 10 east of Bozeman

1930

This small but sophisticated Art Deco building greets the vistor as he or she drives into Bozeman. The central entrance contains several geometric Art Deco motifs: zigzags, vertical pilasters, and so on. Some of the orna-ment is realized in exposed concrete, some in metal. Flanking the entrance is a pair of slender metal light fixtures; these fixtures are V-shaped, with side panels of angled metal and a stepped projection on top.

GREAT FALLS

Fine Arts Building

Montana State Fairgrounds,
   off 6th Street

1938

COTTIER & HERRINGTON

Prominent buttresses rise up and then curve over the parapet of this Streamline Moderne building. The buttresses occur as pairs, and each buttress has slightly paneled sides. Between each pair of buttresses are louvered canopies that provide a horizontal counterplay to the buttresses' verticality. The cornice, decorated with a zigzag pattern, forms a strong horizontal band. The building's other walls also exhibit paired narrow buttresses, which create a pleated effect.

Griffin Apartments, Bozeman, Montana.

Fine Arts Building, Great Falls, Montana. Cascade County Historical Society.

NEVADA

BOULDER CITY

Hoover Dam

U.S. Highway 93 at the
Colorado River

1929–35

U.S. BUREAU OF RECLAMATION; GORDON B.
KAUFMANN, ARCHITECT

If one were compiling a list of the major monuments of the 1930s Streamline Moderne, the Hoover Dam would certainly be included. The great curved concrete dam is surmounted by four Moderne towers; pairs of circular intake towers that project out into the lake have vertically articulated walls and tops capped by small circular lanterns. The powerhouse at the base of the dam, with its series of mammoth generators, conjures up the science fiction stories of H. G. Wells. Kaufmann wrote about the interior of the powerhouse that "the painting of the equipment was studied carefully by Allen True of Denver. Being a mural painter of note, he has a fine sense of the correlation of color and achieved incredible results. He also designed and supervised the terrazzo floors in various places. These designs (very Art Deco) are largely adaptations of Indian motifs, the permanent recording of these being justified by the general locale." The panels of low-relief sculpture over the elevator tower doors were executed by Oskar J. W. Hansen, who also provided the sculpture for the Nevada plaza approach to the dam.

Hoover Dam and Colorado River, Boulder City, Nevada. Bureau of Reclamation, U.S. Department of Interior. *Inset*, Hoover Dam, powerhouse.

Hoover Dam sculpture, Boulder City, Nevada. Manis Collection, University of Nevada.

OREGON

LEABURG

Leaburg Power Plant, City of Eugene

42520 McKensie Highway
1929

ELLIS F. LAWRENCE, ARCHITECT; STEVENS &
    KOONS, ENGINEERS

Lawrence was an important architect (both a practitioner and an educator) on the Oregon scene from the 1910s through the 1930s. He was particularly gifted in his ability to employ a wide range of architectural styles, including the Art Deco. In the Leaburg Power Plant he enlivened a concrete box with a pronounced band of zigzags running along the parapet; a recessed panel on the entrance facade that accommodates three sculptured figures; and, below these figures, large metal doors flanked by curved fluted surfaces that suggest quarter-segments of a classical column. The sculptural panel, dominated by a central male figure of Power, was produced by Harry Camden. The fenestration pattern on three sides of the building consists of repeated rows of elongated openings accented above by a band of horizontal rectangular windows.

MOUNT HOOD

Timberline Lodge

North off of Highway 26, before
    Barlow Pass
1936–38

GILBERT STANLEY UNDERWOOD; W. I. TURNER;
    DEAN WRIGHT; LINN A. FORREST; WARD
    GANNO; INTERIORS BY MARGERY HOFFMAN
    SMITH

The theme of this romantic and impressive wooden building is a return to nature via a rustic handmade image. But the form and massing of the building and its details place it fully within the Art Deco. The central focus of both

Leaburg Power Plant,
Eugene, Oregon.

the exterior and interior is an octagonal tower whose tall roof terminates in a cupola. The interior exhibits a variety of carved animals and birds which occur on the beams and on top of the newels. The building was a labor-intensive Depression project funded by the Federal government. In 1972 a convention space was added to the building (following the projected late 1930s design), and in 1975 the building was restored.

NEWPORT

Yaquina Bay Bridge

Highway 101 over Yaquina Bay
1936

C. B. MCCULLOUGH, ENGINEER

McCullough was a planner and director of construction for the Oregon Highway Commission. He designed several impressive bridges for Highway 101 along Oregon's Pacific coast. These include the Yaquina Bay Bridge, the Coos Bay Bridge (at North Port), the Umpqua Bridge (at Reedport), the Siuslaw Bridge (at Florence), and the Alsea Bridge (at Waldport). All of these bridges were completed at the end of 1936. McCullough's approach for each bridge was to contrast its steel frame with the reinforced-concrete pylons acting as supports. The pylons continue above the road deck of each bridge and assume the form of small setback skyscrapers. The projecting pylons of the Yaquina Bay Bridge are three-tiered, broken in the center by a V-shaped form that at the top forms a pyramid. The walkways that go through the base of the pylons are covered by V-shaped vaults.

Yaquina Bay Bridge,
Newport, Oregon.

PORTLAND

Charles F. Berg Building

615 S. Broadway
1929–30

GRAND RAPIDS DESIGN SERVICE

Here, in a small three-bay retail store, one can sense the sophistication and urbanity of the Art Deco style, and how the style was rapidly adopted for buildings across the country. The Berg Building is sheathed in black terracotta tile, with accents in cream, gold, and blue-green. Between the four narrow pilasters is a rich array of ornament: zigzags, sunbursts, raincloud patterns, and floral motifs.

Eastside Mortuary

537 S.E. Alder
1930

THOMAS & MERCIER

This mortuary appropriates the image of a public building. A three-story volume is balanced on each side by a two-story wing; the entrance corner is cut at 45 degrees. A high contrast is obtained between the multicolored brick of the walls and the vertical cast-stone bands that contain the windows and doors. Art Deco floral motifs occur within panels of cast stone above and below windows, at the parapet edge, and in an exuberant manner above the entrance.

Charles F. Berg Building, Portland, Oregon. Oregon Historical Society.

First Christian Science Church

1722 S.E. Madison Street
1923–26

WILLIAM GRAY PURCELL

Purcell, together with his partner George Grant Elmslie, was one of the principal figures in the Prairie School movement. After World War I, Purcell moved to Portland, where he established an independent practice. The First Christian Science Church was his largest commission of the 1920s. Regrettably, only the Sunday School portion of the church was built. The school consists of a two-story space dominated by a high clerestory. The low pitch of the main roof is perceptible within, as are the trusses supporting the roof and the vertical members that sustain the trusses. On the exterior, the end walls of the side aisles exhibit stepped parapets, as do the end walls of the central nave. The school is devoid of ornament (ornament by Elmslie was projected for the unbuilt main auditorium). While the design of the First Christian Science Church is certainly not typical Art Deco, the building nonetheless displays a close affinity to this mode in its volumes, spaces, and details.

Virgil T. Golden Funeral Service Building

605 Commercial Street S.E.
1949

D. A. HUSTON

This is a Streamline Moderne composition, with the major emphasis placed on two curved walls of glass brick that rise from ground level to the top of the

First Christian Science Church, Portland, Oregon.

parapet. Glass brick occurs also at the entrance, where a thin metal canopy extends from one vertical band of glass brick to another. The building's white stucco volumes ascend the hillside. The concrete retaining wall with a curved corner reinforces the theme of horizontality.

Portland Bottling Company Building

1321 Couch Street N.E.
1941

ARTHUR P. CRAMER

This is one of the West Coast's strongest Streamline Moderne designs. The metal-frame windows of this one- and two-story building are set out as horizontal bands. A central tower, with its arched opening and fluted pilaster, refers back to the Art Deco, but in a clean Streamline manner. The building's dominant note is its curved corner facing the intersection. An immense corner window with rounded upper corners occurs on the first floor; above are two large porthole windows. The entire composition suggests a face, that is, a mouth and eyes.

Temple Beth Israel

1931 N.W. Flanders Street
1924–27

M. H. WHITEHOUSE, HERMAN BROOKMAN, AND HARRY HERZOG

Like the First Christian Science Church, the Temple Beth Israel represents an extension of the 1920s Art Deco sensibility. The Art Deco approach was always to reduce to basic geometric volumes any direct or implied references to traditional forms. In the case of this temple, the octagonal building surmounted by a dome looks to Byzantine architecture, while the entrance facade, with its two abbreviated towers and curved parapeted entrance screen, suggests Hispanic influence. The layered tops and small domes of the two towers convey a Goodhue-esque quality; the ornamental screens on the sides of the towers employ a subtle Art Deco pattern of triangles. The temple exhibits throughout the variety and richness of materials and colors that one associates with the Art Deco. The exterior surfaces are of exposed concrete, salmon-colored brick, and cream terra-cotta and sandstone. Colors on the interior range from deep blue to cream buff.

SALEM

Oregon State Capitol

Between Court and State Streets
1936–39

FRANCIS KEALLY (TROWBRIDGE & LIVINGSTON)

Considering the general scarcity of commissions for architects during the Depression, it should not be surprising that 123 designers submitted drawings when the state of Oregon announced a competition for a new capitol. The entries ranged from versions of the International Style modern (William Lescaze and Harrison & Fouilhoux) to the PWA Moderne (Ralph C. Flewelling and others). The winning design beautifully sums up the best elements of the PWA Moderne.

Keally's three-story structure is dominated by what almost appears to be the fragmented base of a classical fluted column (in place of the traditional drum and dome). The exterior is sheathed in smooth granite at the base and Vermont marble above. The only ornament is the occasional suggestion of fluting within some of the spandrels and the window grilles in the ribbed central tower and small lantern. Delicate sculptured forms occur mounted on the walls over several of the doors, and a large figure stands atop the lantern. On the interior, the rotunda features horizontal bands of murals. The sculpture was executed by Ulric Ellerhusen and Leo Friedlander and the murals by Barry Faulkner and F. H. Schwarz.

Oregon State Capitol, Salem, Oregon.

UTAH

HELPER

Helper Civic Auditorium and Library

19 S. Main

1936–37

SCOTT & WELCH

The brick walls of this one- and two-story PWA Moderne building are dramatically curved, and the themes of horizontality and speed are strongly emphasized by the narrow bands along the cornices and above the windows at the entrance. At the center of the building are three layered pilasters; the stepped pattern of the windows flanking these pilasters reflects the presence of internal staircases. Although the building has a monumental quality, it was certainly meant to be responded to as an incarnation of the Streamline Moderne of the 1930s.

OGDEN

Ogden City and County Building

2549 Washington Boulevard

1938–39

HODGSON & MCCLANAHAN

This late 1930s American Vertical–style skyscraper was funded in part by the Public Works Administration. The structure is 183 feet high and encompasses 12 stories. The exterior is sheathed in pale brick trimmed in terra-cotta. Parts of the base and the front entrance are sheathed in granite. The building reads almost as two separate structures. The lower regions of the base, which con-sists of a raised basement and two floors, exhibit horizontal recessed banding. The floors above the base exhibit indented vertical bands of windows and brick spandrels. The entrance is pulled slightly forward and is dominated by a high recess containing the metal-frame entrance doors and metal grilles. The upper floors of the building contain pilasters that rise to the top of the parapet. Above the eighth floor, the verticality of the rectangular central tower is emphasized by the fenestration; the tower culminates in a row of projecting finials.

Ogden High School

2828 Harrison Boulevard

1935–37

LESLIE S. HODGSON (HODGSON & McCLANAHAN)

Although somewhat late for the style, this building is indeed one of the finest examples of the Art Deco in the American West. The four-story steel-and-reinforced-concrete structure, which is sheathed in brick and terra-cotta, was funded in part by the Public Works Administration. The complex consists of a T-shaped, tower-dominated, four-story academic building, and a large auditorium-and-gymnasium building extending to the right. At the rear is a separate two-story shop building. The overall design is almost Gothic Revival in its linearity and vertical thrust. The building is sheathed in pale brick, with numerous details in smooth stone. The three piers emerge dramatically as layered buttresses above the entrance, and the stepped lintels of the three high windows between the piers have a strong pre-Columbian flavor. The interior is resplendent with Art Deco patterns on the walls, around doorways, and on the ceiling.

Reynolds House

2636 Taylor Avenue

1938

Of the several Streamline Moderne houses in Ogden, the Reynolds House is undoubtedly the most impressive. A one-story wing and a two-story wing project toward the street; each wing has a single curved corner, giving the strong impression that these two volumes are fragments of a whole. The smooth concrete walls are interrupted by round windows, large openings containing glass brick, and wraparound projecting bands just below the parapets.

Another strong Streamline Moderne design is the Behling House (1937) at 1502 27th Street. This house presents almost all of the features typically associated with the Streamline Moderne, but its dramatic entrance looks back to the Art Deco. On either side of the arched door are fluted Doric-like columns that support a flat cantilevered roof. Above are vertically arranged curved bands, the center one of which projects above the parapet.

Union Bus Depot

Grant Avenue at 25th Street

1940

JAMES T. ALLAN AND EBER F. PIERS

The two street facades of this building curve toward the corner entrance tower. The upper section of the round tower is slightly recessed to accommodate the building's name. The terminal's walls are treated as three horizontal bands, with metal-frame windows occupying the center band. Horizontal lines are carried above the window band. The building is an excellent, self-assured example of the late 1930s Streamline Moderne.

Union Bus Depot, Ogden, Utah. University Lithoprinters.

WASHINGTON

BELLINGHAM

Bellingham High School

Cornwall Street between Kentucky
and Ohio Streets
1936–37

NARAMORE & YOUNG

This three-story reinforced-concrete structure presents an essentially Streamline Moderne image, although, as often happens, the entrance pavilion has overtones of the Art Deco. The H-shaped building exhibits three horizontal bands of windows that are terminated at each end by the slight hint of a recessed pavilion. The building's designer seems to have been playing with classical symmetrical assertions, and then introducing odd off-center events. The pavilion to the right of the entrance is recessed at ground level; above is a small projecting concrete box with a large porthole window. On the first floor of the entrance pavilion a pair of wide curved piers separates the three entrances; from a distance these piers read as drum columns. Above the doors is a panel containing the school's name in the typeface Broadway; still higher is the familiar Art Deco pattern of recessed window-and-spandrel bands with intervening pilasters. The right side of the entrance pavilion curves inward at the second and third floors, and here, in low-relief sculpture, are two panels that illustrate aspects of modern education and culture. The building's other delightful, if idiosyncratic, features include the small volume with porthole windows on top of the entrance pavilion and the flagpole/antenna, which is mounted on a segmented curved surface below which a vertical pattern of repeated V's appears.

EVERETT

Everett Public Library

Hoyt Avenue at Everett Avenue,
southwest corner
1934

BEBB & GOULD

Discounting the 1963 additions, this library structure reads as three distinct buildings. The first episode to attract one's attention is a single-story volume with a curved corner that appears to be emerging from the two-story mass behind it. The windows of this entrance pavilion form a horizontal band directly under the projecting edge of the flat roof. Rounded pilasters flank the doors, which feature decorative aluminum grilles. To the left of the entrance pavilion is a small block with three high windows and, below the windows, a central niche. The main building, which lies to the rear, declares itself as a symmetrical design with a slightly convex center. The stepped walls that project from this mass have horizontal bands of brick and a vertical brick pattern above the windows. Sculptured blocks that project forward slightly establish this upper decorative zone. Within the library are murals by J. T. Jacobsen and sculpture by Dudley Pratt.

Everett Public Library, Everett, Washington. Richard Cardwell.

SEATTLE

Exchange Builing

821 2nd Avenue
1929

JOHN GRAHAM, SR. (GRAHAM
   AND GRANT)

This 23-story example of the American Vertical–style skyscraper of the late 1920s was touted at the time as one of the tallest buildings in the country to be constructed of reinforced concrete. The exterior piers are terminated by relief sculpture of flowers. The polished black marble walls of the entrance lobby contrast dramatically with the highly patterned gold ceiling.

Other Art Deco skyscrapers in the downtown Seattle area include:

Olympic Tower (United Shopping Tower)

217 Pine Street
1929

HAROLD ADAMS (HENRY BITTMAN)

Seattle Tower (Northern Life Tower)

1218 3rd Avenue
1928–29

JOSEPH W. WILSON (ALBERTSON, WILSON
   AND RICHARDSON)

Fire Station No. 6

23rd Avenue at E. Yesler Way

1931

DUDLEY STEWART

The facade of this small fire station is inscribed with vertical lines. The parapet is stepped, and passages of horizontal lines hint at traditional horizontal divisions of the surface. The most striking aspect of the design is a central shaft, V-shaped in plan, that supports a flagpole. Adjacent to the shaft, at the base of the parapet, is a pair of grilles containing zigzag lines, similar to the grilles that decorated many late 1920s radios.

Harborview Hospital

325 9th Avenue

1931

THOMAS, GRAINGER & THOMAS

The architect has broken his massive structure into five pieces, starting with a central volume of 12-plus stories and stepping down to 8-story wings at either end. The three central volumes contain pilasters, recessed window-and-spandrel panels, and the suggestion of solid end sections. The central volume is given increased emphasis by groups of four C-shaped finials that project out from all four facades. The slightly projecting entrance screen displays several typical Art Deco motifs.

Saint Joseph's Roman Catholic Church

732 18th Avenue E.

1932

JOSEPH WILSON (A. H. ALBERTSON, JOSEPH WILSON & PAUL D. RICHARDSON)

The tall tower of this reinforced-concrete church is visible from a great distance. The tower exhibits narrow corner buttresses that terminate in small lanterns. Within these four buttresses is the octagonal tower, whose faces are articulated with deep vertical grooves (à la the American Vertical skyscraper style). The upper portions of the tower step back and reveal vertical patterns of Art Deco ornament. The body of the church is roofed with a low

Fire Station No. 6, Seattle, Washington. Seattle Fire Department.

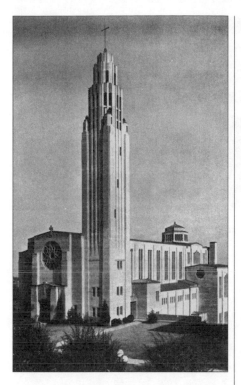

Saint Joseph's Roman Catholic Church, Seattle, Washington. *Architectural Concrete* (1932).

gable, and elongated round-arched windows occur along the sides of the building. Ornament is employed across the gable end and above the entrance. The reinforced-concrete nature of the walls is legible in the rough pattern left by the forms.

Seattle Art Museum

Volunteer Park
1932

BEBB & GOULD

The segmented curved entrance suggests an elegant Art Deco perfume bottle, while the two flanking wings with fluted niches seem to be waiting for equally elegant bottles. The T-shaped building and its rear garden court are pure Beaux Arts in plan and proportion, but the influence of the 1925 Paris Exposition of the Decorative Arts is also evident in the design. The concrete structure is covered with smooth gray-buff sandstone, which (excepting the fluted niches of the end pavilions) has been left plain. Delicate aluminum grilles bearing patterns of diamonds, flowers, and scrolls appear over the entrance and on the doors. The entrance hall has walls of imitation travertine with horizontal bands of gold terra-cotta. The stairway to the basement lecture room has a dramatic stepped pattern that draws one downward.

Tunnel entrances

Highway 90, west end of Murrow
   Bridge
1940

LLOYD LOVEGREN, ARCHITECT; JAMES
   FITZGERALD, SCULPTOR

The deeply recessed concentric rings of this pair of arched tunnel entrances evoke the atmosphere of a Buck Rogers city of the 25th century. The walls, canted slightly inward, feature three projecting sculptured panels. The center panel contains bold lettering (readable even from a moving automobile); the panels on either side reveal a strong but sensitive semi-abstract version of traditional Indian art of the Pacific Northwest. These tunnel entrances easily constitute the most impressive example of a Stream-line Moderne monument (as opposed to building) in the country.

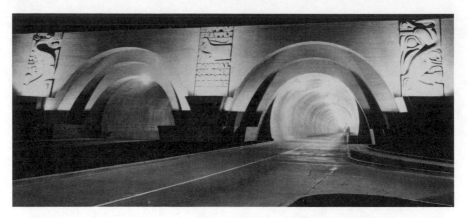

Tunnel Entrance, Murrow Bridge, Seattle, Washington. Special Collections, University of Washington.

United States Public Service Hospital

1131 14th Street S.

1934

BEBB AND GOULD; JOHN GRAHAM, SR.

The essential form of this 16-story building with its central tower pavilion is Art Deco, but the strong horizontal treatment of the walls to each side of the central tower look to the Streamline Moderne. The strongest element of this complex are the officers' and nurses' housing. This group of six 2-story buildings working their way up the hillside play with patterns of brick in an effective Expressionist fashion.

SPANGLE

High School and Grade School

Two blocks north of Cheney
  Spangle Road

1936–37

G. A. PEHRSON

In this two-story concrete box, the architect has grouped the windows within bands of dark masonry that wrap around the building's subtly curved corners. The entrance is stepped slightly forward, with a recess for the ground-floor doors and a second-floor window.

SPOKANE

KFPY Radio Transmission Building (now Radio Station KXLY)

5000 block S. Regal Street

1936

RIGG & VANTYNE

The Streamline Moderne was a favored style for radio stations in the 1930s, for its machine imagery perfectly mirrored the electronic world of radio broadcasting. This small transmission building is not as vigorous today as it originally was, but enough remains to indicate what a beautiful Streamline package the architects provided. A tall narrow door and its grilled transom are tucked between two inward-curving concrete surfaces. Rising from the corner of the station's curved form is a small cylindrical tower surmounted by a metal tripod that originally contained a ship's searchlight. To the right of the entrance was a glass-brick wall that curved around the corner; this wall is now red brick with small glazed openings. Another Spokane radio transmission tower, for station KHQ, is also Streamline Moderne.

Kirk Thompson House

E. 1413 Overbluff
1935

G. A. PEHRSON

When constructed, this house was described in the Spokane newspaper as "extreme in modernistic architecture." The house is of reinforced concrete and incorporates many of the forms and details associated with the Streamline Moderne. A series of one-story volumes work their way to a two-story section that features curved corners. A pair of indented horizontal bands extends around the parapet. The metal-frame casement windows are horizontally oriented. There are abundant corner windows and, of course, glass brick. Pehrson was an advocate of reinforced-concrete construction and of the Streamline Moderne style, which he employed for residences, commercial buildings, and schools. The Thompson House is one of several Streamline Moderne houses on Overbluff.

TACOMA

Rhodes Medical Arts Building (now the Tacoma City Hall)

Between Market Street
    and St. Helens Avenue
1929–30

JOHN GRAHAM, SR.

The architect arranged this American Vertical–style skyscraper as three distinct blocks: a 16-story central section, a 12-story section to the left, and a 6-story section to the right. The top two floors of the left volume are set back on the side, and the central tower exhibits a top floor set far back from the front of

Spangle High School and Grade School, Spangle, Washington. Washington State Historic Preservation Office, Spokane.

the building. The St. Helens Avenue elevations are similar to the Market Street elevations except that, because of the angle of the street, a 2-story volume runs in front of the 16- and 12-story towers. Narrow pilasters rise from the second floor to the respective parapets of the building's three sections. Characteristic Art Deco ornament occurs at the parapet level both within the recessed window-and-spandrel zone and on the intervening pilasters. The principal entrance on Market Street, set within a deep recess, features a stepped arch and lintel. Rich floral, zigzag, and spiral patterns embellish the upper section of the entrance. At the base of the building is an elegant band of polished black marble. The lobby also contains abundant decoration, as well as an elaborate three-story staircase.

Tacoma City Hall (Rhodes Medical Arts Building), Tacoma, Washington.
Tacoma Planning Department, City of Tacoma.

INFORMATION SOURCES

Visual fascination, augmented in some instances by nostalgia, has led to the emergence of several organizations interested in Art Deco and Streamline Modern design and architecture. Since new Art Deco Societies are constantly being formed, it is difficult to compile anything approaching a complete list. The largest and most active of these groups include the Miami Design Preservation League (P.O. Bin L, Miami Beach, Florida 33119); the Art Deco Society of New York (c/o Ryan Gibson Bauer Komblath, 90 West Street, New York, New York 10006); the Art Deco Society of Washington (P.O. Box 11090, Washington, D.C. 20008); the Art Deco Society of Boston (1 Murdock Terrace, Brighton, Massachusetts 02135); the Chicago Art Deco Society (5801 N. Lincoln, Chicago, Illinois 60659); the Detroit Area Art Deco Society (P.O. Box 458, Royal Oak, Michigan 48068 0458); the Art Deco Society of the Palm Beaches (820 Lavers Circle, G203, Delray Beach, Florida 33444); the Art Deco Society of California (109 Minna Street, San Francisco, California 95105); the Art Deco Society of Los Angeles (P.O. Box 972, Hollywood, California 90078); the Art Deco Society of Sacramento (P.O. Box 102836, Sacramento, California 95816-2836); San Diego Art Deco Society (P.O. Box 33762, San Diego, California 92103); the Art Deco Society of South Carolina, Charleston Chapter (856-A Linope Lane, Mount Pleasant, South Carolina 29464); Art Deco Society of Northern Ohio (3439 West Brainard Road, Room 260, Woodmere, Ohio 44122); and the Art Deco Society of Philadelphia (1924 Arch Street, Philadelphia, Pennsylvania 19103). All of these societies publish newsletters (and occasionally guidebooks), sponsor lectures, and conduct tours.

Also quite involved with Streamline Moderne buildings (especially those of the road, street, and highway) is the Society for Commercial Archaeology (Room 5010, National Museum of American History, Washington, D.C. 20560). The national Society of Architectural Historians has held sessions on Art Deco/Streamline Moderne at its annual meeting, and many of the society's regional chapters conduct tours of Art Deco and Streamline Moderne buildings. Other national groups involved with the Art Deco and Streamline Moderne are Friends of Terra Cotta (771 West End Avenue, Apt. 10-E, New York, New York 10025); Tile Heritage Foundation (P.O. Box 1850, Healdsburg, California 95448); and the National Coalition of Art Deco Societies (1 Murdock Terrace, Brighton, Maine 02135).

FURTHER READING

Since the early 1970s there has been an impressive array of articles, exhibition catalogs, and books published on the Art Deco. Much of this literature—most of it concerned with the decorative arts rather than with architecture—is listed in Mary Vance, *Art Deco Monographs* (Monticello, Illinois: Vance Bibliographies, January 1985) and in Lamia Doumato, *A Bibliography on Art Deco* (Monticello, Illinois: Vance Bibliographies, July 1986). Two volumes relating to the Paris exposition that were originally published in 1925 have been reissued: *Architectural Ornament and Sculpture: Exposition Internationale des Arts Décoratifs et Industriels Modernes* (New York: Garland, 1977), and *Architecture: Exposition Internationale des Arts Décoratifs et Industriels Modernes* (New York: Garland, 1977). By far the best and most comprehensive volume on American Art Deco is Barbara Capitman, Michael D. Kinerk, and Dennis W. Wilhelm *Rediscovering Art Deco U.S.A.*, published in 1994 (New York: Viking Studio Books). Several regional Art Deco societies across the country publish impressive newsletters, and this is especially true of the Chicago Art Deco Society (*Quarterly Publication of the Chicago Art Deco Society*). In addition, roadside examples of the Art Deco and Streamline Moderne frequently occur in publications of The Society for Commercial Archaeology (*News Journal* and *News*). Anyone searching out Art Deco and Streamline Moderne buildings should also consult the various state and city architectural guidebooks, particularly those issued from the 1970s on. Factual information about Art Deco, PWA Moderne, and Streamline Moderne buildings (and even occasional critical assessments of Moderne architecture) are to be found in almost all of the books in the series of WPA guides published in the 1930s. The most useful of these WPA guides are the editions published up through 1942; later, revised editions often eliminated illustrations and even text relating to Art Deco and Streamline Moderne buildings.

The most rewarding approach to researching Art Deco and Streamline Moderne architecture is to look back at the professional architectural journals and the shelter magazines of the 1920s through the 1940s (not only for the articles and illustrations but also for the advertisements). The professional journals include: *Architectural Forum, Architectural Record, Pencil Points* (now *Progressive Architecture*), *American Architect, The Architect,* and *Architecture,* as well as such regional journals as *Western Architect, Inland Architect,* and *Architect and Engineer.* The principal shelter magazines were *Country Life, Arts and Decoration, House and Garden, House Beautiful, Better Homes and Gardens,* and *American Home.*

Adams, Rayne. "Thoughts on Modern, and Other Ornament." *Pencil Points* 10 (January 1929): 3–16.

Agard, Walter Raymond. *The New Architectural Sculpture.* New York: Oxford University Press, 1935.

Albrecht, Donald. *Designing Dreams: Modern Architecture in the Movies.* New York: Harper and Row, 1986.

Alexander, Hartley. *The Architectural Sculpture of the State Capitol at Lincoln, Nebraska.* Washington, D.C.: American Institute of Architects, 1926.

—————. "Symbolism and Inscriptions." *American Architect* 145 (October 1934): 24–28.

Appelbaum, Stanley. *The New York World's Fair 1939/40.* New York: Dover Publications, 1977.

Architectural Forum. "Design Decade." *Architectural Forum* 73 (October 1940): 211–320.

Architectural League of New York. *1930 Yearbook of the Architectural League of New York.* New York: Architectural League of New York, 1930.

Architectural Record. "Streamline Buildings Next?" *Architectural Record* 114 (July 3, 1918): 23–24.

Balfour, Alan. *Rockefeller Center Architecture as Theater.* New York: McGraw-Hill, 1978.

Barr, Alfred, Jr. *Machine Art.* New York: Museum of Modern Art, 1934.

Battersby, Martin. *The Decorative Twenties.* New York: Walker & Co., 1969.

—————. *The Decorative Thirties.* New York: Walker & Co., 1971.

Bayer, Patricia. *Art Deco Interiors: Decoration and Design Classics of the 1920s and 1930s.* Boston: Bulfinch Press Division, Little Brown Company, 1990.

Bletter, Rosemarie Haag. "1930–1945: The World of Tomorrow: The Future With a Past." In *High Styles: Twentieth-Century American Design,* edited by Lisa Phillips. New York: Whitney Museum of American Art, 1985, pp. 84–127.

Bossom, Alfred C. "Alfred Bossom Develops a New Skyscraper." *Arts and Decoration* 22 (April 1925): 34.

Boston Architectural Club. *The Book of the Boston Architectural Club, 1929.* Boston: Boston Architectural Club, 1929.

Bragdon, Claude. "Ornament From Platonic Solids." *Architectural Record* 63 (June 1928): 505–510.

————. *The Frozen Fountain.* New York: Alfred A. Knopf, 1932.

Brannach, Frank E. *Church Architecture: Building for a Living Faith.* Milwaukee: Bruce Publishing Co., 1932.

Breeze, Carla. *Pueblo Deco.* New York: Rizzoli, 1990.

————. *L. A. Deco.* New York: Rizzoli, 1991.

————. *New York Deco.* New York: Rizzoli, 1993.

Burleigh, Manferd, and Charles M. Adams. *Modern Bus Terminals and Post Houses.* Ypsilanti, Michigan: University Lithoprinters, 1941.

Bush, Donald J. *The Streamline Decade.* New York: George Braziller, 1975.

Capitman, Barbara. "Coming of Age: The Art Deco District [Miami Beach, Florida]." *Portfolio.* Miami Beach, 1979.

————. *Deco Delights: Preserving the Beauty and Joy of Miami Beach.* New York: E. P. Dutton, 1988.

Capitman, Barbara, Michael D. Kinerk, and Dennis W. Wilhelm. *Redisovering Art Deco U.S.A.* New York: Viking Studio Books, 1994.

Cerwinske, Laura, and David Kaminsky. *Tropical Deco: The Architecture and Design of Old Miami Beach.* New York: Rizzoli, 1981.

Chase, Stuart. *Men and Machines.* New York: Macmillan, 1935.

Cheney, Howard Lovewell. "Post Office for Miami Beach." *Architectural Concrete* 5 (March 1939): 3–4.

Cheney, Sheldon. *The New World Architecture.* New York: Longman, Green, 1930.

Cheney, Sheldon and Martha. *Art and the Machine.* New York: Whittlesey, 1936.

Cohen, Judith Singer. *Cowtown Moderne: Art Deco Architecture of Fort Worth, Texas.* College Station, Texas A & M Press, 1988.

Corbett, Harvey Wiley. "Expo Discussed at Meeting of New York Architectural League." *Western Architect* 35 (March 1926): 30.

Crane, Theodore. "The Future of American Design." *Pencil Points* 18 (October 1937): 651–658.

Cret, Paul Philippe. "Ten Years of Modernism." *Architectural Forum* 59 (August 1933): 91–94.

Crowe, Michael F. *Deco by the Bay: Art Deco Architecture in the San Francisco Bay Area.* New York: Viking Studio Books, 1995.

Cucchiella, Sheryl R. *Baltimore Deco.* Baltimore: Maclay & Associates, Inc., 1984.

Dilemme, Philip, and Rudi Stern. *American Streamline: A Handbook of Neon Advertising Design.* New York: Van Nostrand Reinhold, 1984.

Duncan, Alastair. *Art Deco.* London: Thames and Hudson, 1988.

Eberhard, Ernest. "Architectural Use of Aluminum." *American Architect* 137 (May 1930): 48–57.

Eckert, Kathryn Bishop. *Buildings of Michigan*. New York: Oxford University Press, 1993.

Emanuel, Jay, Publications. *The 1941 Theatre Catalogue*. Vol. 2. Philadelphia: Jay Emanuel Publications, Inc., 1941.

Ehrlich, George. *Kansas City, Missouri: An Architectural History, 1826–1976*. Kansas City, Missouri: Historic Kansas City Foundation with the Lowell Press, 1979.

Etter, Don. Denver Going Modern. Denver: Graphic Impressions, 1977.

Ferriss, Hugh. *The Metropolis of Tomorrow*. New York: Ives Washburn, 1929.

————. *Power in Building*. New York: Columbia University Press, 1953.

Francisco, Charles. *The Radio City Music Hall: An Affectionate History of the World's Greatest Theatre*. New York: E. P. Dutton, 1979.

Frankl, Paul T. *New Dimensions*. New York: Payson and Clarke, 1928.

————. *Form and Reform*. New York: Harper, 1930.

————. *Space for Living*. New York: Doubleday, Doran & Co., 1938.

Gebhard, David. *The Richfield Building, 1928–1968*. New York: Atlantic Richfield, 1969.

————. *Tulsa Art Deco*. Tulsa: Junior League of Tulsa, 1980.

————. "1915–1930: Traditionalism and Design: Old Models for the New." In *High Styles: Twentieth-Century American Design*, edited by Lisa Phillips. New York: Whitney Museum of American Art, 1985, pp. 48–81.

————. *Robert Stacy-Judd: Maya Architecture and the Creation of a New Style*. Santa Barbara: Capra Press, 1993.

Gebhard, David, and Gerald Mansheim. *The Buildings of Iowa*. New York: Oxford University Press, 1993.

Gebhard, David, and Hariette Von Breton. *Kem Weber: The Moderne in Southern California, 1920–1941*. Santa Barbara, California: University Museum, University of California, 1969.

Gebhard, David, and Robert Winter. *Los Angeles: An Architectural Guide*. Salt Lake City: Peregrine Smith Books, 1994.

Gifford, Denis. *Science Fiction Film*. London: Studio Vista/Dutton, 1971.

Gill, Harrison. "Copper Alloys." *American Architect* 129 (September 1930): 52–55, 98.

Goldberger, Paul. *The Skyscraper*. New York: Borzoi Book Division Knopf, 1981.

Greif, Martin. *Depression Modern*. New York: Universe Books, 1975.

Gutman, Richard J. S., and Elliot Kaufman. *American Diner*. New York: Harper & Row, 1979.

Hamlin, Talbot F. "New Victorianism." *American Architect* 141 (February 1932): 18–19, 70–74.

————. "A Contemporary American Style." *Pencil Points* 19 (February 1938): 99–106.

Hanks, David. *Donald Deskey*. New York: E. P. Dutton, 1987.

Haskell, Douglas. "Building or Sculpture: The Architecture of Mass." *Architectural Record* 67 (April 1930): 366–367.

Haslam, Malcolm. *Art Deco, Collector's Style Guide*. New York: Ballantine Books, 1987.

Herman, Lloyd E., and Lois Frieman Brand. *The Designs of Raymond Loewy.* Washington, D.C.: Renwick Gallery, Smithsonian Institution, 1975.

Hillier, Bevis. *Art Deco.* London: Studio Vista/Dutton, 1968.

————. *Art Deco.* Minneapolis: Minneapolis Institute of Arts, 1971.

Hirshorn, Paul, and Steven Izenour. *White Towers.* Cambridge, Massachusetts: MIT Press, 1979.

Hitchcock, Henry-Russell. "Some American Interiors in the Moderne Style." *Architectural Record* 64 (September 1928): 235–243.

Hitchcock, Henry-Russell, and Philip Johnson. *The International Style: Architecture Since 1922.* New York: Museum of Modern Art, 1932.

Hopper, Parker Morse. "Modern Architectural Decoration." *Architectural Forum* 48 (February 1928): 153–160.

Ingle, Marjorie. *Mayan Revival Style.* Salt Lake City: Peregrine Smith Books, 1984.

Jackson, Donald C. *Great American Bridges and Dams.* Washington, D.C.: Preservation Press, 1988.

Jakle, John A., and Keith A. Sculle. *The Gas Station in America.* Baltimore: The Johns Hopkins University Press, 1995.

Jennings, Jan, editor. *Roadside America: The Automobile in Design and Culture.* Ames, Iowa: Iowa State University Press, 1990.

Johnson, Philip. "The Skyscraper School of Modern Architecture." *The Arts* 17 (March 1931): 569–575.

Kahn, Ely Jacques. "Sources of Inspiration." *Architecture* 60 (November 1929): 249–255.

————. "The Province of Decoration in Modern Design." *Creative Art* 5 (December 1929): 885–889.

————. *Contemporary American Architects: Ely Jacques Kahn.* (New York: Whittlesey House Division, McGraw-Hill, 1931).

Kaplan, Donald, and Alan Bellink. *Diners of the Northeast.* Stockbridge, Massachusetts: Berkshire Traveller Press, 1980.

Kiesler, Frederick. "Space House." *Architectural Forum* 60 (February 1934): 17.

Kilham, Walter H., Jr. *Raymond Hood, Architect: Form Through Function in the American Skyscraper.* New York: Architectural Book Publishing Company, 1973.

King, Edith Morgan. "Modernism?" *Vogue* 73 (May 11, 1929): 104–105, 162, 164, 166, 170, 172.

Kingsley, Karen. *Modernism in Louisiana: A Decade of Progress 1930–1940.* New Orleans: School of Architecture, Tulane University, 1984.

Kittel, Gerd and Richard F. Snow. *Diners: People and Places.* New York: Thames and Hudson, 1990.

Klein, Dan, Nancy A. McClelland, and Malcolm Haslam. *In the Deco Style.* New York: Rizzoli, 1986.

Kreisman, Lawrence, and Victor Gardaya. *Art Deco Seattle.* Seattle: Allied Arts of Seattle, 1979.

Krinsky, Carol Herselle. *Rockefeller Center.* New York: Oxford University Press, 1978.

Kubly, Vincent F. *The Louisiana Capitol: Its Art and Architecture*. Gretna, Lousiana: Pelican Publishing Co., 1977.

Le Corbusier. *Towards a New Architecture*. London: Architectural Press, 1946. The original French edition was published in Paris in 1923.

Leich, Jean Ferriss. *Architectural Visions: The Drawings of Hugh Ferriss*. New York: Whitney Library of Design, Watson-Guptill Publications, 1980.

Lesieutre, Alain. *The Spirit and Splendor of Art Deco*. London: Paddington Press, 1974.

Liebs, Chester H. *Main Street to Miracle Mile*. Boston: Little, Brown & Company, 1985.

Loewy, Raymond. *Never Leave Nature Alone*. New York: Simon and Schuster, 1951.

————. *Industrial Design*. Woodstock, New York: Overlook Press, 1979.

Longstreth, Richard. *The Buildings of Main Street*. Washington, D.C.: Preservation Press, 1987.

Loos, Adolf. "The Black Bottom and the Charleston . . . ." *Pencil Points* 8 (July 1927): 435.

Mandelbaum, Howard, and Eric Myers. *Screen Deco: A Celebration of High Style in Hollywood*. New York: St. Martin's Press, 1985.

Margolies, John, and Emily Gwathmey. *Ticket to Paradise: American Movie Theatres and How We Had Fun*. Boston: Bulfinch Press Division, Little Brown & Company, 1991.

————. *Signs of Our Times*. New York: Abbeville Press, 1993.

————. *Home Away From Home*. New York: Bulfinch Press Division, Little Brown & Company, 1995.

McClinton, Katharine Morrison. *Art Deco: A Guide for Collectors*. New York: Clarkson N. Potter, 1972.

McGarry, Bernard J. "Porcelain Enameled Metal." *American Architect* 141 (April 1932): 34–35, 82.

McMillan, Elizabeth. *Bullocks Wilshire*. Los Angeles: Privately published, 1977.

Meikle, Jeffrey L. *Twentieth Century Limited: Industrial Design in America, 1925–1939*. Philadelphia: Temple University Press, 1972.

Menten, Theodore. *The Art Deco Style*. New York: Dover Publications, 1972.

Messler, Norbert. *The Art Deco Skyscraper in New York*. New York: Peter Lang, 1986.

Mock, Elizabeth. *Built in the USA*. New York: Museum of Modern Art, 1944.

Moskowitz, Sam. *Explorers of the Infinite*. New York: World, 1963.

Mumford, Lewis. "American Architecture Today." *Architecture* 58 (October 1928): 189–198.

————. "The American Dwelling House." *Architect and Engineer* 101 (June 1930): 83–92.

————. "Machines for Living." *Fortune* 7 (February 1933): 87–88.

————. "Mr. Rockefeller's Center." *The New Yorker* 9 (December 19, 1933): 27, 30.

Nakamura, Toshio. "New York Art Deco Skyscrapers, 1924–1939," *Architecture and Urbanism*, special no. (April 1987).

Naylor, David. *Great American Movie Theatres*. Washington, D.C.: Preservation Press, 1987.

Newcomb, Rexford. "Modernism Yesterday, Today, and Tomorrow." *Architecture* 68 (November 1933): 253–258.

Nimmons, George C. "The New American Renaissance in Architecture." *American Architect* 134 (August 5, 1928): 141–148.

Pildas, Ave. *Art Deco Los Angeles*. Los Angeles: Ave Pildas, 1977.

Plummer, Kathleen Church. "The Streamline Moderne." *Art in America* 62 (January/February 1974): 46–54.

Radde, Bruce. *The Merritt Parkway*. New Haven, Connecticut: Yale University Press, 1993.

Reinhardt, Richard. *Treasure Island 1939–1940*. San Francisco: Square Books, 1978.

Roberts, Jennifer Davis. *Norman Bel Geddes*. Austin, Texas: University of Texas, 1979.

Robinson, Cervin, and Rosemarie Haag Bletter. *Skyscraper Style: Art Deco New York*. New York: Oxford University Press, 1975.

Root, Keith. *Miami Beach Art Deco Guide*. Miami Beach: Miami Design Preservation League, 1987.

Rosenblum, Robert, Rosemarie Haag Bletter, et al. *Remembering the Future: The New York World's Fair from 1939–1964*. New York: Rizzoli, 1989.

Sasser, Elizabeth Skidmore. *Dugout to Deco: Buildings in West Texas, 1880–1930*. (Lubbock, Texas: Texas Tech University Press, 1993).

Sawtelle, Mark C. "Diner." *Historic Preservation* 31 (September/October 1979): 28–35.

Scarlett, Frank and Majorie Townley, Arts Decoratifs 1925, *A Personal Recollection of the Paris Exposition*. (New York: St. Martin's Press, 1975).

Scheffauer, Herman George. "Dynamic Architecture: New Forms of the Future." *Dial* 70 (March 1921): 323–328.

Segrave, Kerry. *Drive-in Theaters: A History From Their Inception in 1933*. Jefferson, North Carolina: McFarland & Co., 1992.

Sexton, R. W. *The Logic of Modern Architecture*. New York: Architectural Book Publishing Co., 1929

————. "Style in Modern Architectural Ornament." *American Architect* 137 (April 1930): 48–53.

Short, C. W., and R. Stanley Brown. *Public Buildings: A Survey of Architecture of Projects Constructed by Federal and Other Governmental Bodies Between the Years 1933 and 1939*. Washington, D.C.: U.S. Government Printing Office, 1939.

Solon, Leon V. "Will the Exposition Regain Artistic Leadership for France?" *Architectural Record* 67 (October 1925): 391–393.

Stires, Arthur McK. "Glass." *American Architect* 146 (March 1935): 48–69.

————. "Metal." *American Architect* 146 (May 1935): 73–91.

Striner, Richard. "Art Deco, Polemics and Synthesis." *Winterthur Portfolio* 25, no. 1 (Spring, 1990): 21–34.

Teague, Walter Dorwin. *Design This Day*. New York: Harcourt Brace and Co., 1940.

Tennyson, Jeffrey. *Hamburger Heaven: The Illustrated History of the Hamburger.* New York: Hyperion Press, 1993.

Valentine, Maggie. *The Show Starts on the Sidewalk: An Architectural History of the Movie Theatre.* New Haven, Connecticut: Yale University Press, 1994.

Van Doren, Harold. *Industrial Design.* New York: McGraw-Hill, 1940.

Van Trump, James. "The Skyscraper Style in Pittsburgh: Deco Form and Ornament: 1920–1940." *Carnegie Magazine,* May 1977, 198–219.

Varian, Elayne H. *American Art Deco Architecture.* New York: Finch College Museum of Art, 1975.

Vieyra, Daniel I. *"Fill'er Up": An Architectural History of America's Gas Stations.* New York: Collier Macmillan Publishers, 1979.

Vlack, Don. *Art Deco Architecture in New York.* New York: Harper & Row, 1974.

Ward, Arthur, Jr. "Architecture Moderne." *Architecture* 58 (July 1928): 1–8.

Weber, Eva. *Art Deco in America.* New York: Exeter Books, 1985.

————. *Art Deco.* New York: Gallery Book Division, W. H. Smith, 1989.

Weiss, Peg. *The Art Deco Environment.* Syracuse: Everson Museum of Art, 1976.

Werntz, Carl N. "Revolution in Decorative Styles." *Literary Digest,* April 25, 1925, 29–30.

Whiffen, Marcus, with Carla Breeze. *Pueblo Deco: The Art Deco Architecture of the Southwest.* Albuquerque: University of New Mexico Press, 1984.

Wileman, Edgar Harrison. "These Modern Homes." *Sunset Magazine* 62 (September 1929): 26–27.

Wilson, Richard Guy. "Machine Age Iconography in the American West: The Design of Hoover Dam," *Historical Review* 54, no. 1 (November 1985): 463–493.

Wilson, Richard Guy, with Dianne H. Pilgrim and Dickran Tashjian. *Machine Age in America, 1918–1941.* New York: Harry Abrams, 1986.

Wirz, Hans, and Richard Striner. *Washington Deco: Art Deco in the Nation's Capital.* Washington, D.C.: Smithsonian Institution Press, 1984.

Wood, Clifford. *Science Fiction: A Bibliography.* Sacramento: Library, California State University, 1973.

Wurts, Richard, et. al. *The New York World's Fair, 1939/1940.* New York: Dover, 1977.

Youtz, Philip N. "American Architecture Emerges from the Stone Age." *Creative Art* 10 (January 1932): 16–21.

Zim, Larry, with Mel Lemer and Herbert Rolfes. *The World of Tomorrow: The 1939 New York's World's Fair.* New York: Main Street Press, 1988.

INDEX